DEADPOOL'S
Art of War

COLLECTION EDITOR
ALEX STARBUCK
ASSOCIATE EDITOR
SARAH BRUNSTAD
EDITOR, SPECIAL PROJECTS
MARK D. BEAZLEY
SENIOR EDITOR, SPECIAL PROJECTS
JENNIFER GRÜNWALD
VP, PRODUCTION & SPECIAL PROJECTS
JEFF YOUNGQUIST
SVP PRINT, SALES & MARKETING
DAVID GABRIEL
BOOK DESIGNER
RODOLFO MURAGUCHI

EDITOR IN CHIEF
AXEL ALONSO
CHIEF CREATIVE OFFICER
JOE QUESADA
PUBLISHER
DAN BUCKLEY
EXECUTIVE PRODUCER
ALAN FINE

DEADPOOL'S ART OF WAR. Contains material originally published in magazine form as DEADPOOL'S ART OF WAR #1-4. Second printing 2016. ISBN# 978-0-7851-9097-4. Published by MARVEL WORLDWIDE, INC., a subsidiary of MARVEL ENTERTAINMENT, LLC. OFFICE OF PUBLICATION: 135 West 50th Street, New York, NY 10020. Copyright © 2015 MARVEL No similarity between any of the names, characters, persons, and/or institutions in this magazine with those of any living or dead person or institution is intended, and any such similarity which may exist is purely coincidental. **Printed in the U.S.A.** ALAN FINE, President, Marvel Entertainment; DAN BUCKLEY, President, TV, Publishing & Brand Management; JOE QUESADA, Chief Creative Officer; TOM BREVOORT, SVP of Publishing; DAVID BOGART, SVP of Business Affairs & Operations, Publishing & Partnership; C.B. CEBULSKI, VP of Brand Management & Development, Asia; DAVID GABRIEL, SVP of Sales & Marketing, Publishing; JEFF YOUNGQUIST, VP of Production & Special Projects; DAN CARR, Executive Director of Publishing Technology; ALEX MORALES, Director of Publishing Operations; SUSAN CRESPI, Production Manager; STAN LEE, Chairman Emeritus. For information regarding advertising in Marvel Comics or on Marvel.com, please contact Vit DeBellis, Integrated Sales Manager, at vdebellis@marvel.com. For Marvel subscription inquiries, please call 888-511-5480. **Manufactured between 6/8/2016 and 7/11/2016 by HESS PRINT SOLUTIONS, A DIVISION OF BANG PRINTING, BRIMFIELD, OH, USA.**

DEADPOOL'S Art of War

WRITER
PETER DAVID

ARTIST
SCOTT KOBLISH

COLORS
VAL STAPLES

LETTERER
VC'S JOE SABINO

COVER ARTIST
SCOTT KOBLISH
ASSISTANT EDITOR
CHARLES BEACHAM
EDITOR
JORDAN D. WHITE
X-MEN GROUP EDITOR
MIKE MARTS

SPECIAL THANKS TO *RAUNAK*

DEADPOOL CREATED BY *ROB LIEFELD* & *FABIAN NICIEZA*

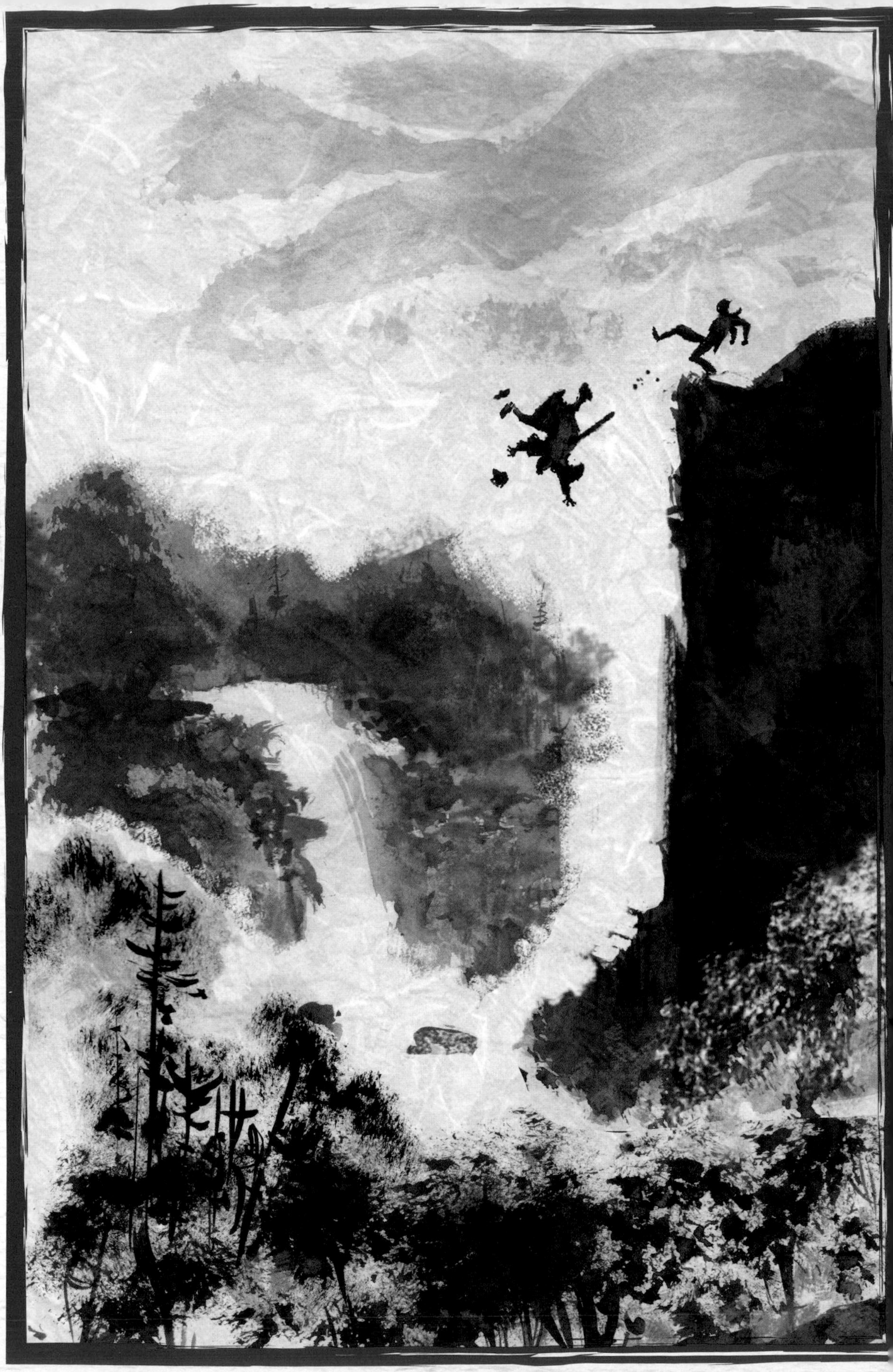

CHAPTER ONE

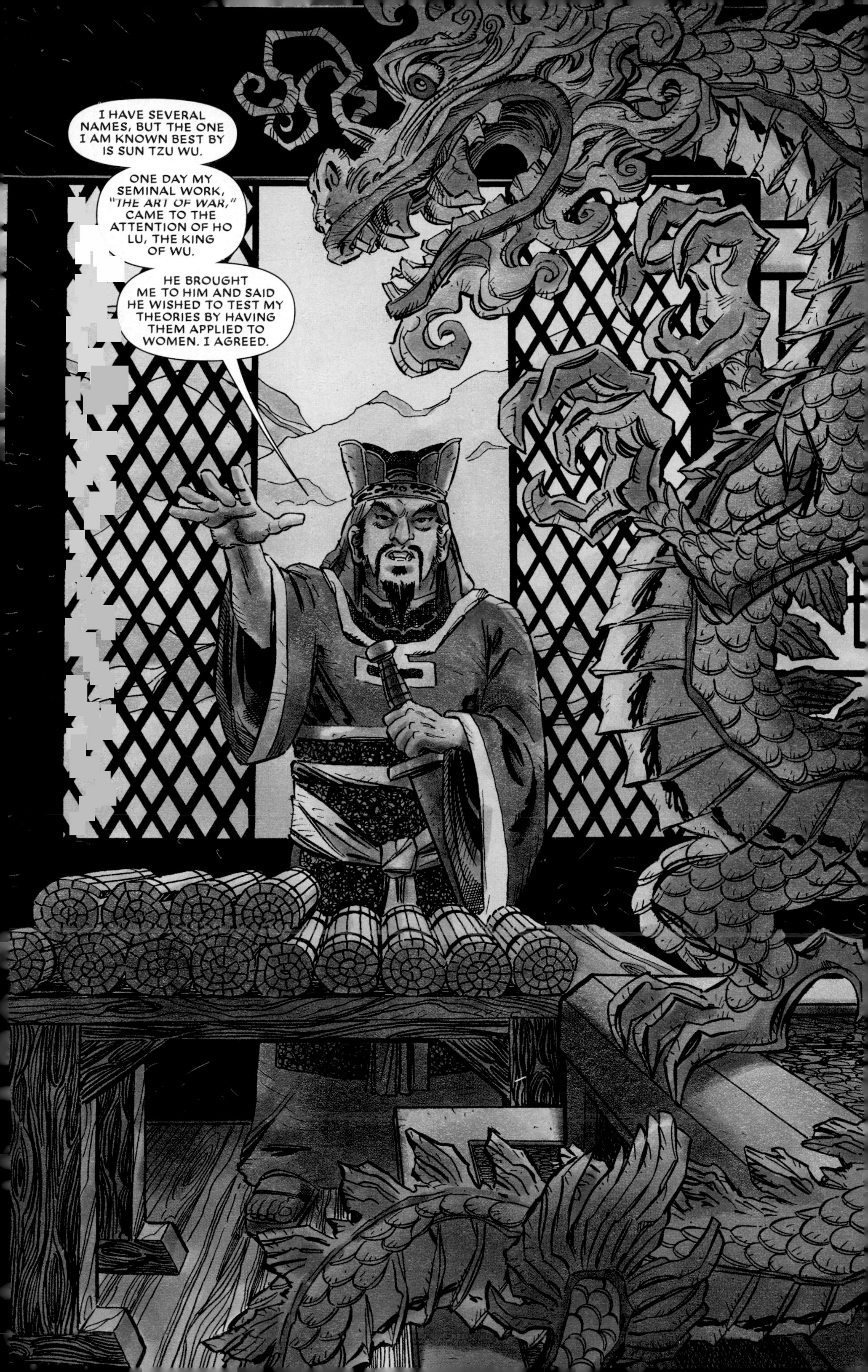
I HAVE SEVERAL NAMES, BUT THE ONE I AM KNOWN BEST BY IS SUN TZU WU.
ONE DAY MY SEMINAL WORK, *"THE ART OF WAR,"* CAME TO THE ATTENTION OF HO LU, THE KING OF WU.
HE BROUGHT ME TO HIM AND SAID HE WISHED TO TEST MY THEORIES BY HAVING THEM APPLIED TO WOMEN. I AGREED.

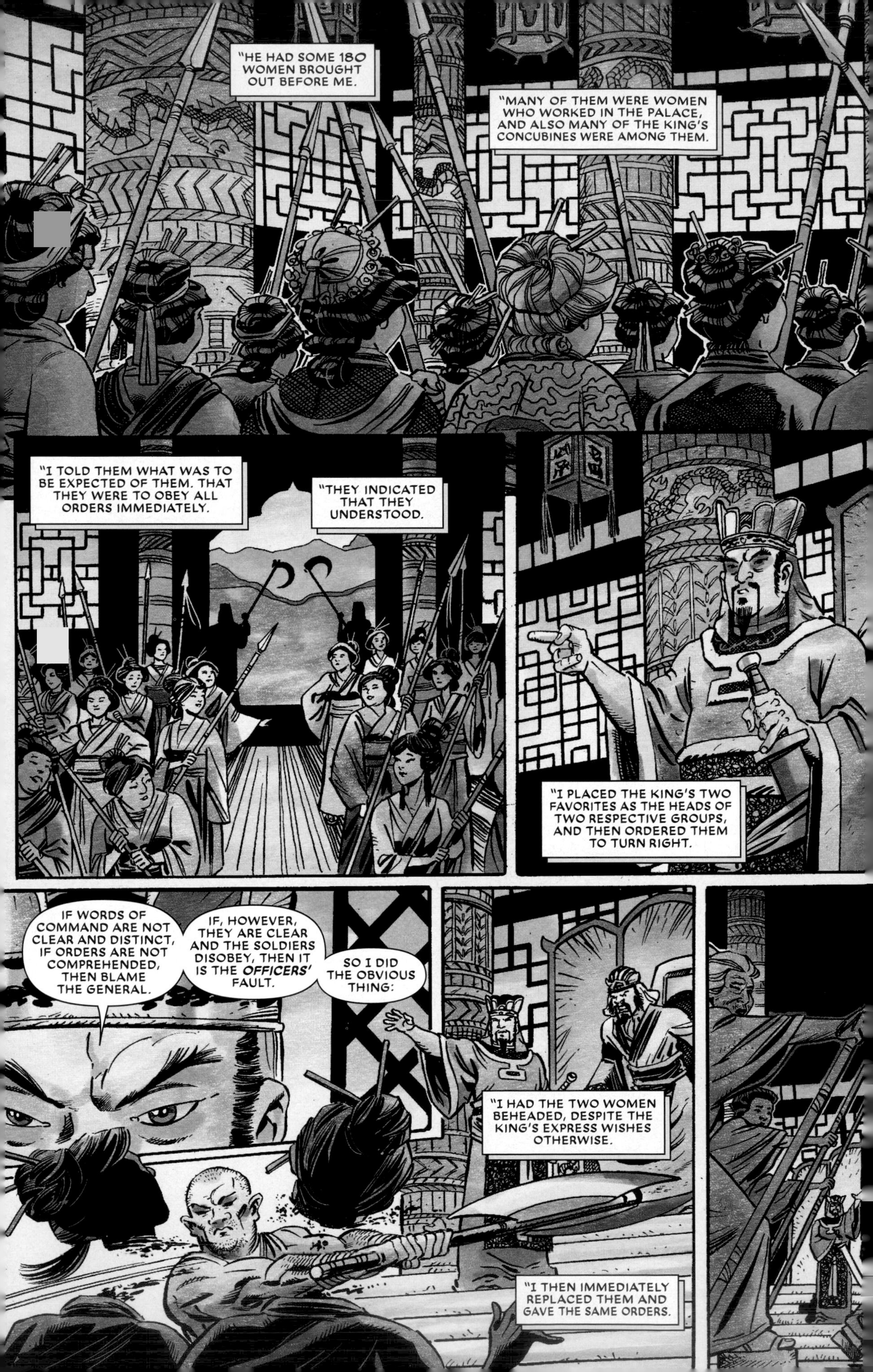
"HE HAD SOME 180 WOMEN BROUGHT OUT BEFORE ME.
"MANY OF THEM WERE WOMEN WHO WORKED IN THE PALACE, AND ALSO MANY OF THE KING'S CONCUBINES WERE AMONG THEM.
"I TOLD THEM WHAT WAS TO BE EXPECTED OF THEM. THAT THEY WERE TO OBEY ALL ORDERS IMMEDIATELY.
"THEY INDICATED THAT THEY UNDERSTOOD.
"I PLACED THE KING'S TWO FAVORITES AS THE HEADS OF TWO RESPECTIVE GROUPS, AND THEN ORDERED THEM TO TURN RIGHT.
IF WORDS OF COMMAND ARE NOT CLEAR AND DISTINCT, IF ORDERS ARE NOT COMPREHENDED, THEN BLAME THE GENERAL.
IF, HOWEVER, THEY ARE CLEAR AND THE SOLDIERS DISOBEY, THEN IT IS THE *OFFICERS'* FAULT.
SO I DID THE OBVIOUS THING:
"I HAD THE TWO WOMEN BEHEADED, DESPITE THE KING'S EXPRESS WISHES OTHERWISE.
"I THEN IMMEDIATELY REPLACED THEM AND GAVE THE SAME ORDERS.

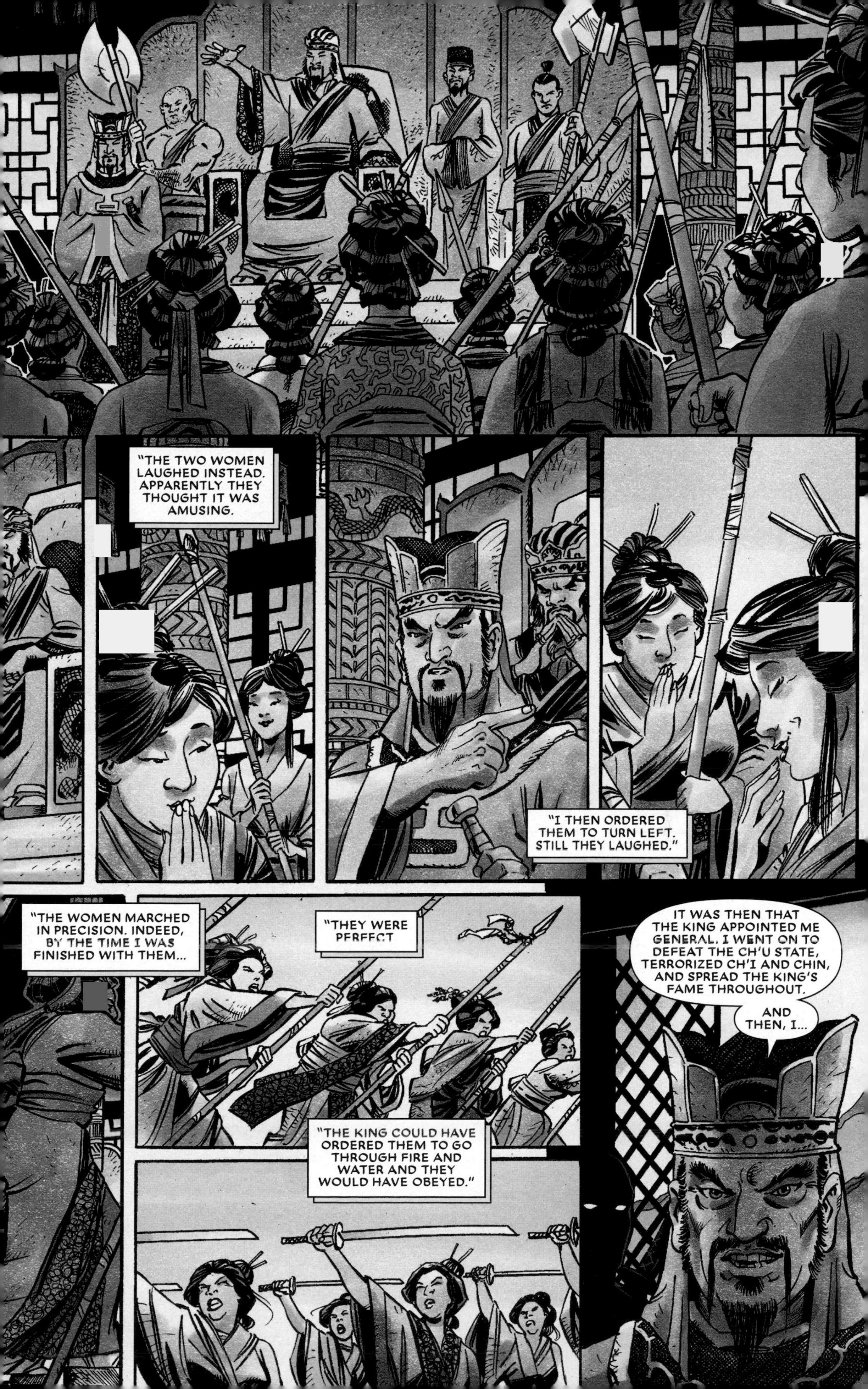
"THE TWO WOMEN LAUGHED INSTEAD. APPARENTLY THEY THOUGHT IT WAS AMUSING.
"I THEN ORDERED THEM TO TURN LEFT. STILL THEY LAUGHED."
"THE WOMEN MARCHED IN PRECISION. INDEED, BY THE TIME I WAS FINISHED WITH THEM...
"THEY WERE PERFECT
"THE KING COULD HAVE ORDERED THEM TO GO THROUGH FIRE AND WATER AND THEY WOULD HAVE OBEYED."
IT WAS THEN THAT THE KING APPOINTED ME GENERAL. I WENT ON TO DEFEAT THE CH'U STATE, TERRORIZED CH'I AND CHIN, AND SPREAD THE KING'S FAME THROUGHOUT.
AND THEN, I...

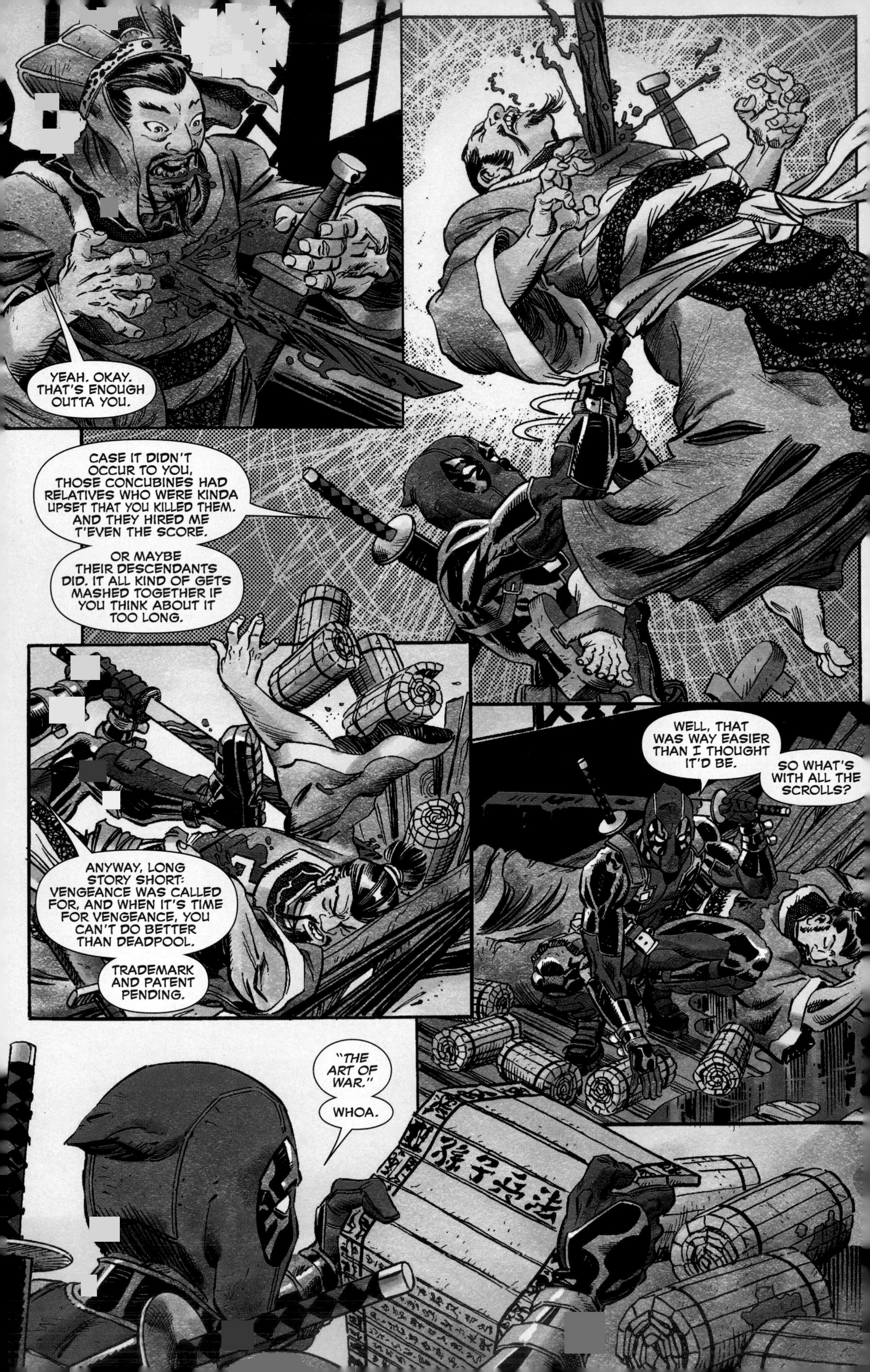
YEAH. OKAY. THAT'S ENOUGH OUTTA YOU.
CASE IT DIDN'T OCCUR TO YOU, THOSE CONCUBINES HAD RELATIVES WHO WERE KINDA UPSET THAT YOU KILLED THEM. AND THEY HIRED ME T'EVEN THE SCORE.
OR MAYBE THEIR DESCENDANTS DID. IT ALL KIND OF GETS MASHED TOGETHER IF YOU THINK ABOUT IT TOO LONG.
ANYWAY, LONG STORY SHORT: VENGEANCE WAS CALLED FOR, AND WHEN IT'S TIME FOR VENGEANCE, YOU CAN'T DO BETTER THAN DEADPOOL.
TRADEMARK AND PATENT PENDING.
WELL, THAT WAS WAY EASIER THAN I THOUGHT IT'D BE.
SO WHAT'S WITH ALL THE SCROLLS?
"THE ART OF WAR."
WHOA.
孫子兵法

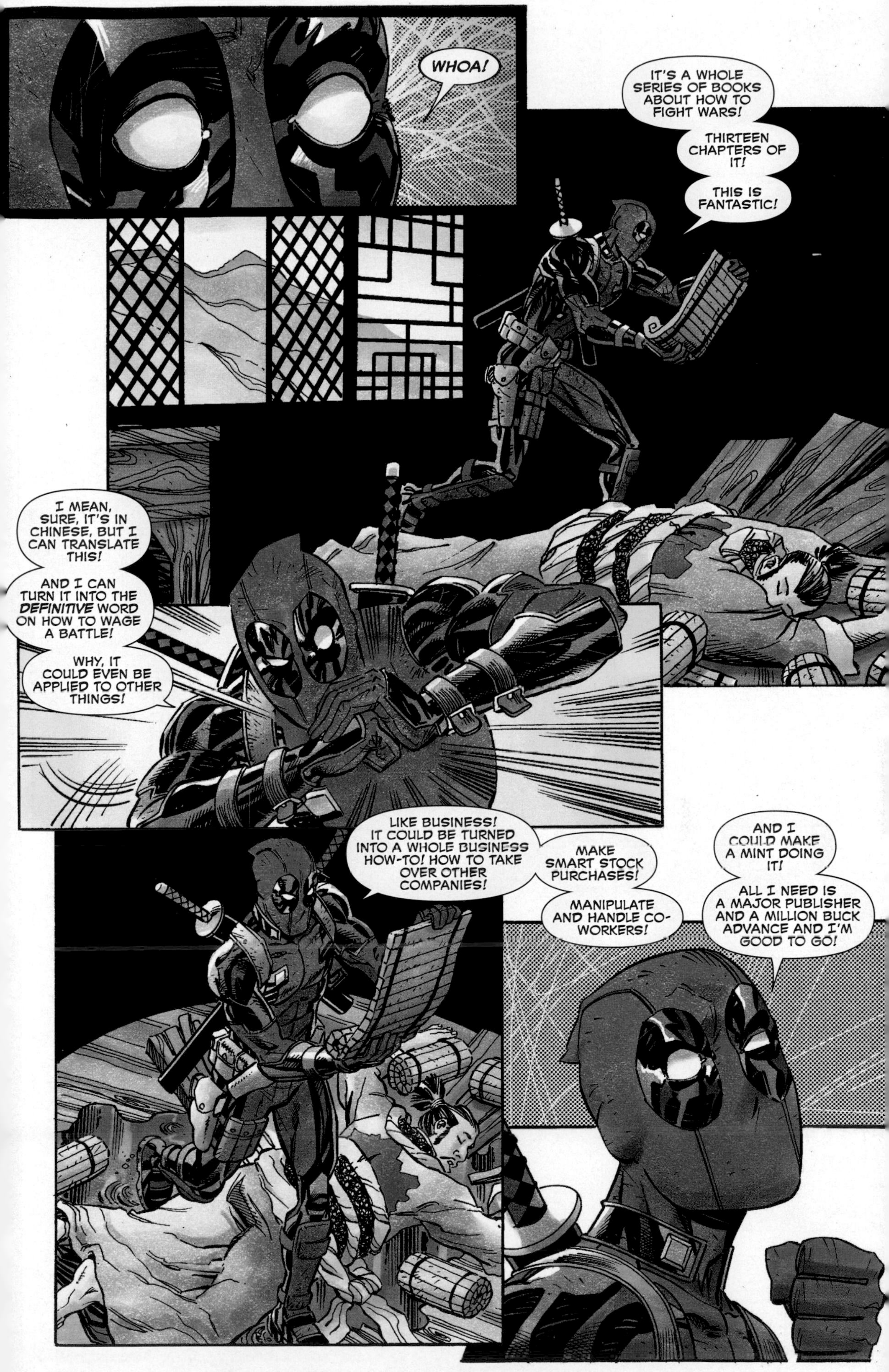
WHOA!
IT'S A WHOLE SERIES OF BOOKS ABOUT HOW TO FIGHT WARS!
THIRTEEN CHAPTERS OF IT!
THIS IS FANTASTIC!
I MEAN, SURE, IT'S IN CHINESE, BUT I CAN TRANSLATE THIS!
AND I CAN TURN IT INTO THE DEFINITIVE WORD ON HOW TO WAGE A BATTLE!
WHY, IT COULD EVEN BE APPLIED TO OTHER THINGS!
LIKE BUSINESS! IT COULD BE TURNED INTO A WHOLE BUSINESS HOW-TO! HOW TO TAKE OVER OTHER COMPANIES!
MAKE SMART STOCK PURCHASES!
MANIPULATE AND HANDLE CO-WORKERS!
AND I COULD MAKE A MINT DOING IT!
ALL I NEED IS A MAJOR PUBLISHER AND A MILLION BUCK ADVANCE AND I'M GOOD TO GO!

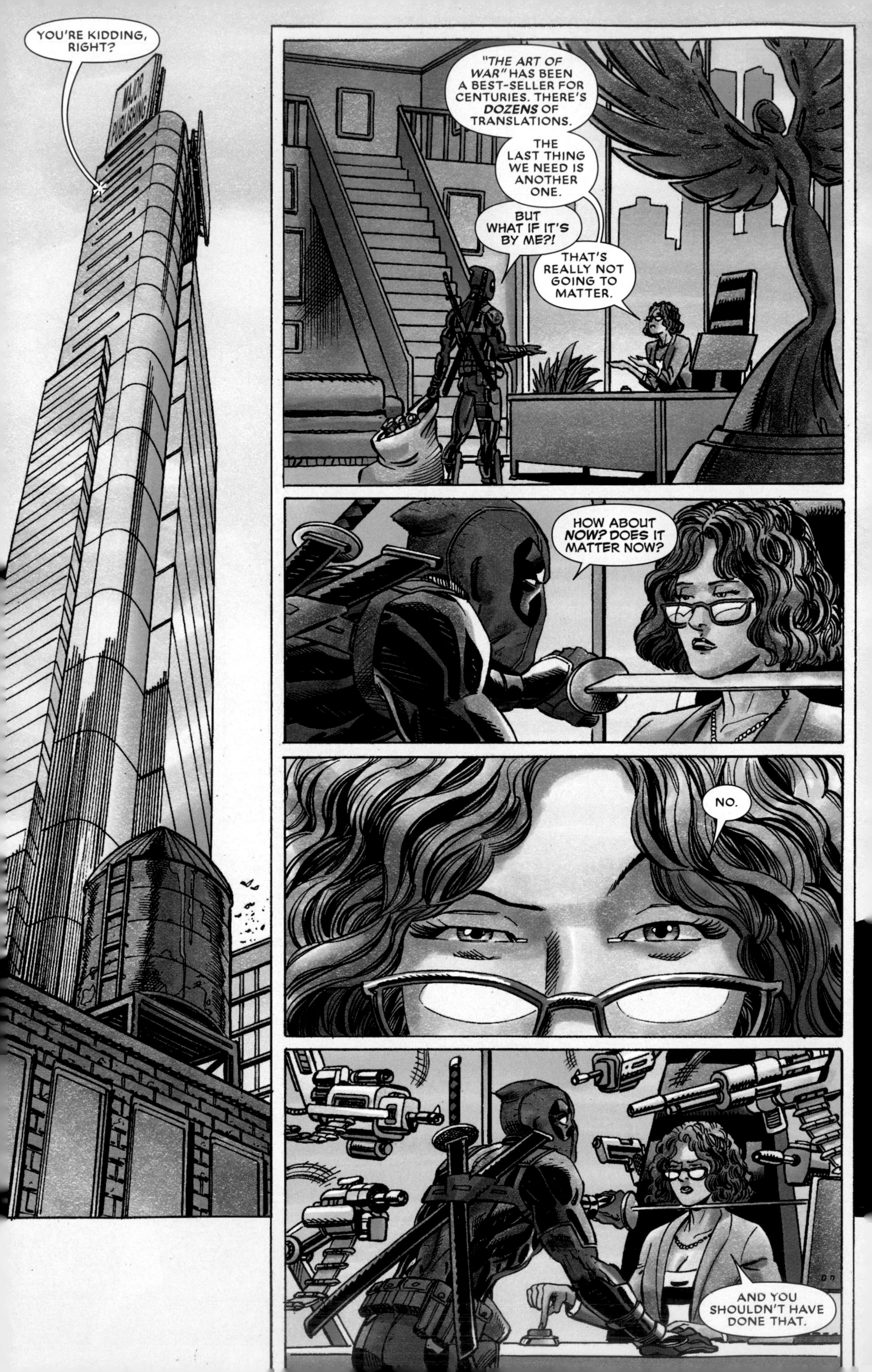
YOU'RE KIDDING, RIGHT?
MAJOR PUBLISHING
"THE ART OF WAR" HAS BEEN A BEST-SELLER FOR CENTURIES. THERE'S DOZENS OF TRANSLATIONS.
THE LAST THING WE NEED IS ANOTHER ONE.
BUT WHAT IF IT'S BY ME?!
THAT'S REALLY NOT GOING TO MATTER.
HOW ABOUT NOW? DOES IT MATTER NOW?
NO.
AND YOU SHOULDN'T HAVE DONE THAT.

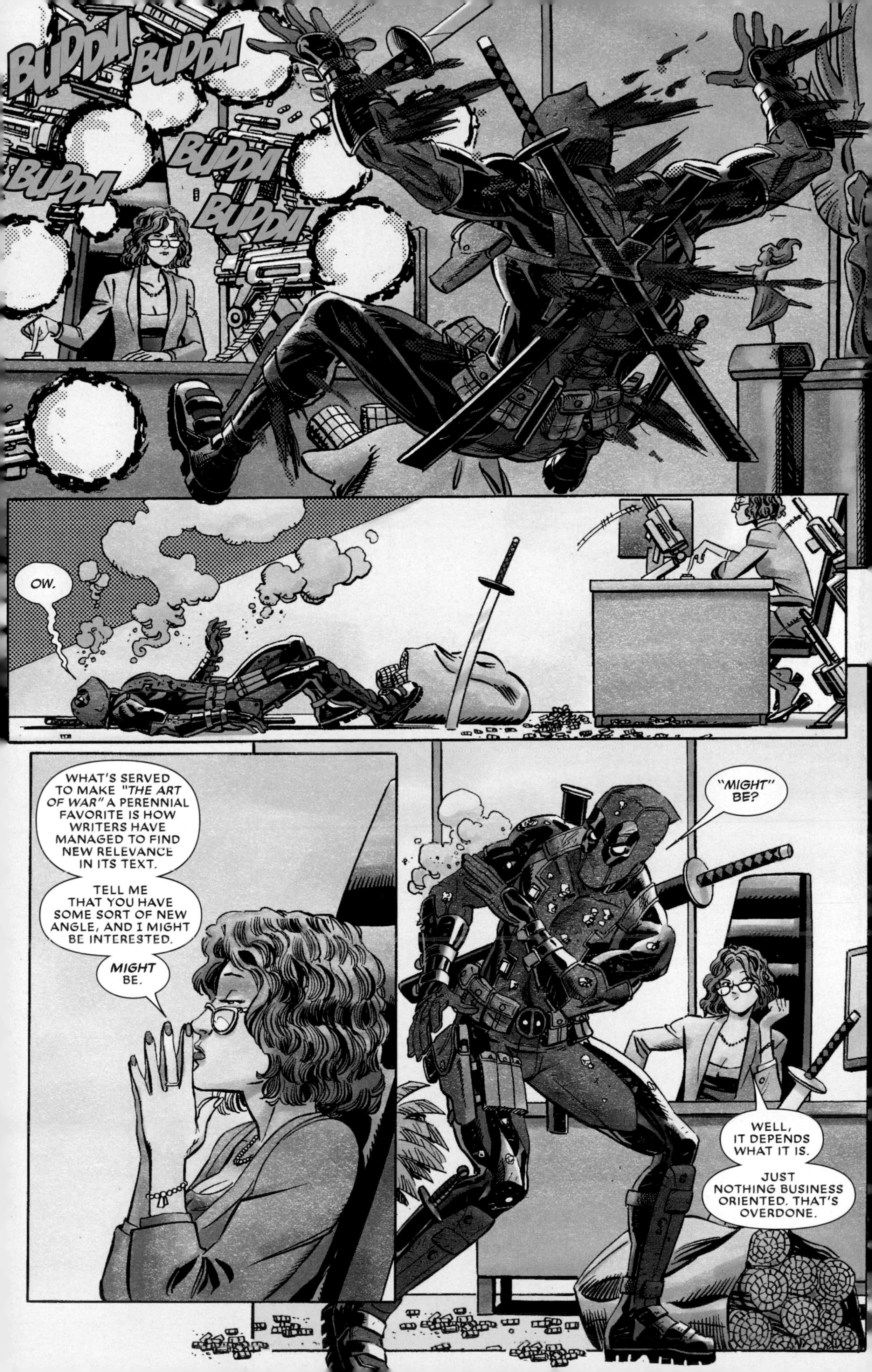
BUDDA BUDDA
BUDDA
BUDDA
BUDDA
OW.
WHAT'S SERVED TO MAKE "THE ART OF WAR" A PERENNIAL FAVORITE IS HOW WRITERS HAVE MANAGED TO FIND NEW RELEVANCE IN ITS TEXT.
TELL ME THAT YOU HAVE SOME SORT OF NEW ANGLE, AND I MIGHT BE INTERESTED.
MIGHT BE.
"MIGHT" BE?
WELL, IT DEPENDS WHAT IT IS.
JUST NOTHING BUSINESS ORIENTED. THAT'S OVERDONE.

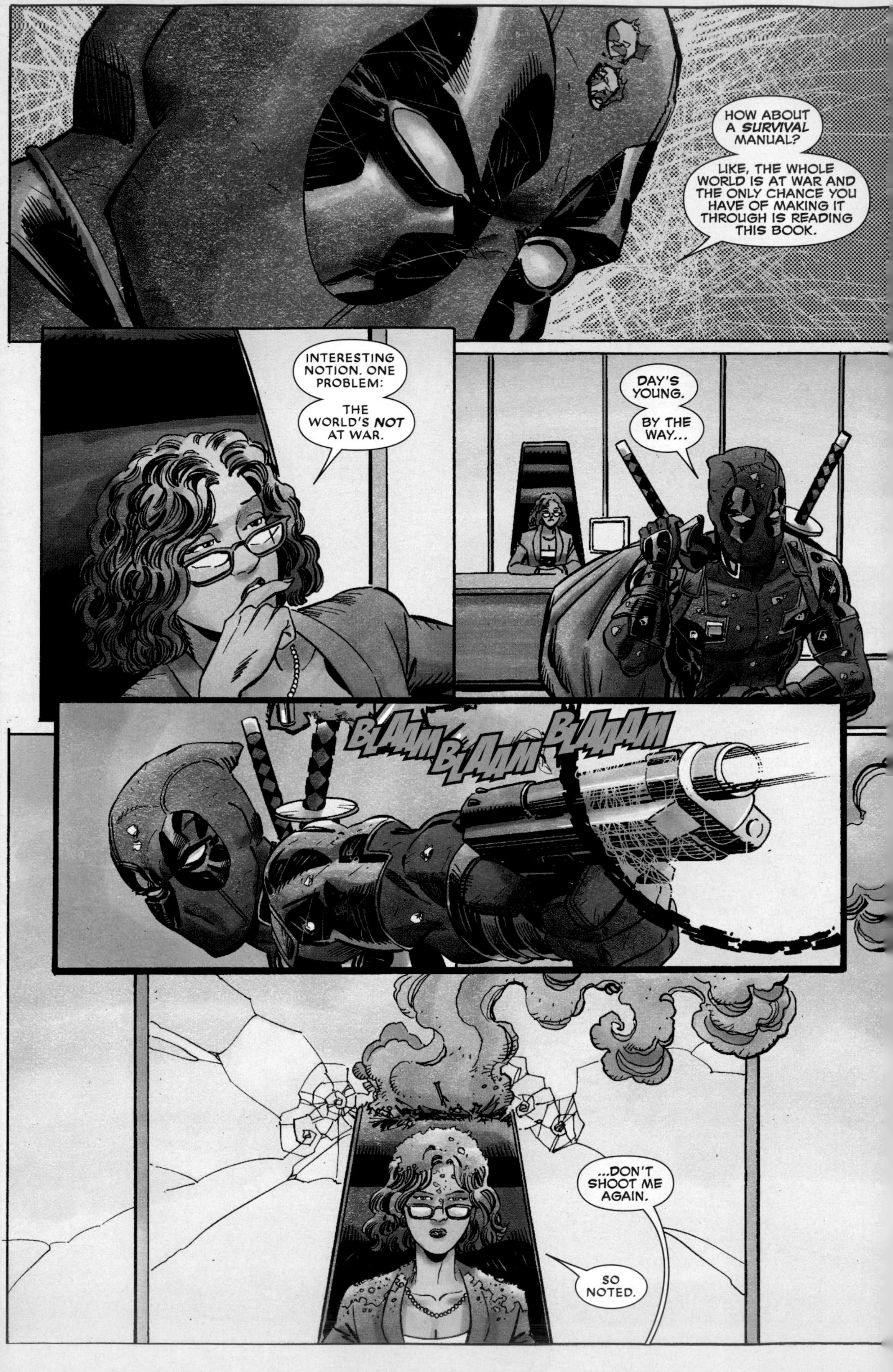

HOW ABOUT A *SURVIVAL* MANUAL?
LIKE, THE WHOLE WORLD IS AT WAR AND THE ONLY CHANCE YOU HAVE OF MAKING IT THROUGH IS READING THIS BOOK.
INTERESTING NOTION. ONE PROBLEM:
THE WORLD'S *NOT* AT WAR.
DAY'S YOUNG.
BY THE WAY...
BLAAM BLAAM BLAAAM
...DON'T SHOOT ME AGAIN.
SO NOTED.

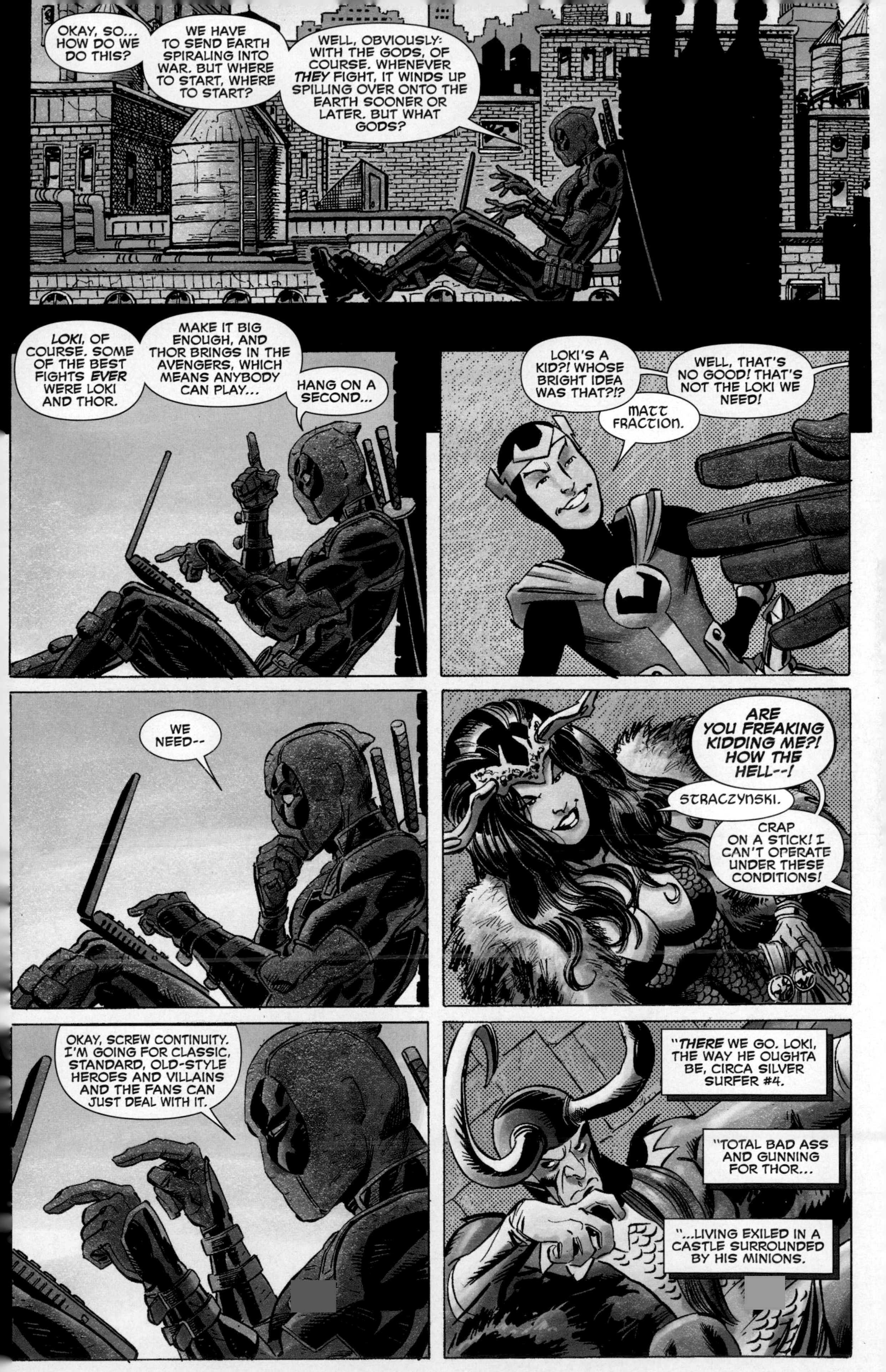
OKAY, SO... HOW DO WE DO THIS?
WE HAVE TO SEND EARTH SPIRALING INTO WAR. BUT WHERE TO START, WHERE TO START?
WELL, OBVIOUSLY: WITH THE GODS, OF COURSE. WHENEVER THEY FIGHT, IT WINDS UP SPILLING OVER ONTO THE EARTH SOONER OR LATER. BUT WHAT GODS?
LOKI, OF COURSE. SOME OF THE BEST FIGHTS EVER WERE LOKI AND THOR.
MAKE IT BIG ENOUGH, AND THOR BRINGS IN THE AVENGERS, WHICH MEANS ANYBODY CAN PLAY...
HANG ON A SECOND...
LOKI'S A KID?! WHOSE BRIGHT IDEA WAS THAT?!?
MATT FRACTION.
WELL, THAT'S NO GOOD! THAT'S NOT THE LOKI WE NEED!
WE NEED--
ARE YOU FREAKING KIDDING ME?! HOW THE HELL--!
STRACZYNSKI.
CRAP ON A STICK! I CAN'T OPERATE UNDER THESE CONDITIONS!
OKAY, SCREW CONTINUITY. I'M GOING FOR CLASSIC, STANDARD, OLD-STYLE HEROES AND VILLAINS AND THE FANS CAN JUST DEAL WITH IT.
"THERE WE GO. LOKI, THE WAY HE OUGHTA BE, CIRCA SILVER SURFER #4.
"TOTAL BAD ASS AND GUNNING FOR THOR...
"...LIVING EXILED IN A CASTLE SURROUNDED BY HIS MINIONS.

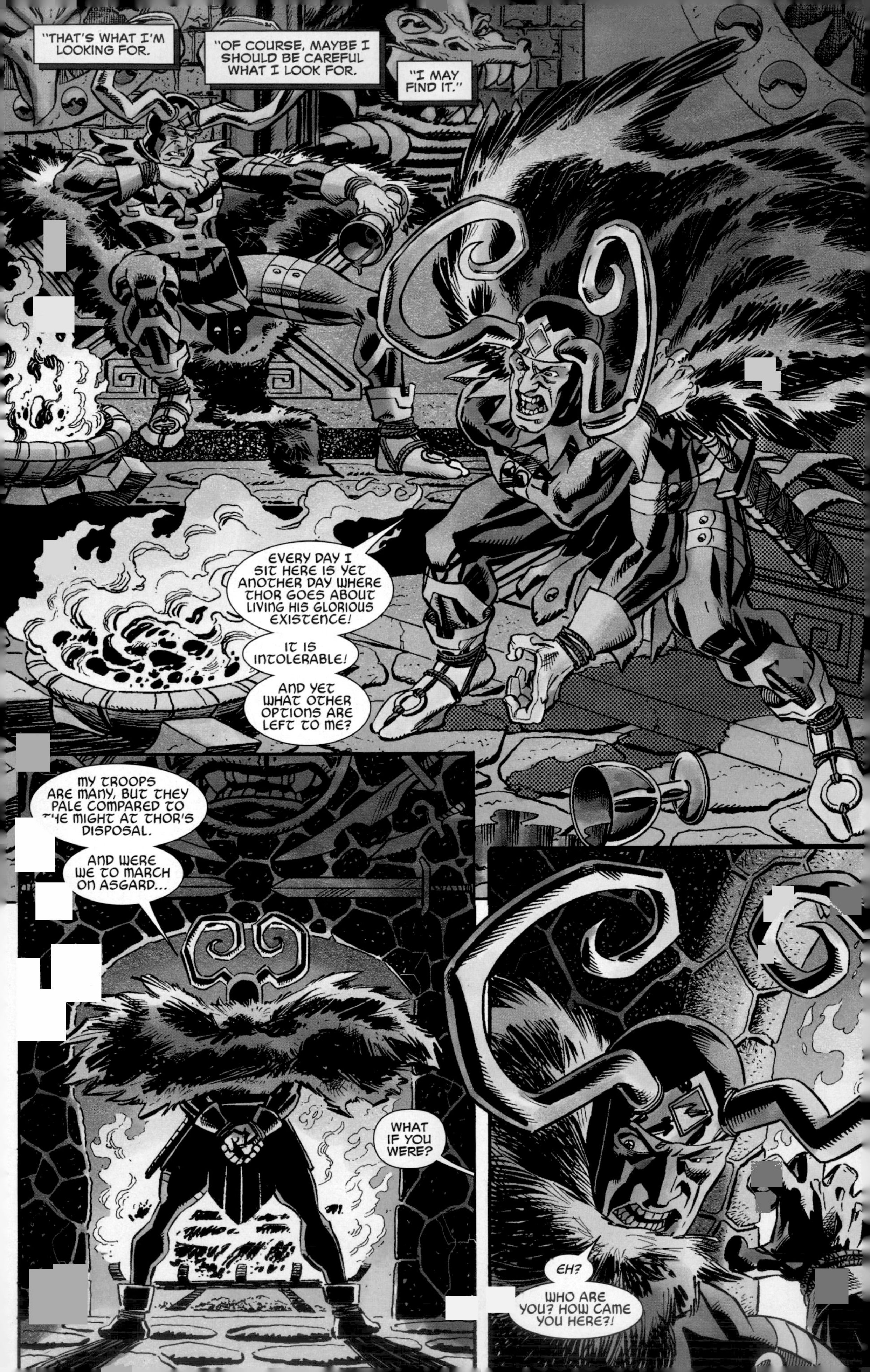
"THAT'S WHAT I'M LOOKING FOR.
"OF COURSE, MAYBE I SHOULD BE CAREFUL WHAT I LOOK FOR.
"I MAY FIND IT."
EVERY DAY I SIT HERE IS YET ANOTHER DAY WHERE THOR GOES ABOUT LIVING HIS GLORIOUS EXISTENCE!
IT IS INTOLERABLE!
AND YET WHAT OTHER OPTIONS ARE LEFT TO ME?
MY TROOPS ARE MANY, BUT THEY PALE COMPARED TO THE MIGHT AT THOR'S DISPOSAL.
AND WERE WE TO MARCH ON ASGARD...
WHAT IF YOU WERE?
EH?
WHO ARE YOU? HOW CAME YOU HERE?!

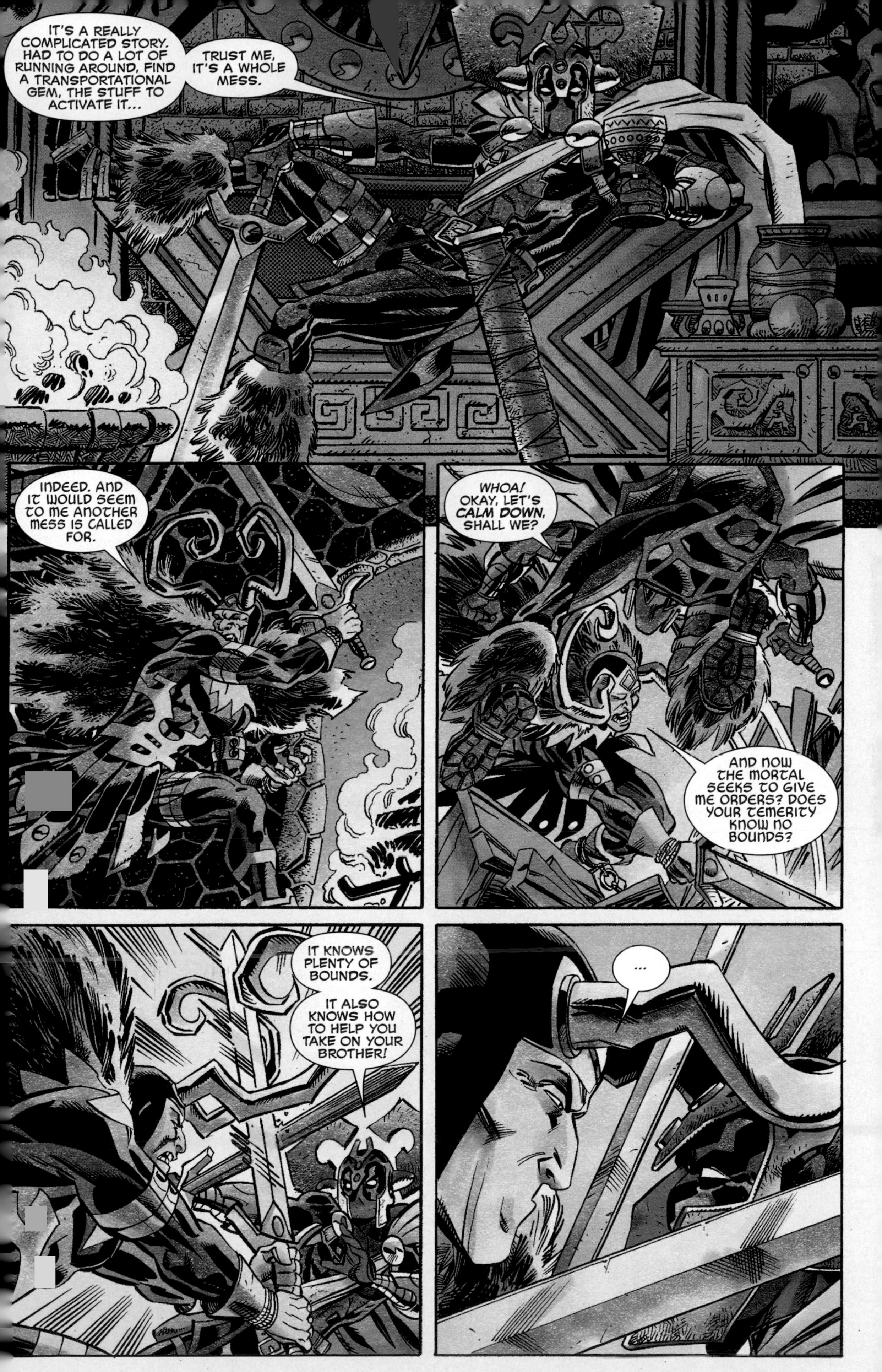

IT'S A REALLY COMPLICATED STORY. HAD TO DO A LOT OF RUNNING AROUND, FIND A TRANSPORTATIONAL GEM, THE STUFF TO ACTIVATE IT...
TRUST ME, IT'S A WHOLE MESS.
INDEED. AND IT WOULD SEEM TO ME ANOTHER MESS IS CALLED FOR.
WHOA! OKAY, LET'S CALM DOWN, SHALL WE?
AND NOW THE MORTAL SEEKS TO GIVE ME ORDERS? DOES YOUR TEMERITY KNOW NO BOUNDS?
IT KNOWS PLENTY OF BOUNDS.
IT ALSO KNOWS HOW TO HELP YOU TAKE ON YOUR BROTHER!
...

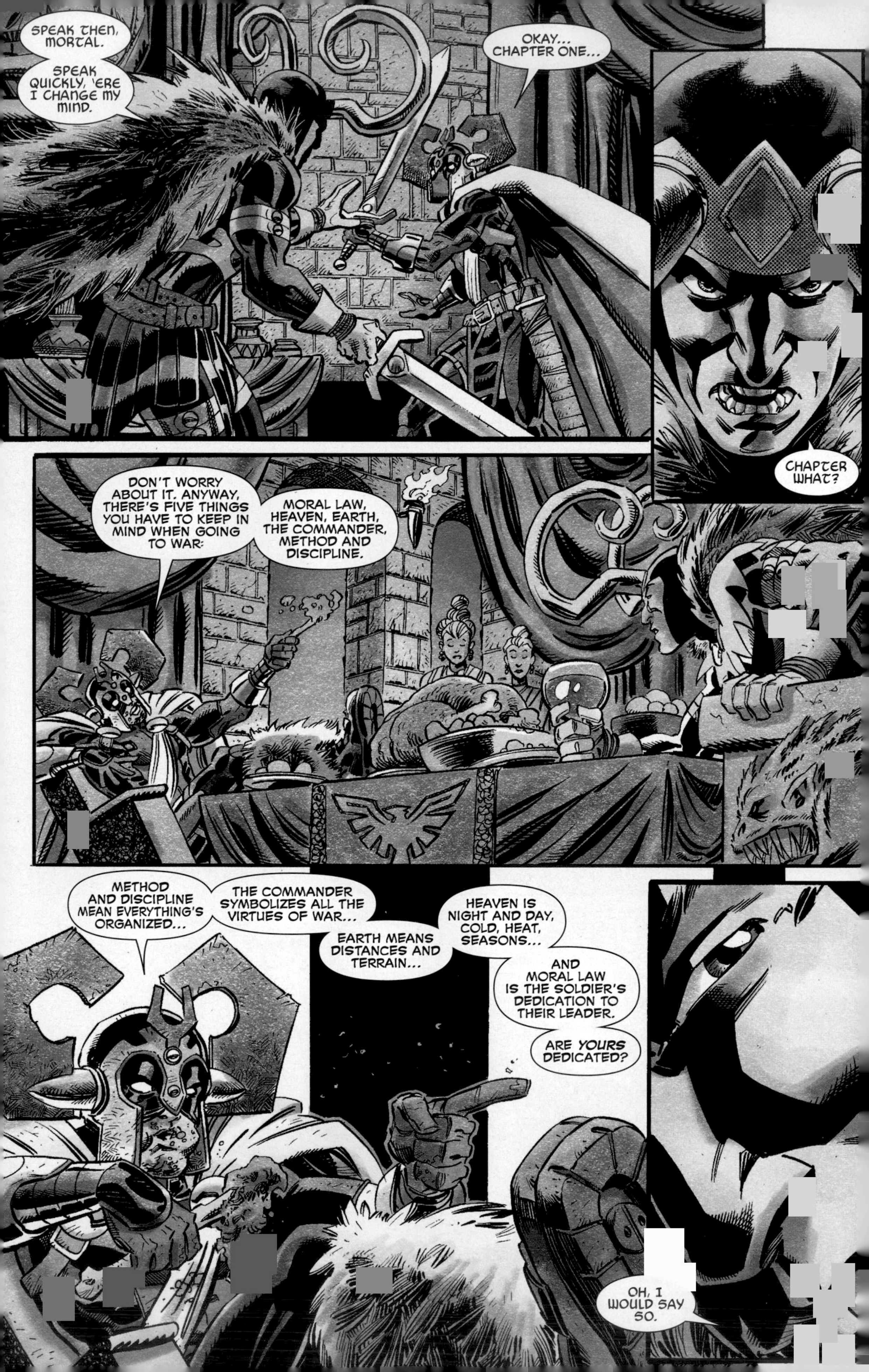
SPEAK THEN, MORTAL.
SPEAK QUICKLY, 'ERE I CHANGE MY MIND.
OKAY... CHAPTER ONE...
CHAPTER WHAT?
DON'T WORRY ABOUT IT. ANYWAY, THERE'S FIVE THINGS YOU HAVE TO KEEP IN MIND WHEN GOING TO WAR:
MORAL LAW, HEAVEN, EARTH, THE COMMANDER, METHOD AND DISCIPLINE.
METHOD AND DISCIPLINE MEAN EVERYTHING'S ORGANIZED...
THE COMMANDER SYMBOLIZES ALL THE VIRTUES OF WAR...
EARTH MEANS DISTANCES AND TERRAIN...
HEAVEN IS NIGHT AND DAY, COLD, HEAT, SEASONS...
AND MORAL LAW IS THE SOLDIER'S DEDICATION TO THEIR LEADER.
ARE *YOURS* DEDICATED?
OH, I WOULD SAY SO.

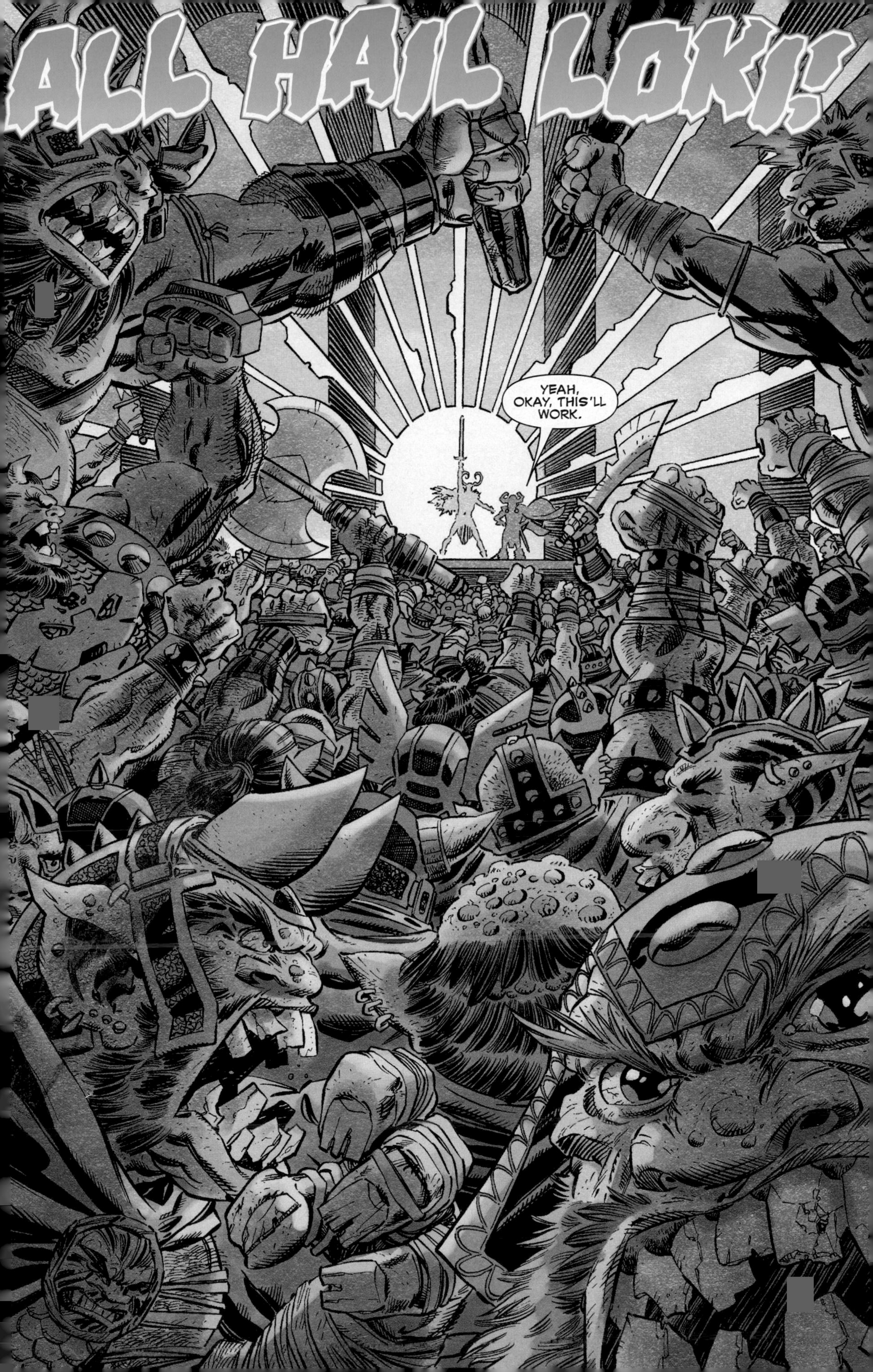
ALL HAIL LOKI!
YEAH, OKAY, THIS'LL WORK.

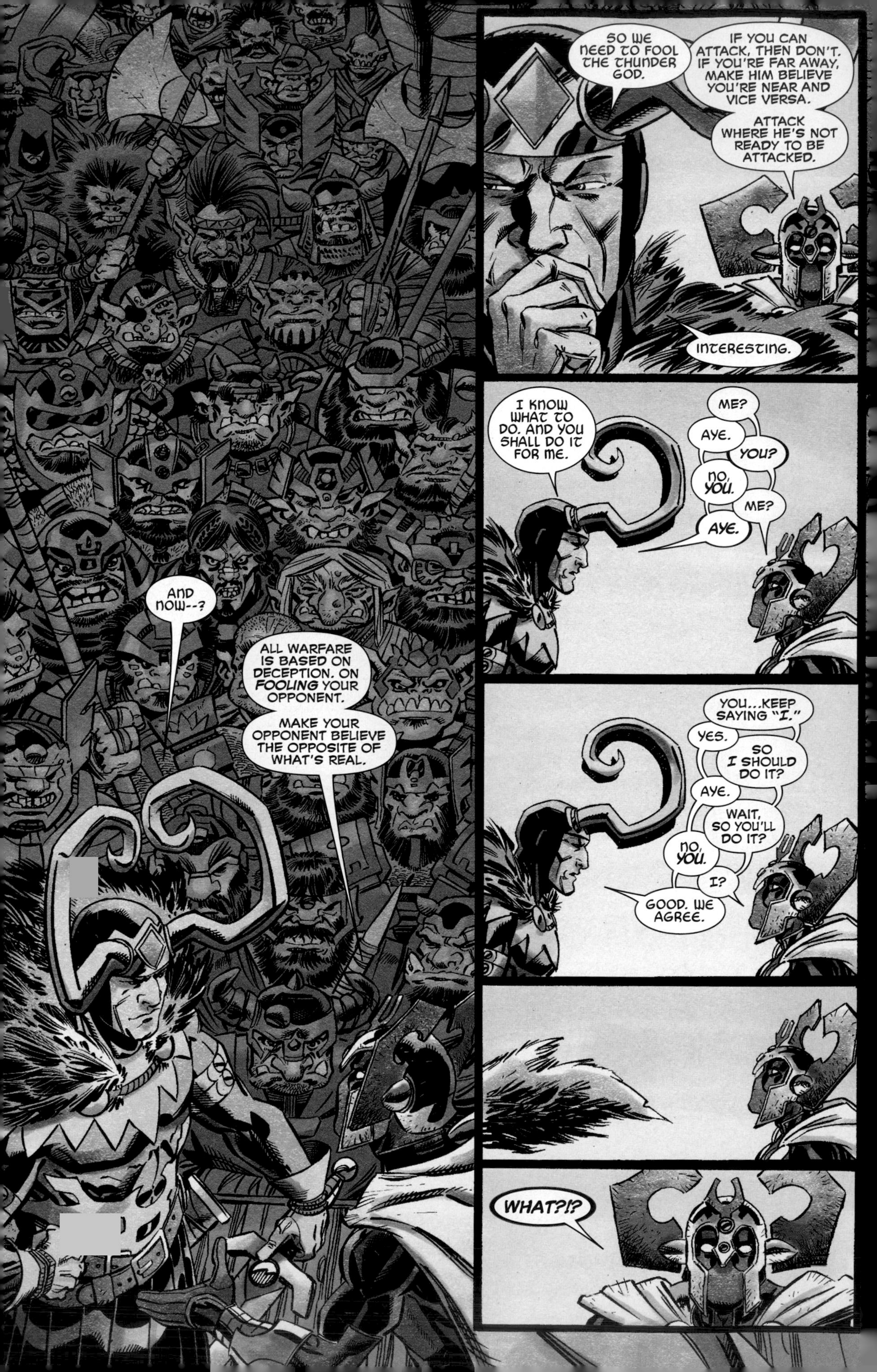
AND NOW--?
ALL WARFARE IS BASED ON DECEPTION. ON FOOLING YOUR OPPONENT.
MAKE YOUR OPPONENT BELIEVE THE OPPOSITE OF WHAT'S REAL.
SO WE NEED TO FOOL THE THUNDER GOD.
IF YOU CAN ATTACK, THEN DON'T. IF YOU'RE FAR AWAY, MAKE HIM BELIEVE YOU'RE NEAR AND VICE VERSA.
ATTACK WHERE HE'S NOT READY TO BE ATTACKED.
INTERESTING.
I KNOW WHAT TO DO. AND YOU SHALL DO IT FOR ME.
ME?
AYE.
YOU?
NO, YOU.
ME?
AYE.
YOU...KEEP SAYING "I."
YES.
SO I SHOULD DO IT?
AYE.
WAIT, SO YOU'LL DO IT?
NO, YOU.
I?
GOOD. WE AGREE.
WHAT?!?

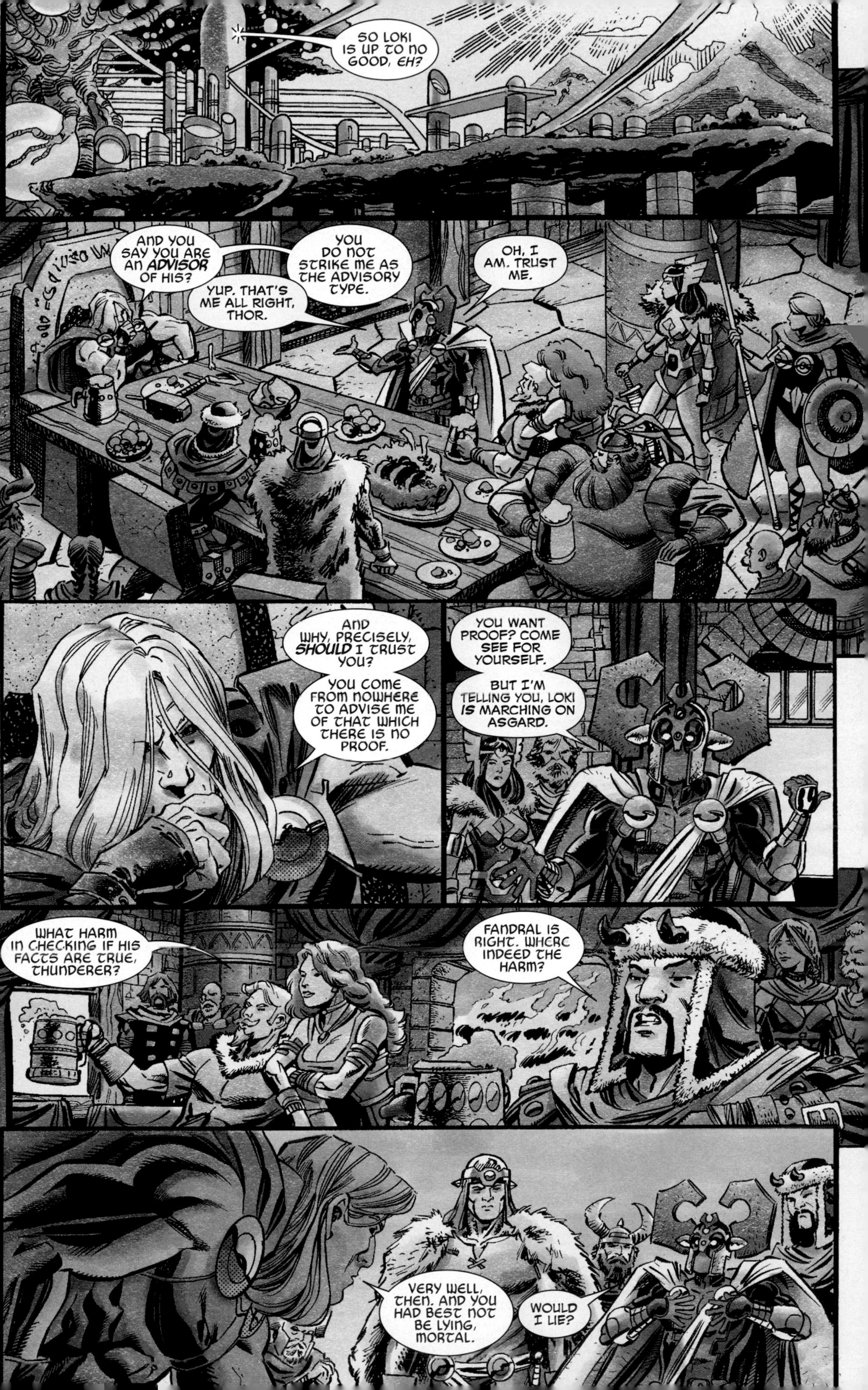
SO LOKI IS UP TO NO GOOD, EH?
AND YOU SAY YOU ARE AN ADVISOR OF HIS?
YUP. THAT'S ME ALL RIGHT, THOR.
YOU DO NOT STRIKE ME AS THE ADVISORY TYPE.
OH, I AM. TRUST ME.
AND WHY, PRECISELY, SHOULD I TRUST YOU?
YOU COME FROM NOWHERE TO ADVISE ME OF THAT WHICH THERE IS NO PROOF.
YOU WANT PROOF? COME SEE FOR YOURSELF.
BUT I'M TELLING YOU, LOKI IS MARCHING ON ASGARD.
WHAT HARM IN CHECKING IF HIS FACTS ARE TRUE, THUNDERER?
FANDRAL IS RIGHT. WHERE INDEED THE HARM?
VERY WELL, THEN. AND YOU HAD BEST NOT BE LYING, MORTAL.
WOULD I LIE?

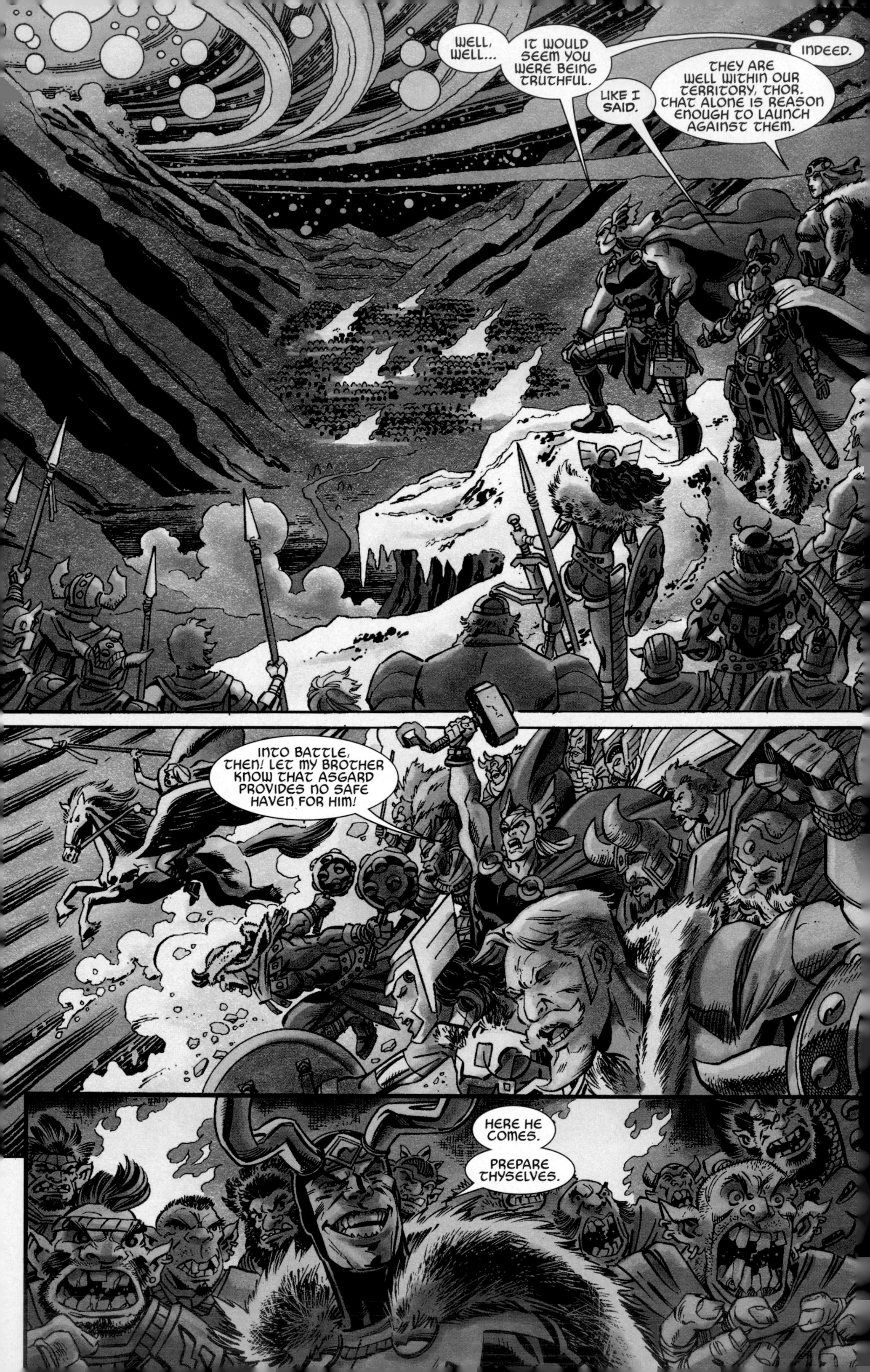
WELL, WELL...
IT WOULD SEEM YOU WERE BEING TRUTHFUL.
INDEED.
LIKE I SAID.
THEY ARE WELL WITHIN OUR TERRITORY, THOR. THAT ALONE IS REASON ENOUGH TO LAUNCH AGAINST THEM.
INTO BATTLE, THEN! LET MY BROTHER KNOW THAT ASGARD PROVIDES NO SAFE HAVEN FOR HIM!
HERE HE COMES.
PREPARE THYSELVES.

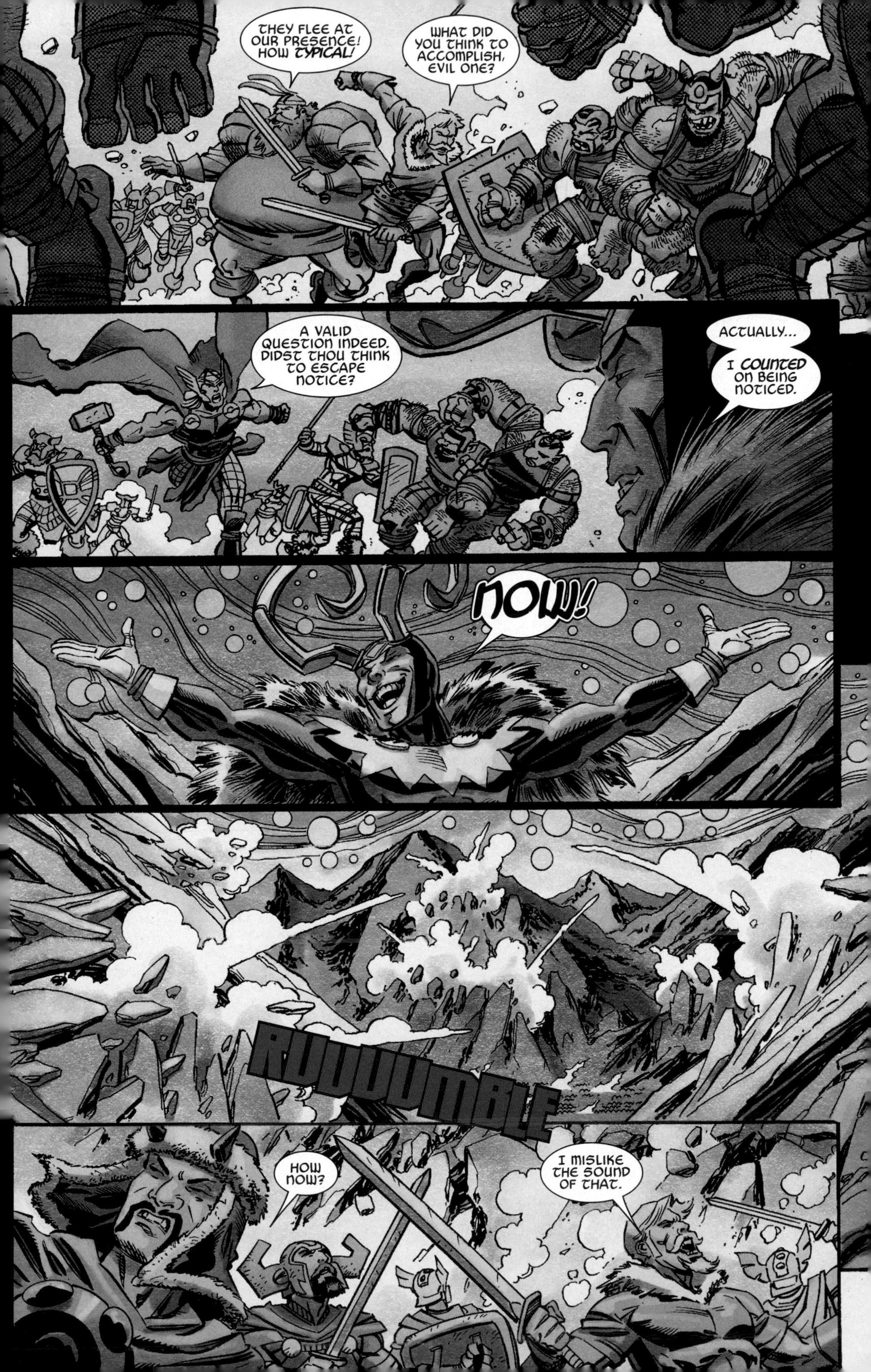
THEY FLEE AT OUR PRESENCE! HOW TYPICAL!
WHAT DID YOU THINK TO ACCOMPLISH, EVIL ONE?
A VALID QUESTION INDEED. DIDST THOU THINK TO ESCAPE NOTICE?
ACTUALLY...
I COUNTED ON BEING NOTICED.
NOW!
RUUUUMBLE
HOW NOW?
I MISLIKE THE SOUND OF THAT.

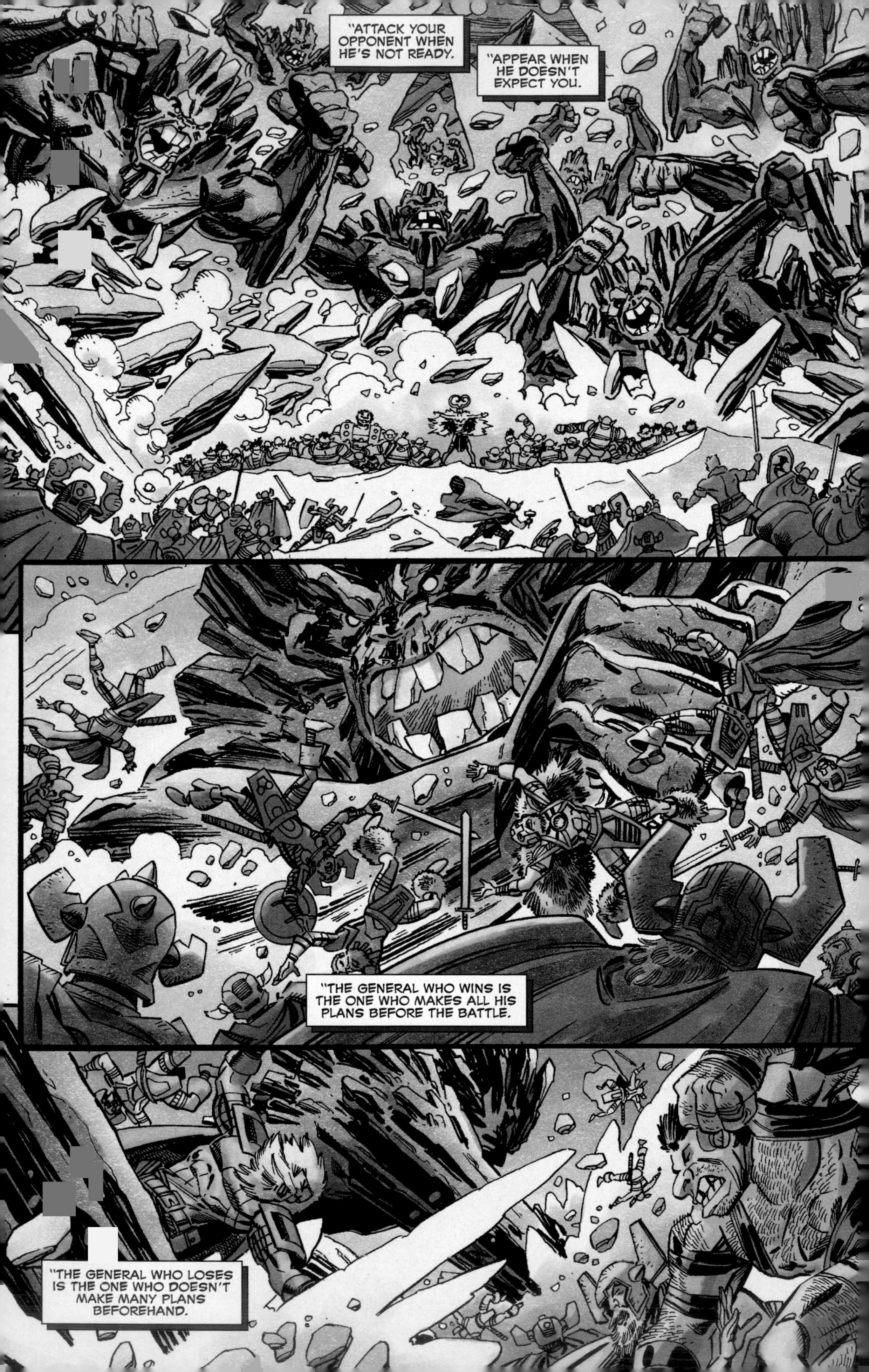
"ATTACK YOUR OPPONENT WHEN HE'S NOT READY.
"APPEAR WHEN HE DOESN'T EXPECT YOU.
"THE GENERAL WHO WINS IS THE ONE WHO MAKES ALL HIS PLANS BEFORE THE BATTLE.
"THE GENERAL WHO LOSES IS THE ONE WHO DOESN'T MAKE MANY PLANS BEFOREHAND.

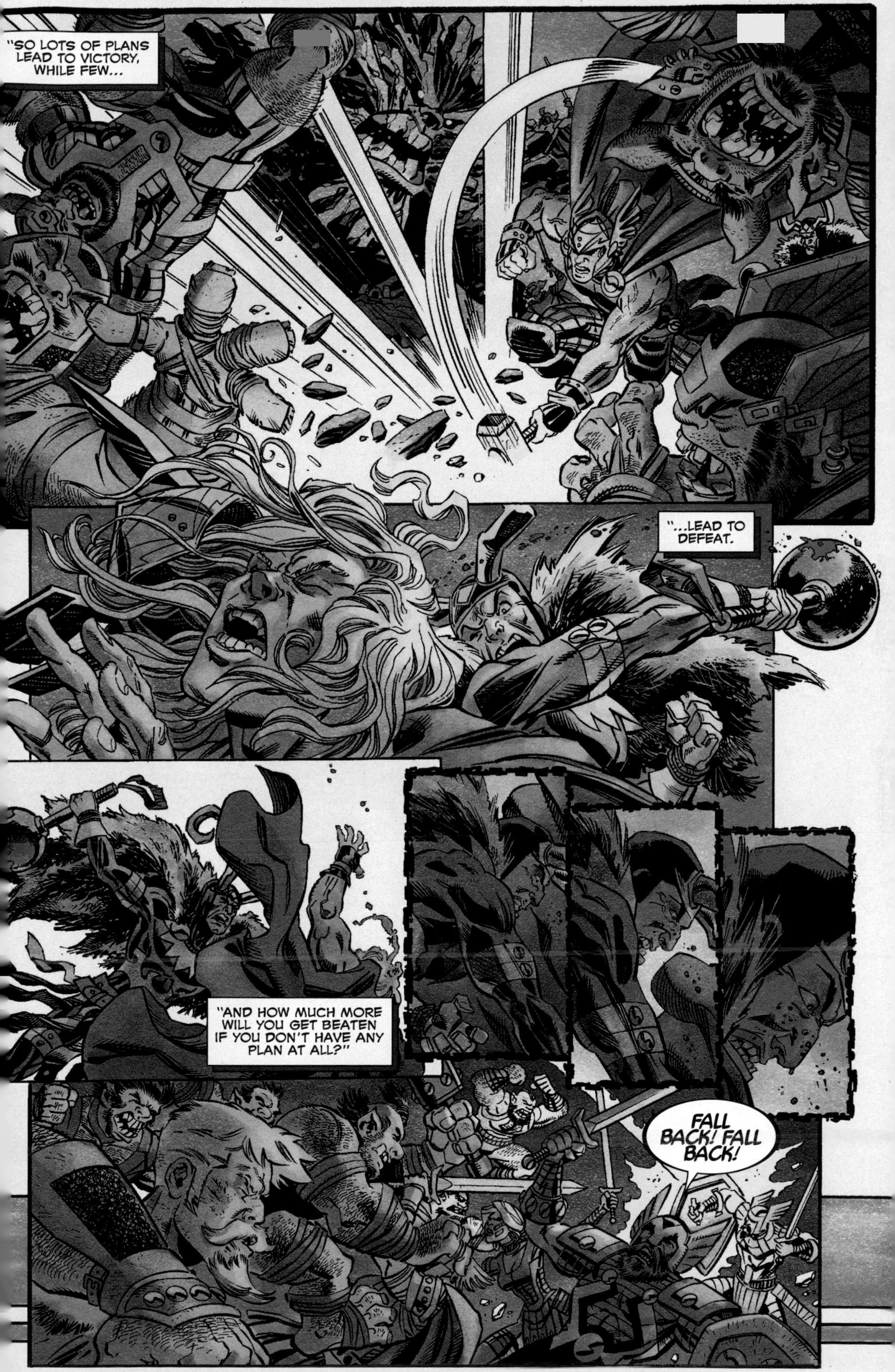
"SO LOTS OF PLANS LEAD TO VICTORY, WHILE FEW...
"...LEAD TO DEFEAT.
"AND HOW MUCH MORE WILL YOU GET BEATEN IF YOU DON'T HAVE ANY PLAN AT ALL?"
FALL BACK! FALL BACK!

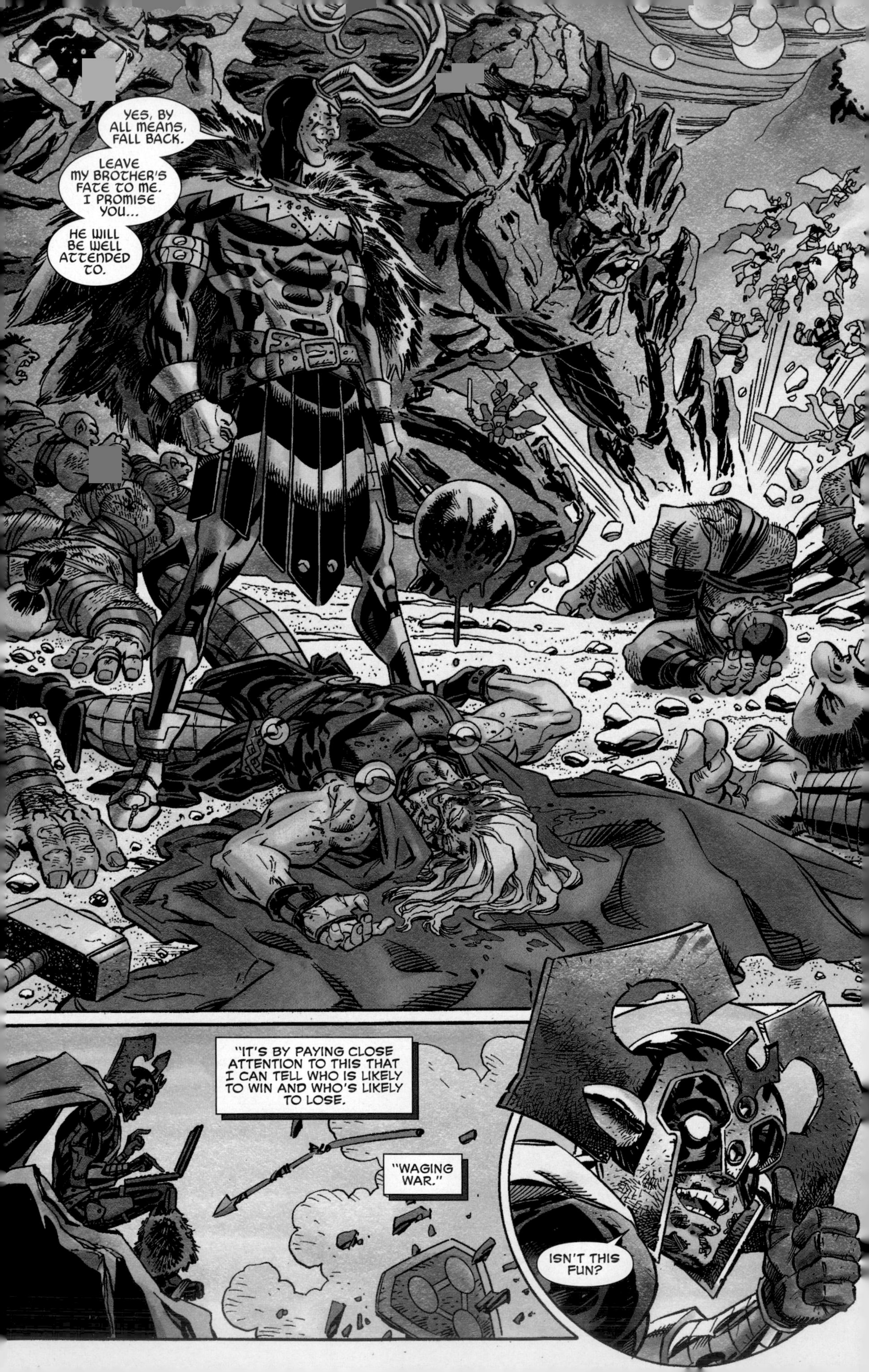
YES, BY ALL MEANS, FALL BACK.
LEAVE MY BROTHER'S FATE TO ME. I PROMISE YOU...
HE WILL BE WELL ATTENDED TO.
"IT'S BY PAYING CLOSE ATTENTION TO THIS THAT I CAN TELL WHO IS LIKELY TO WIN AND WHO'S LIKELY TO LOSE.
"WAGING WAR."
ISN'T THIS FUN?

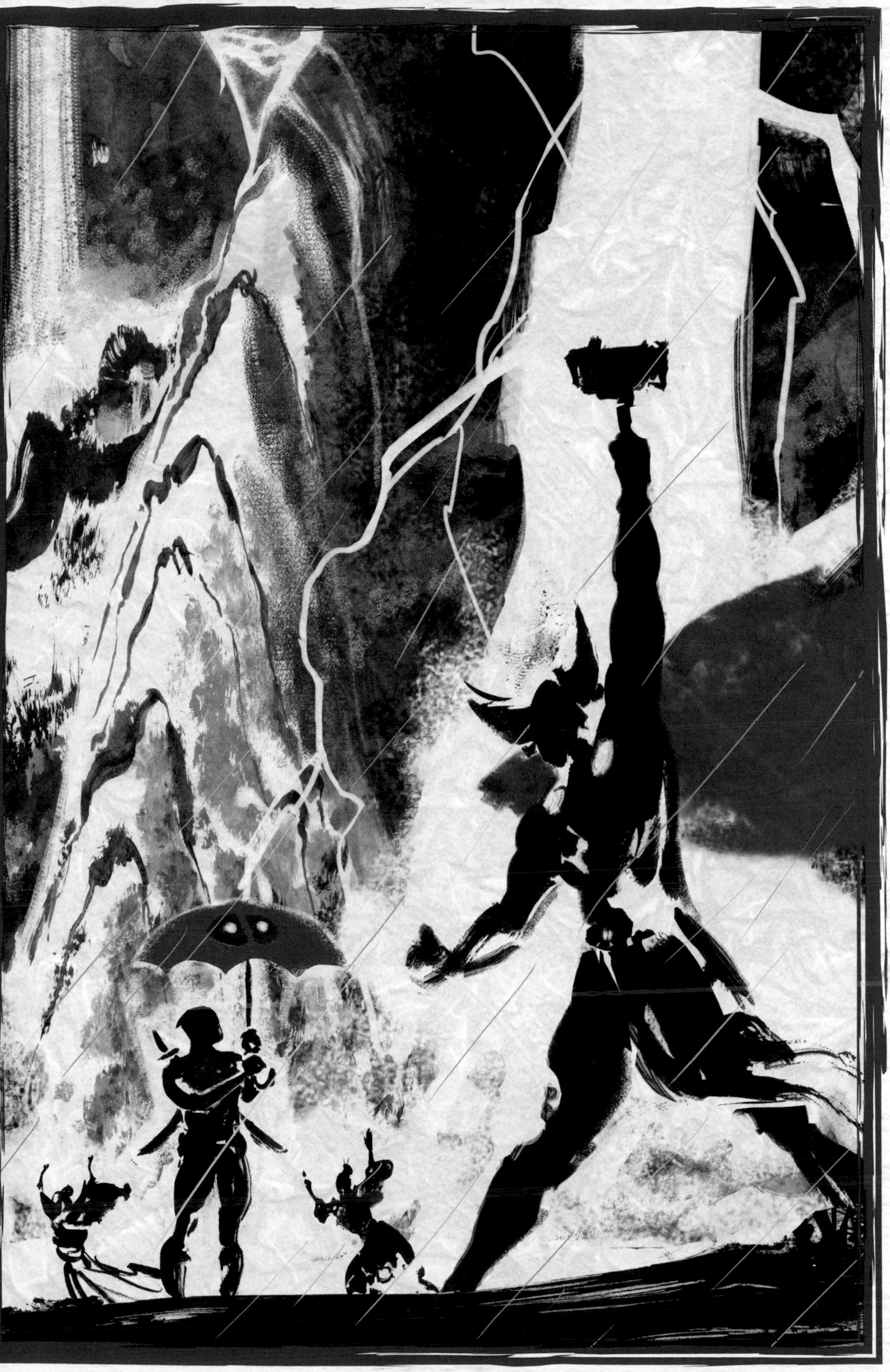

CHAPTER *TWO*

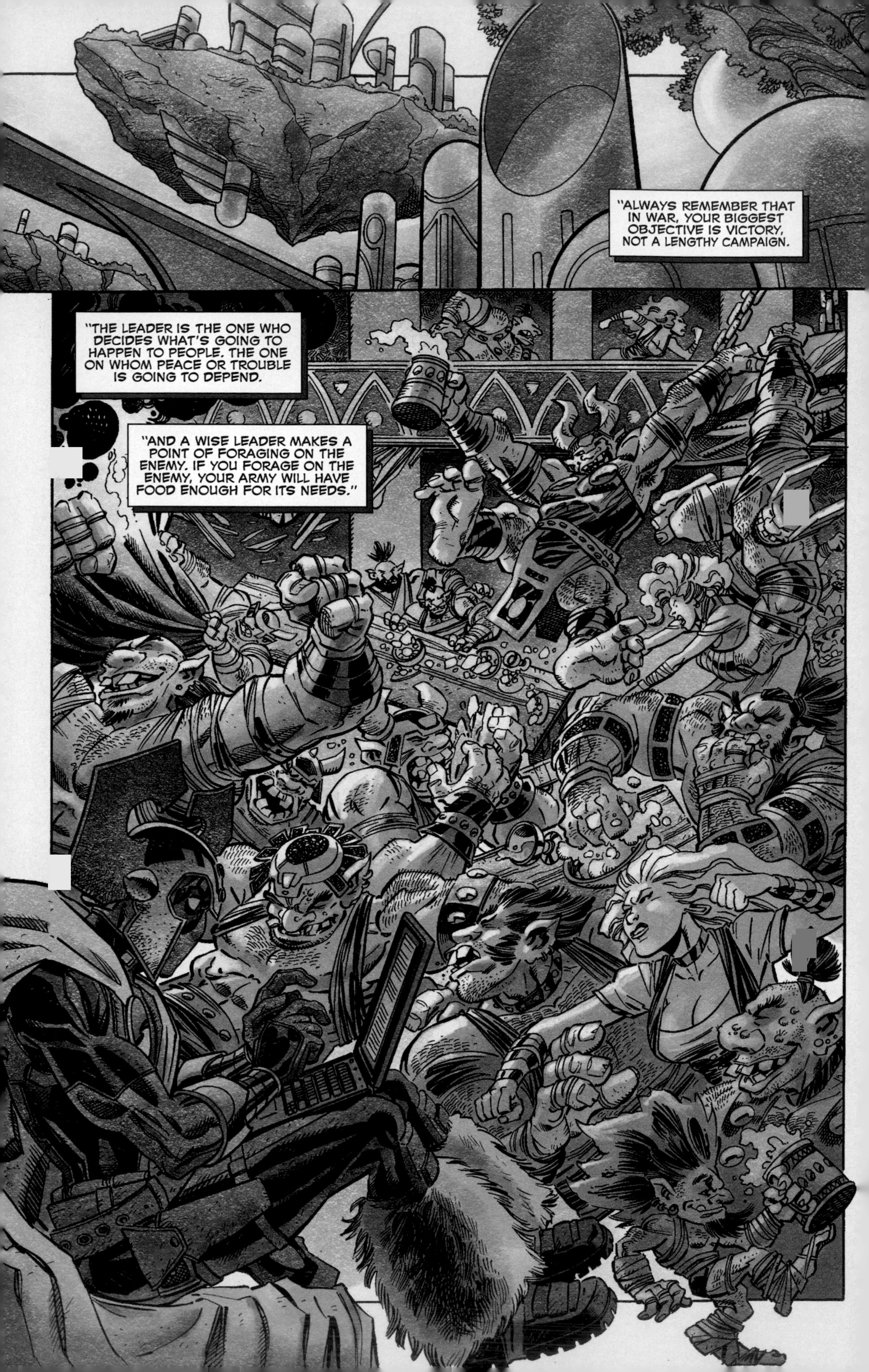
"ALWAYS REMEMBER THAT IN WAR, YOUR BIGGEST OBJECTIVE IS VICTORY, NOT A LENGTHY CAMPAIGN.
"THE LEADER IS THE ONE WHO DECIDES WHAT'S GOING TO HAPPEN TO PEOPLE. THE ONE ON WHOM PEACE OR TROUBLE IS GOING TO DEPEND.
"AND A WISE LEADER MAKES A POINT OF FORAGING ON THE ENEMY. IF YOU FORAGE ON THE ENEMY, YOUR ARMY WILL HAVE FOOD ENOUGH FOR ITS NEEDS."

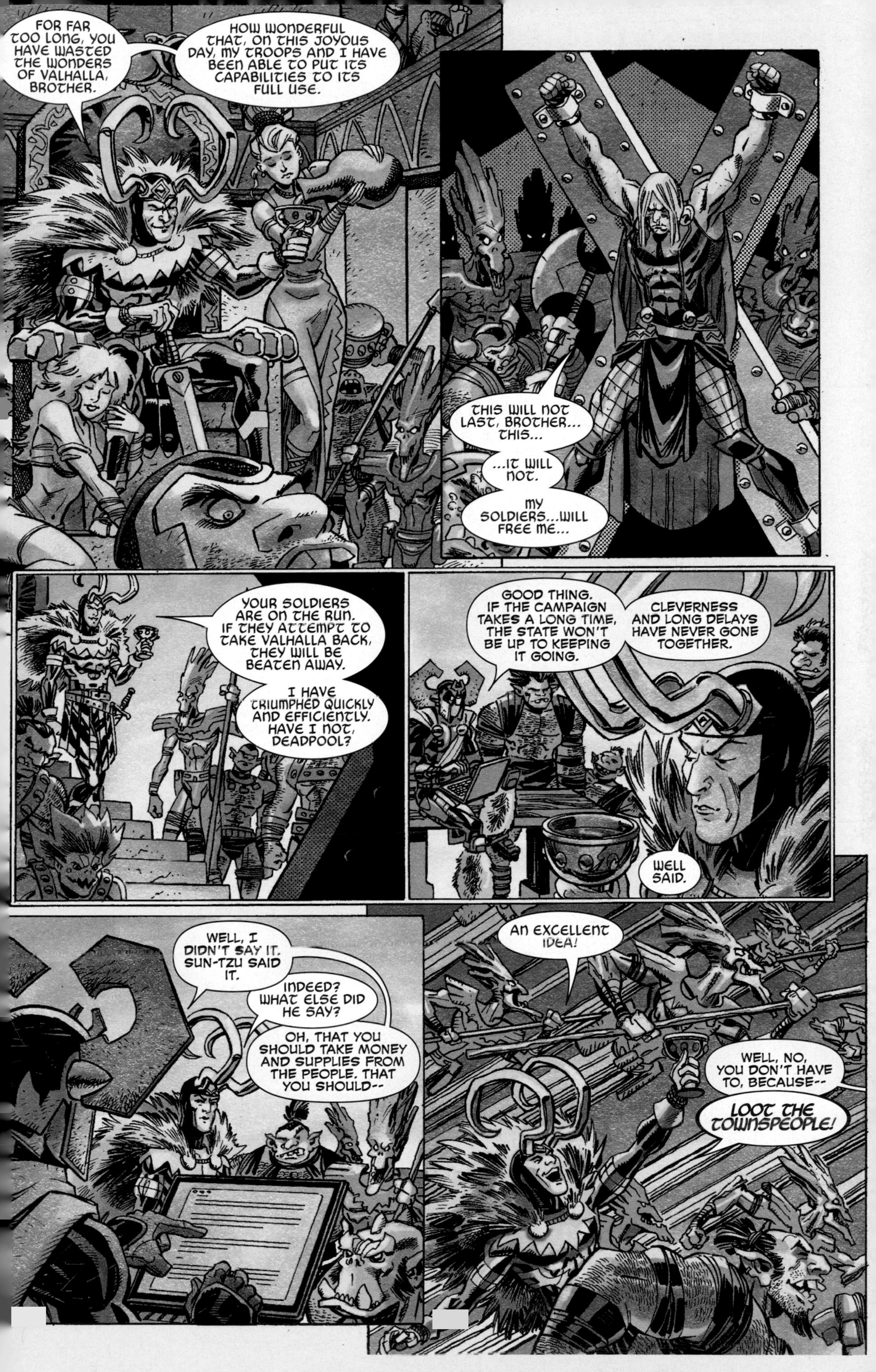
FOR FAR TOO LONG, YOU HAVE WASTED THE WONDERS OF VALHALLA, BROTHER.
HOW WONDERFUL THAT, ON THIS JOYOUS DAY, MY TROOPS AND I HAVE BEEN ABLE TO PUT ITS CAPABILITIES TO ITS FULL USE.
THIS WILL NOT LAST, BROTHER... THIS...
...IT WILL NOT.
MY SOLDIERS...WILL FREE ME...
YOUR SOLDIERS ARE ON THE RUN. IF THEY ATTEMPT TO TAKE VALHALLA BACK, THEY WILL BE BEATEN AWAY.
I HAVE TRIUMPHED QUICKLY AND EFFICIENTLY. HAVE I NOT, DEADPOOL?
GOOD THING. IF THE CAMPAIGN TAKES A LONG TIME, THE STATE WON'T BE UP TO KEEPING IT GOING.
CLEVERNESS AND LONG DELAYS HAVE NEVER GONE TOGETHER.
WELL SAID.
WELL, I DIDN'T SAY IT. SUN-TZU SAID IT.
INDEED? WHAT ELSE DID HE SAY?
OH, THAT YOU SHOULD TAKE MONEY AND SUPPLIES FROM THE PEOPLE. THAT YOU SHOULD--
AN EXCELLENT IDEA!
WELL, NO, YOU DON'T HAVE TO, BECAUSE--
LOOT THE TOWNSPEOPLE!

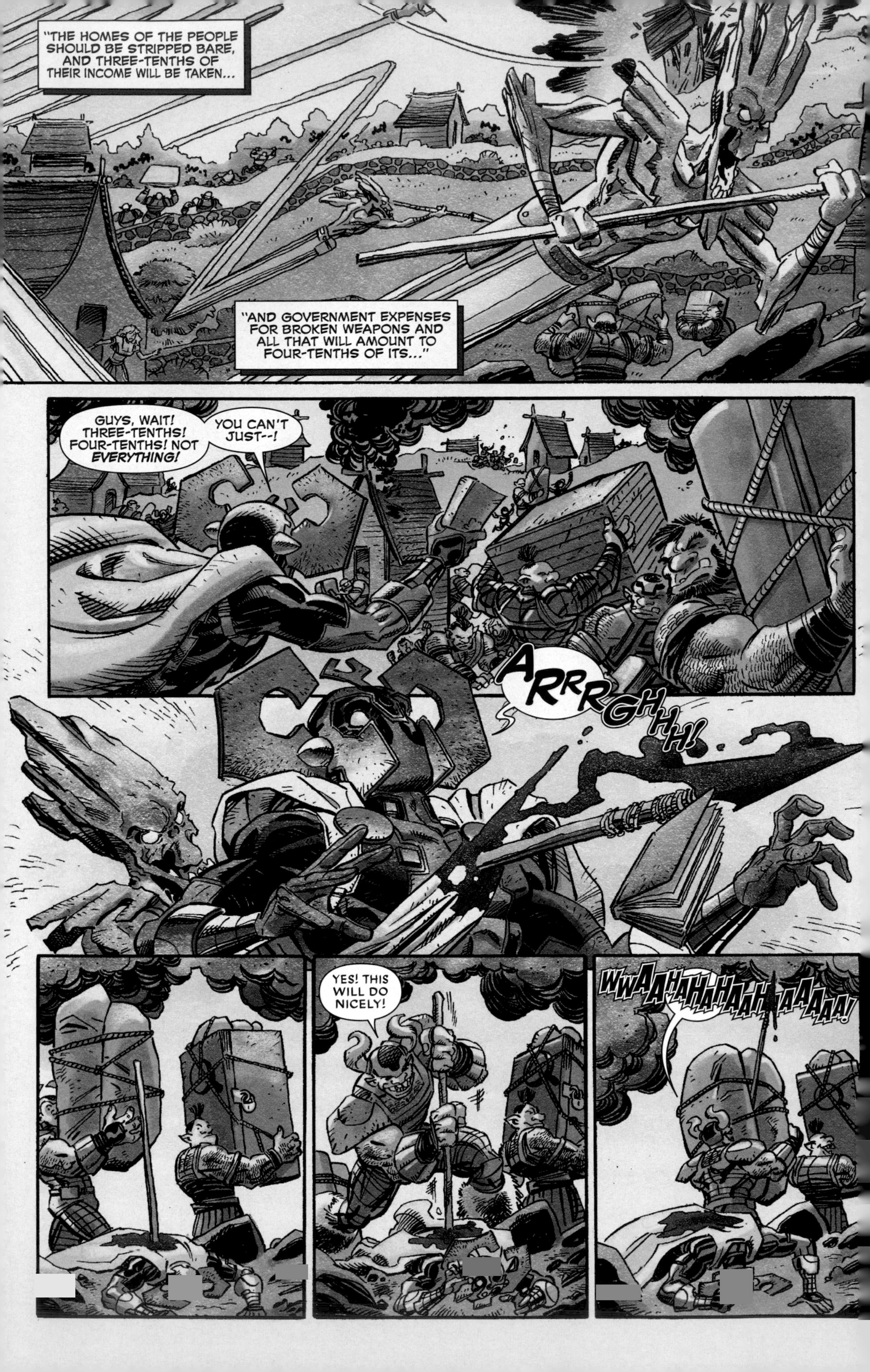

"THE HOMES OF THE PEOPLE SHOULD BE STRIPPED BARE, AND THREE-TENTHS OF THEIR INCOME WILL BE TAKEN...
"AND GOVERNMENT EXPENSES FOR BROKEN WEAPONS AND ALL THAT WILL AMOUNT TO FOUR-TENTHS OF ITS..."
GUYS, WAIT! THREE-TENTHS! FOUR-TENTHS! NOT EVERYTHING!
YOU CAN'T JUST--!
ARRRGHHH!
YES! THIS WILL DO NICELY!
WWAAHAHAHAAHAAAAA!

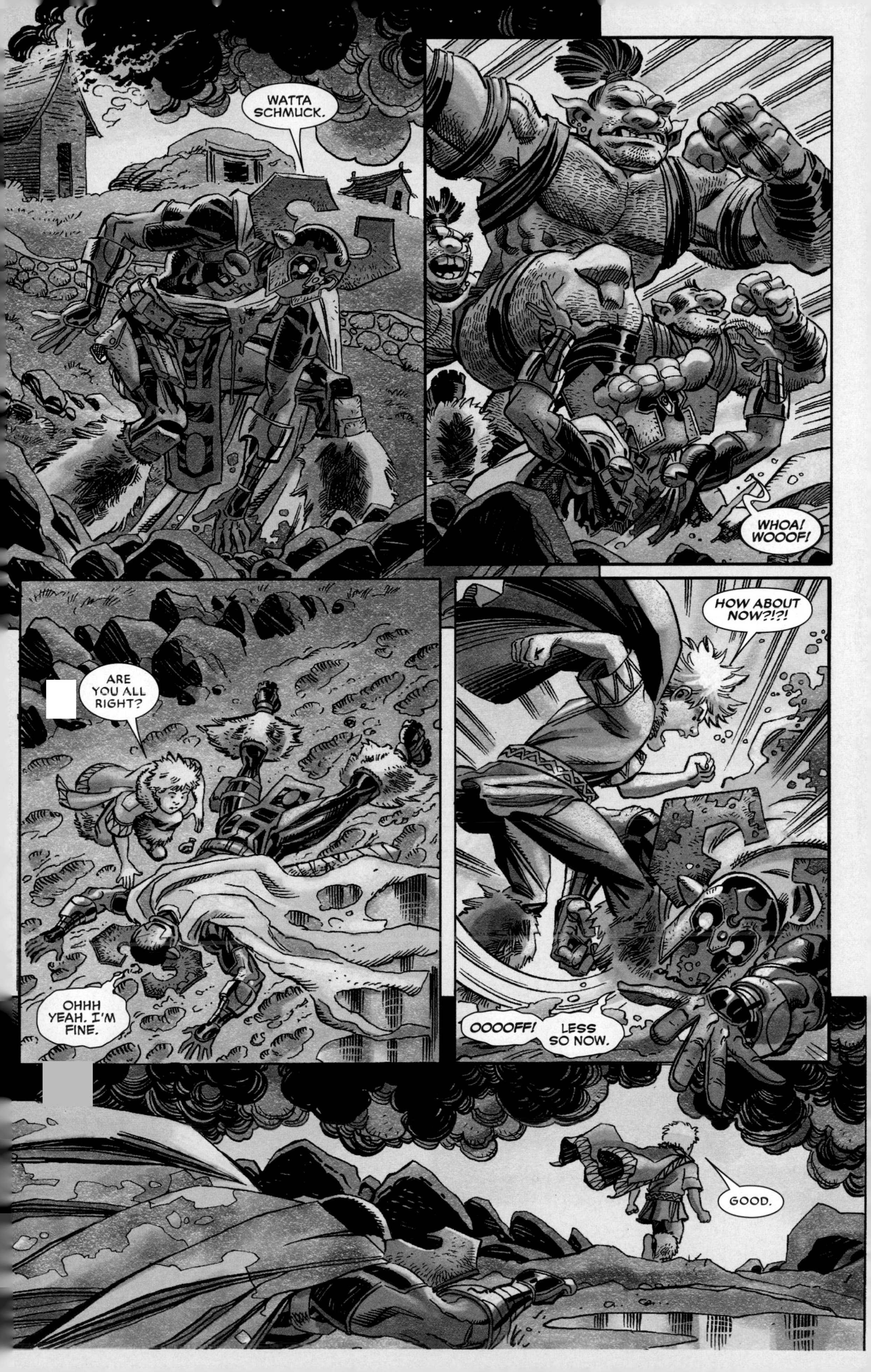
WATTA SCHMUCK.
WHOA! WOOOF!
ARE YOU ALL RIGHT?
OHHH YEAH. I'M FINE.
HOW ABOUT NOW?!?!
OOOOFF!
LESS SO NOW.
GOOD.

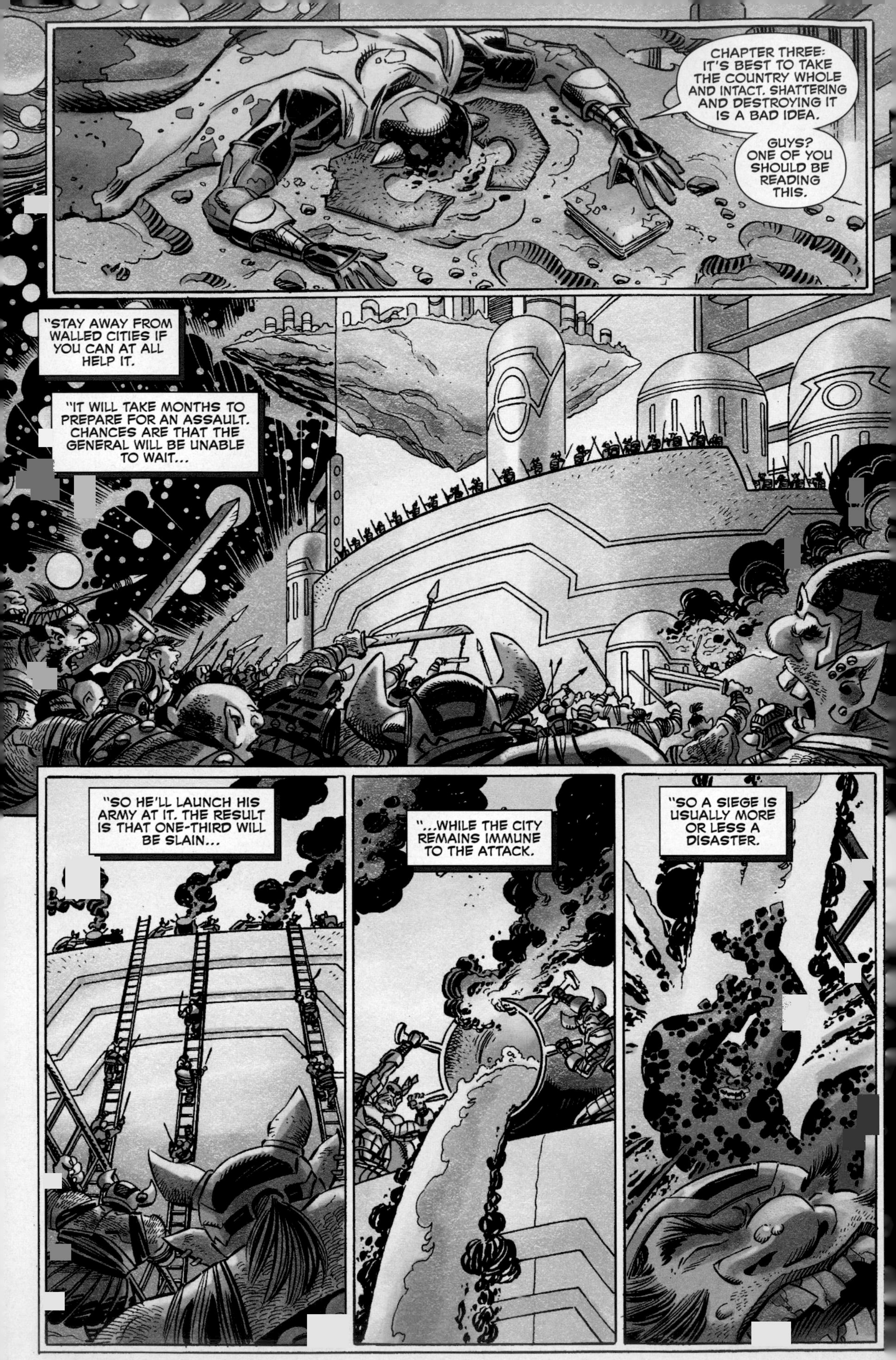
CHAPTER THREE: IT'S BEST TO TAKE THE COUNTRY WHOLE AND INTACT. SHATTERING AND DESTROYING IT IS A BAD IDEA.
GUYS? ONE OF YOU SHOULD BE READING THIS.
"STAY AWAY FROM WALLED CITIES IF YOU CAN AT ALL HELP IT.
"IT WILL TAKE MONTHS TO PREPARE FOR AN ASSAULT. CHANCES ARE THAT THE GENERAL WILL BE UNABLE TO WAIT...
"SO HE'LL LAUNCH HIS ARMY AT IT. THE RESULT IS THAT ONE-THIRD WILL BE SLAIN...
"...WHILE THE CITY REMAINS IMMUNE TO THE ATTACK.
"SO A SIEGE IS USUALLY MORE OR LESS A DISASTER.

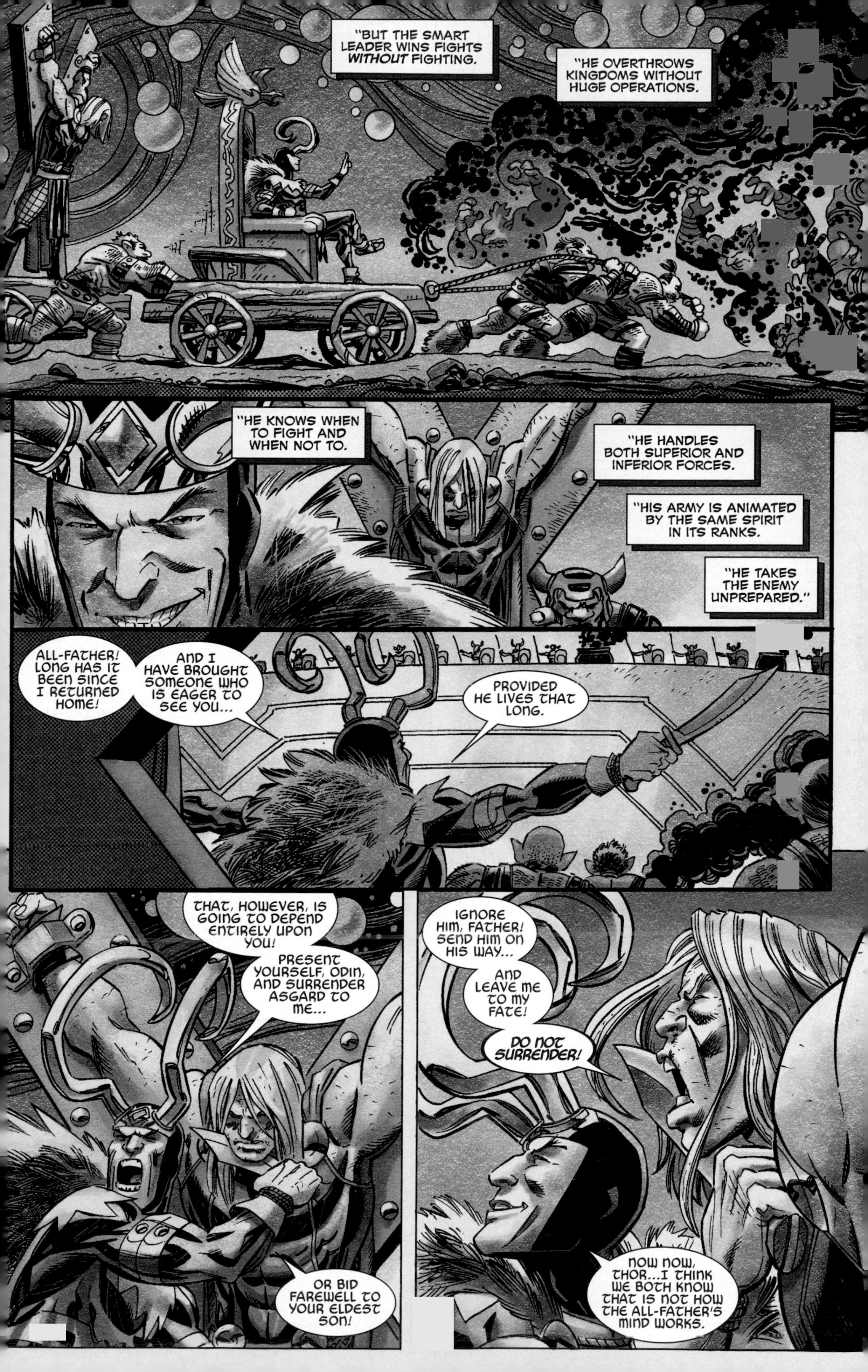
"BUT THE SMART LEADER WINS FIGHTS WITHOUT FIGHTING.
"HE OVERTHROWS KINGDOMS WITHOUT HUGE OPERATIONS.
"HE KNOWS WHEN TO FIGHT AND WHEN NOT TO.
"HE HANDLES BOTH SUPERIOR AND INFERIOR FORCES.
"HIS ARMY IS ANIMATED BY THE SAME SPIRIT IN ITS RANKS.
"HE TAKES THE ENEMY UNPREPARED."
ALL-FATHER! LONG HAS IT BEEN SINCE I RETURNED HOME!
AND I HAVE BROUGHT SOMEONE WHO IS EAGER TO SEE YOU...
PROVIDED HE LIVES THAT LONG.
THAT, HOWEVER, IS GOING TO DEPEND ENTIRELY UPON YOU!
PRESENT YOURSELF, ODIN, AND SURRENDER ASGARD TO ME...
OR BID FAREWELL TO YOUR ELDEST SON!
IGNORE HIM, FATHER! SEND HIM ON HIS WAY...
AND LEAVE ME TO MY FATE!
DO NOT SURRENDER!
NOW NOW, THOR...I THINK WE BOTH KNOW THAT IS NOT HOW THE ALL-FATHER'S MIND WORKS.

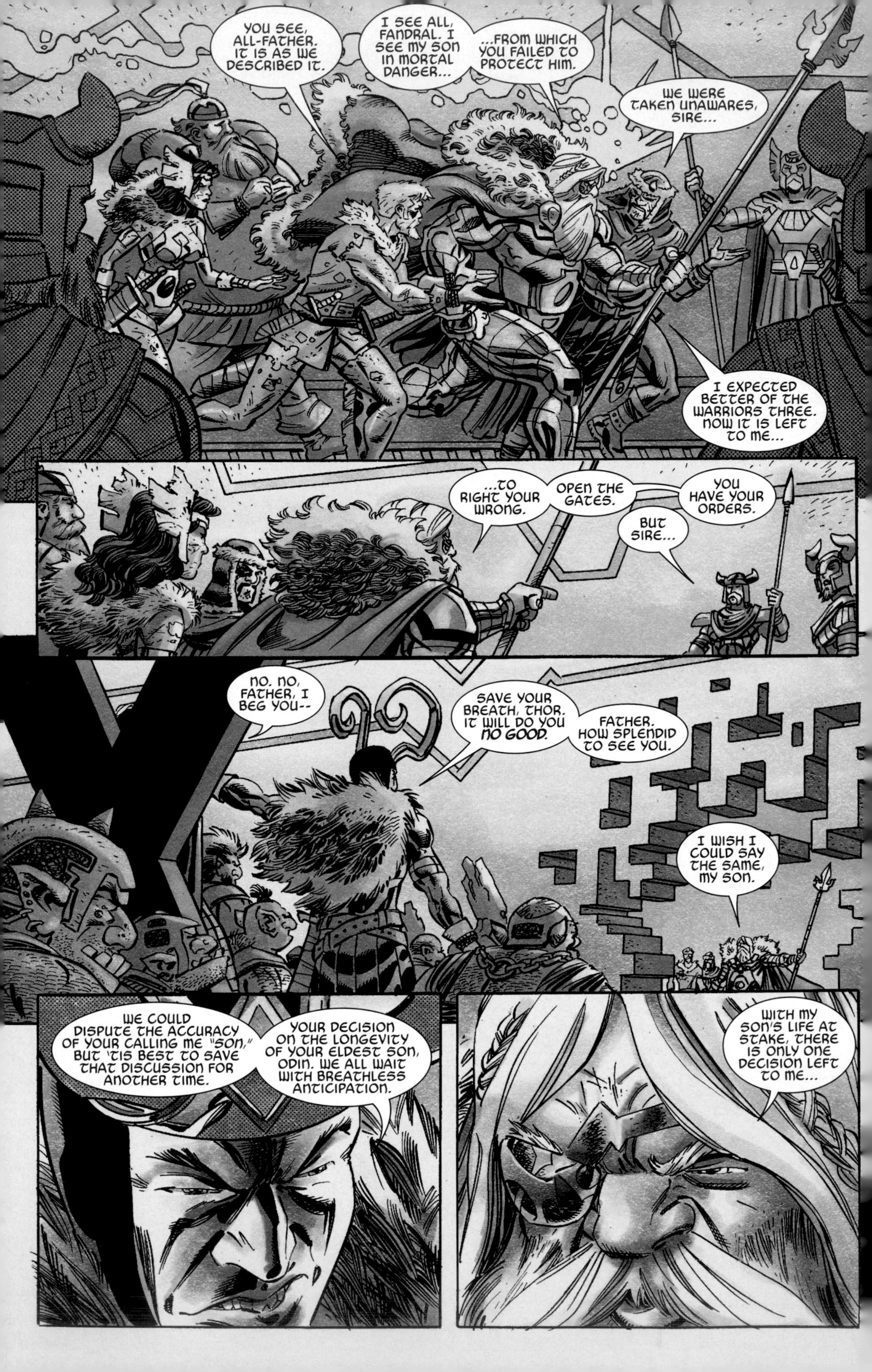

YOU SEE, ALL-FATHER. IT IS AS WE DESCRIBED IT.
I SEE ALL, FANDRAL. I SEE MY SON IN MORTAL DANGER...
...FROM WHICH YOU FAILED TO PROTECT HIM.
WE WERE TAKEN UNAWARES, SIRE...
I EXPECTED BETTER OF THE WARRIORS THREE. NOW IT IS LEFT TO ME...
...TO RIGHT YOUR WRONG.
OPEN THE GATES.
YOU HAVE YOUR ORDERS.
BUT SIRE...
NO. NO, FATHER, I BEG YOU--
SAVE YOUR BREATH, THOR. IT WILL DO YOU **NO GOOD.**
FATHER. HOW SPLENDID TO SEE YOU.
I WISH I COULD SAY THE SAME, MY SON.
WE COULD DISPUTE THE ACCURACY OF YOUR CALLING ME "SON," BUT 'TIS BEST TO SAVE THAT DISCUSSION FOR ANOTHER TIME.
YOUR DECISION ON THE LONGEVITY OF YOUR ELDEST SON, ODIN. WE ALL WAIT WITH BREATHLESS ANTICIPATION.
WITH MY SON'S LIFE AT STAKE, THERE IS ONLY ONE DECISION LEFT TO ME...

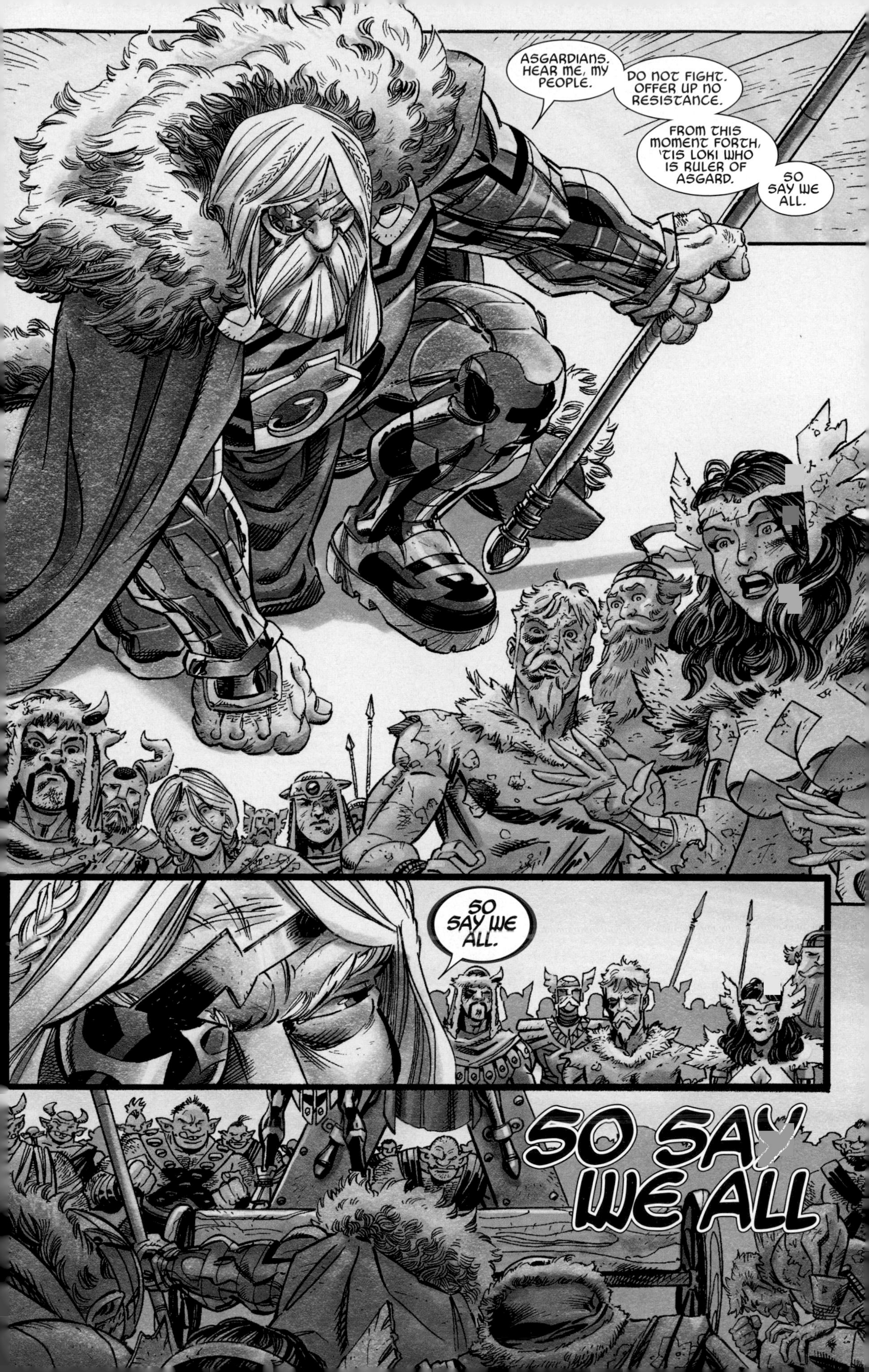
ASGARDIANS. HEAR ME, MY PEOPLE.
DO NOT FIGHT. OFFER UP NO RESISTANCE.
FROM THIS MOMENT FORTH, 'TIS LOKI WHO IS RULER OF ASGARD.
SO SAY WE ALL.
SO SAY WE ALL.
SO SAY WE ALL

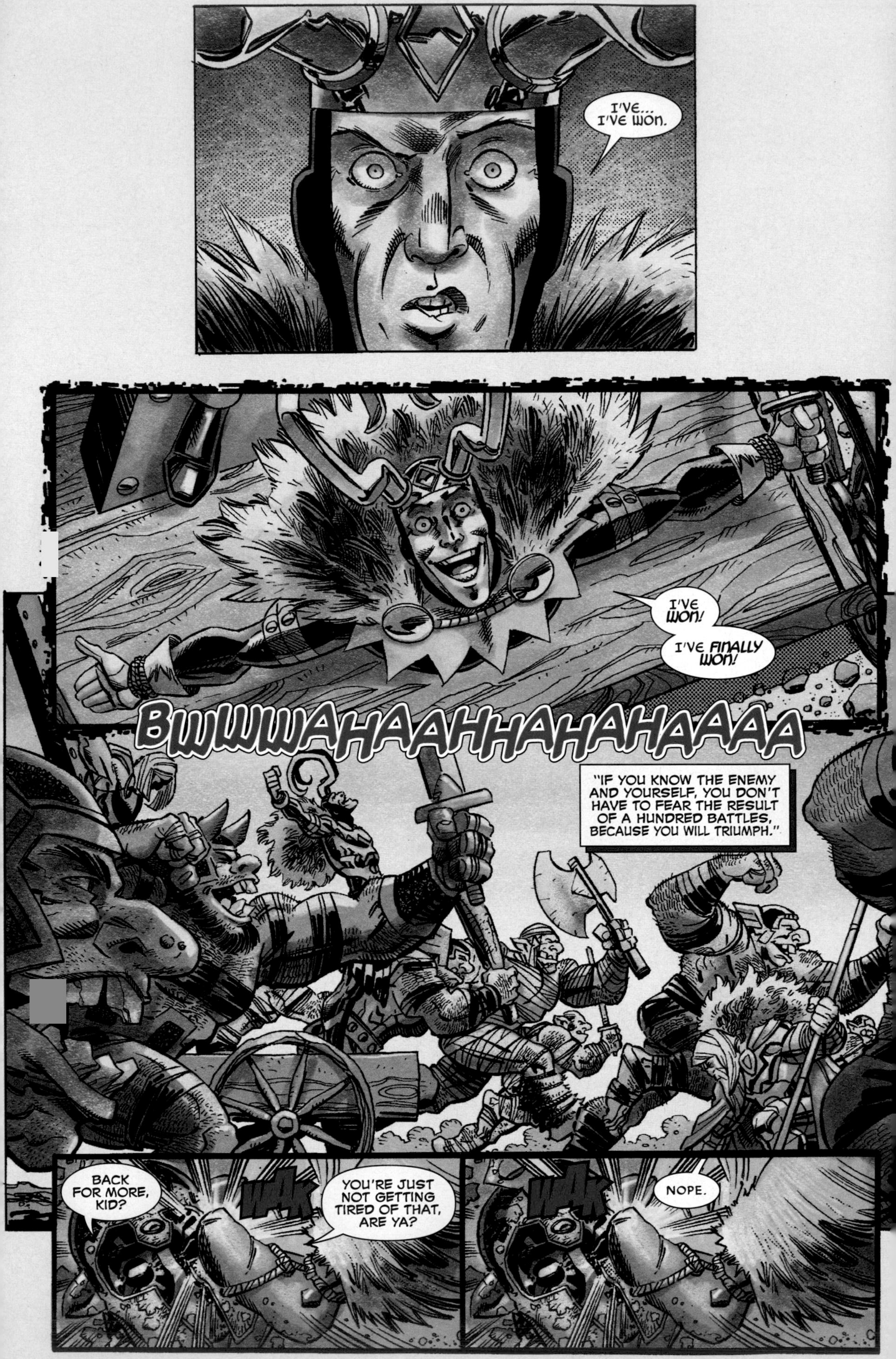
I'VE... I'VE WON.
I'VE WON!
I'VE FINALLY WON!
BWWWAHAAHHAHAHAAAA
"IF YOU KNOW THE ENEMY AND YOURSELF, YOU DON'T HAVE TO FEAR THE RESULT OF A HUNDRED BATTLES, BECAUSE YOU WILL TRIUMPH."
BACK FOR MORE, KID?
WAK
YOU'RE JUST NOT GETTING TIRED OF THAT, ARE YA?
WAK
NOPE.

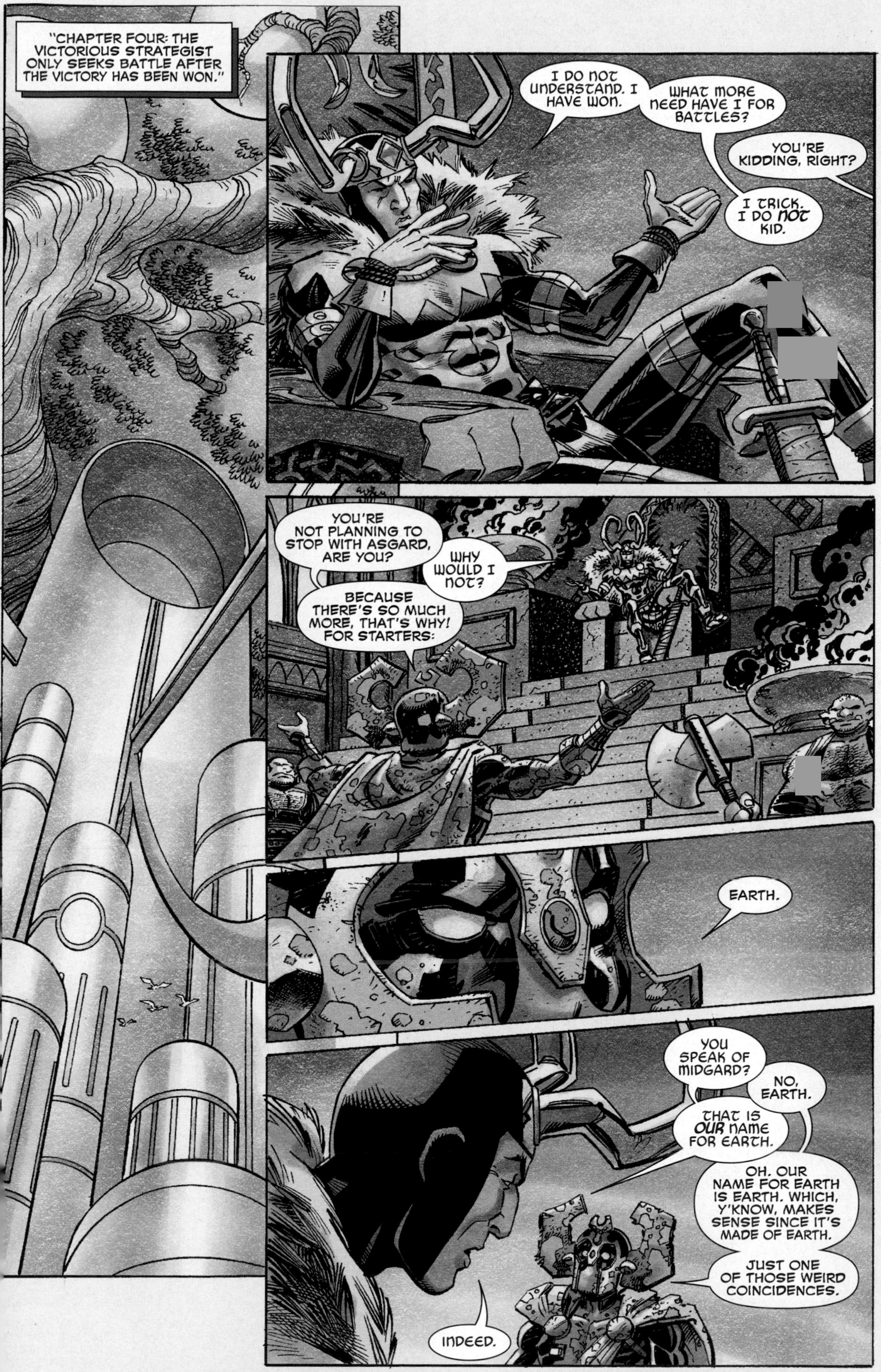
"CHAPTER FOUR: THE VICTORIOUS STRATEGIST ONLY SEEKS BATTLE AFTER THE VICTORY HAS BEEN WON."
I DO NOT UNDERSTAND. I HAVE WON.
WHAT MORE NEED HAVE I FOR BATTLES?
YOU'RE KIDDING, RIGHT?
I TRICK. I DO NOT KID.
YOU'RE NOT PLANNING TO STOP WITH ASGARD, ARE YOU?
WHY WOULD I NOT?
BECAUSE THERE'S SO MUCH MORE, THAT'S WHY! FOR STARTERS:
EARTH.
YOU SPEAK OF MIDGARD?
NO, EARTH.
THAT IS OUR NAME FOR EARTH.
OH. OUR NAME FOR EARTH IS EARTH. WHICH, Y'KNOW, MAKES SENSE SINCE IT'S MADE OF EARTH.
JUST ONE OF THOSE WEIRD COINCIDENCES.
INDEED.

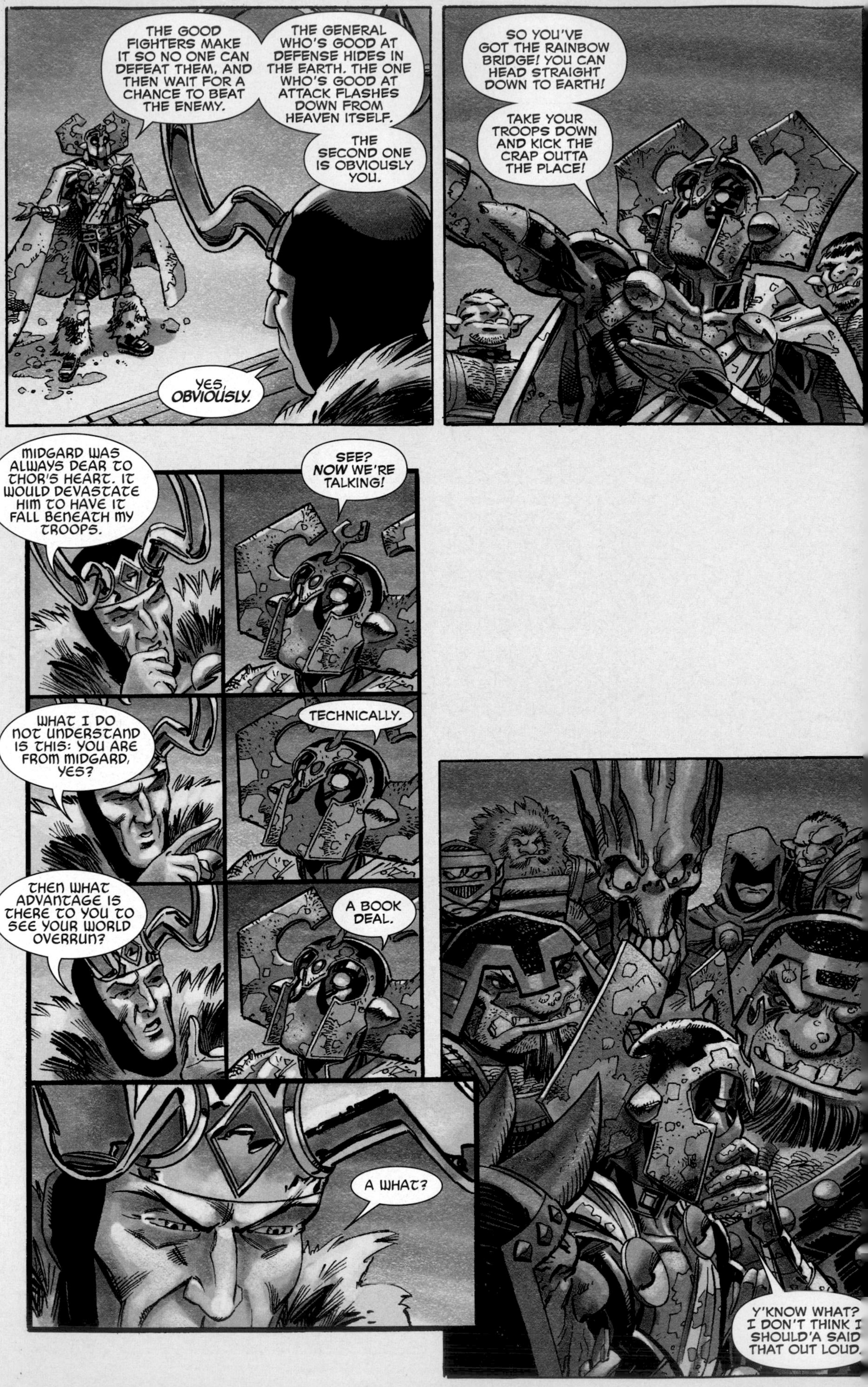
THE GOOD FIGHTERS MAKE IT SO NO ONE CAN DEFEAT THEM, AND THEN WAIT FOR A CHANCE TO BEAT THE ENEMY.
THE GENERAL WHO'S GOOD AT DEFENSE HIDES IN THE EARTH. THE ONE WHO'S GOOD AT ATTACK FLASHES DOWN FROM HEAVEN ITSELF.
THE SECOND ONE IS OBVIOUSLY YOU.
YES, OBVIOUSLY.
SO YOU'VE GOT THE RAINBOW BRIDGE! YOU CAN HEAD STRAIGHT DOWN TO EARTH!
TAKE YOUR TROOPS DOWN AND KICK THE CRAP OUTTA THE PLACE!
MIDGARD WAS ALWAYS DEAR TO THOR'S HEART. IT WOULD DEVASTATE HIM TO HAVE IT FALL BENEATH MY TROOPS.
SEE? NOW WE'RE TALKING!
WHAT I DO NOT UNDERSTAND IS THIS: YOU ARE FROM MIDGARD, YES?
TECHNICALLY.
THEN WHAT ADVANTAGE IS THERE TO YOU TO SEE YOUR WORLD OVERRUN?
A BOOK DEAL.
A WHAT?
Y'KNOW WHAT? I DON'T THINK I SHOULD'A SAID THAT OUT LOUD.

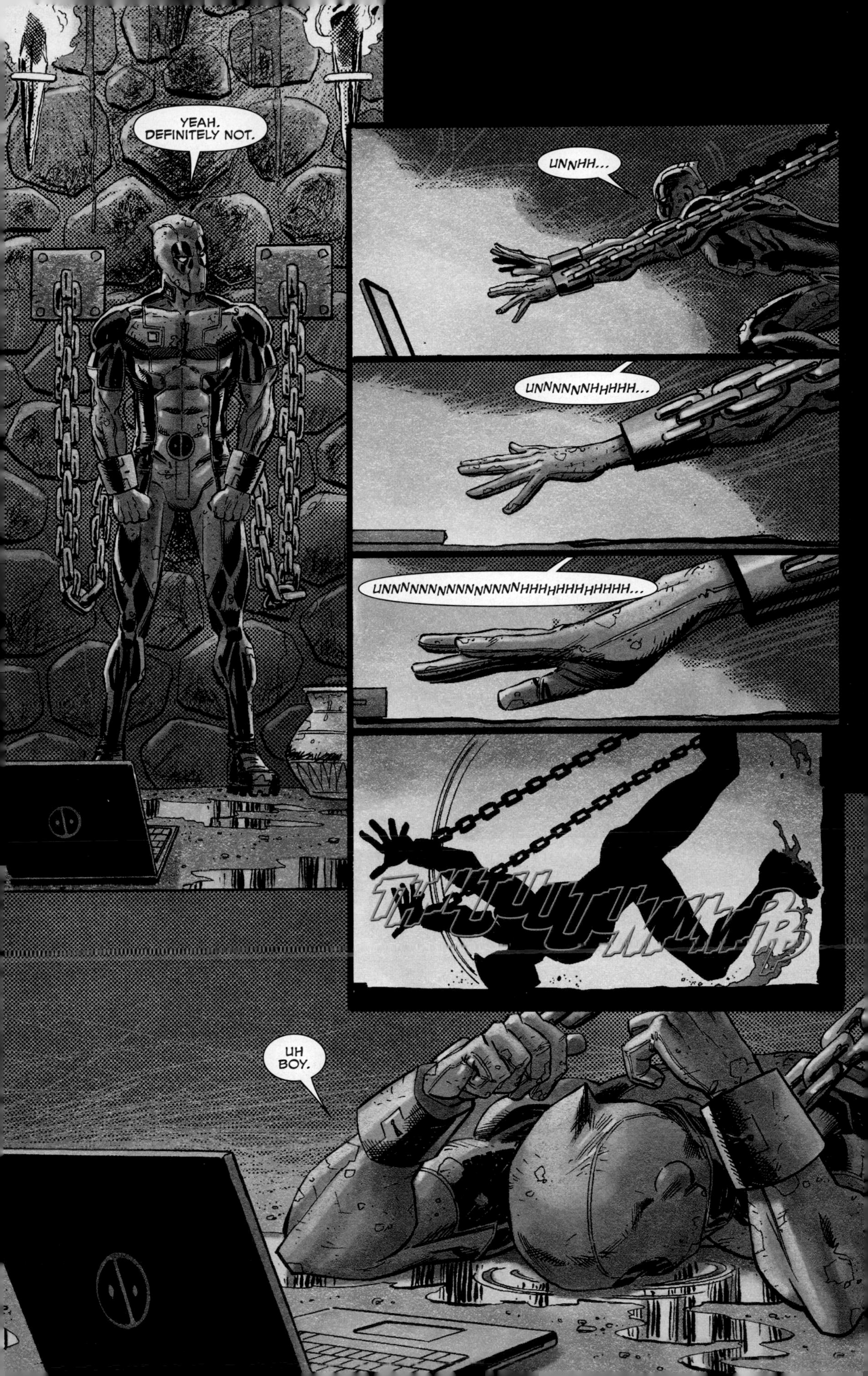
YEAH. DEFINITELY NOT.
UNNHH...
UNNNNNNHHHHH...
UNNNNNNNNNNNNNNNHHHHHHHHHHHH...
THKUUUMMB
UH BOY.

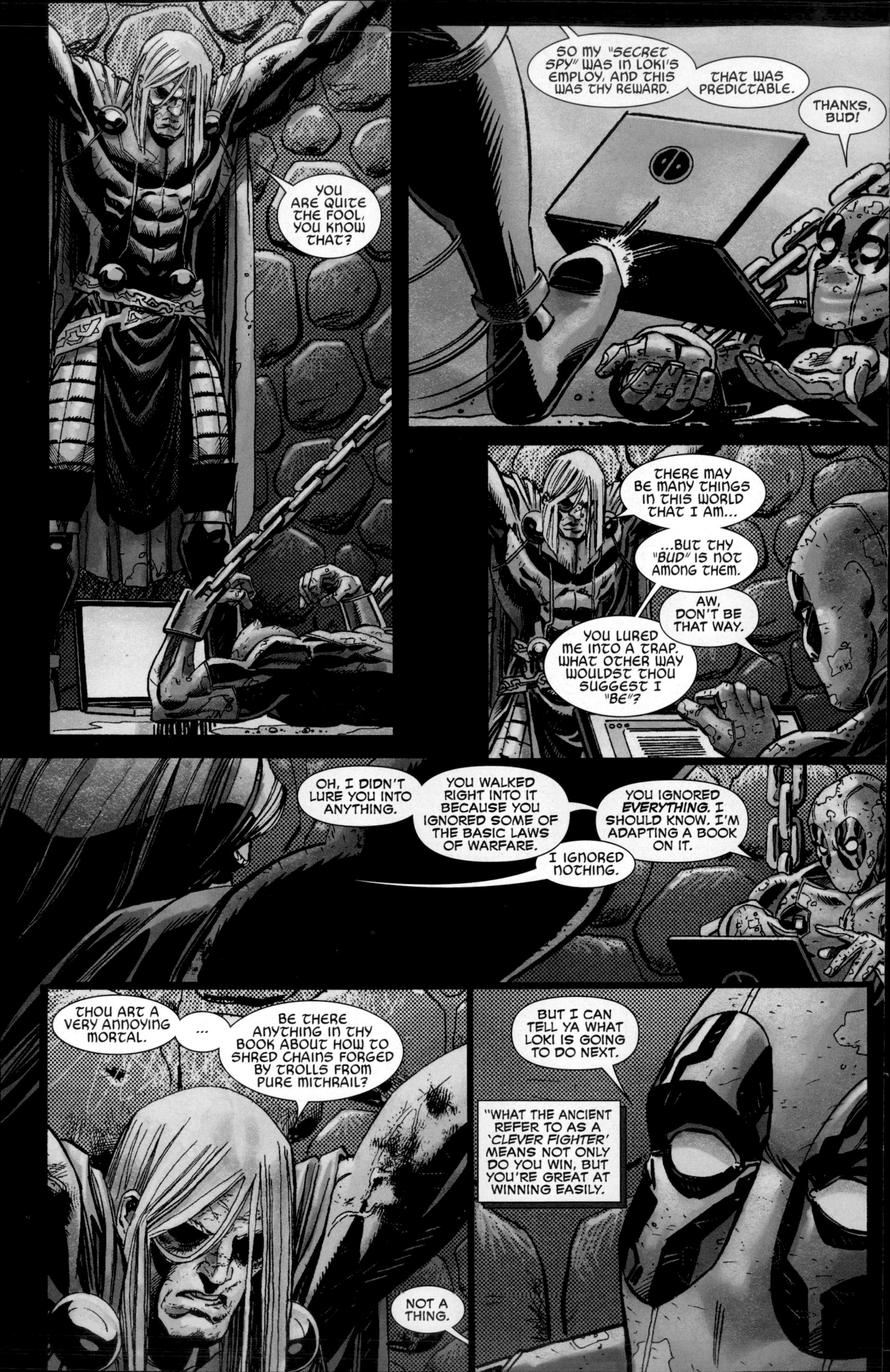
YOU ARE QUITE THE FOOL, YOU KNOW THAT?
SO MY "SECRET SPY" WAS IN LOKI'S EMPLOY, AND THIS WAS THY REWARD.
THAT WAS PREDICTABLE.
THANKS, BUD!
THERE MAY BE MANY THINGS IN THIS WORLD THAT I AM...
...BUT THY "BUD" IS NOT AMONG THEM.
AW, DON'T BE THAT WAY.
YOU LURED ME INTO A TRAP. WHAT OTHER WAY WOULDST THOU SUGGEST I "BE"?
OH, I DIDN'T LURE YOU INTO ANYTHING.
YOU WALKED RIGHT INTO IT BECAUSE YOU IGNORED SOME OF THE BASIC LAWS OF WARFARE.
I IGNORED NOTHING.
YOU IGNORED EVERYTHING. I SHOULD KNOW. I'M ADAPTING A BOOK ON IT.
THOU ART A VERY ANNOYING MORTAL.
...
BE THERE ANYTHING IN THY BOOK ABOUT HOW TO SHRED CHAINS FORGED BY TROLLS FROM PURE MITHRAIL?
NOT A THING.
BUT I CAN TELL YA WHAT LOKI IS GOING TO DO NEXT.
"WHAT THE ANCIENT REFER TO AS A 'CLEVER FIGHTER' MEANS NOT ONLY DO YOU WIN, BUT YOU'RE GREAT AT WINNING EASILY.

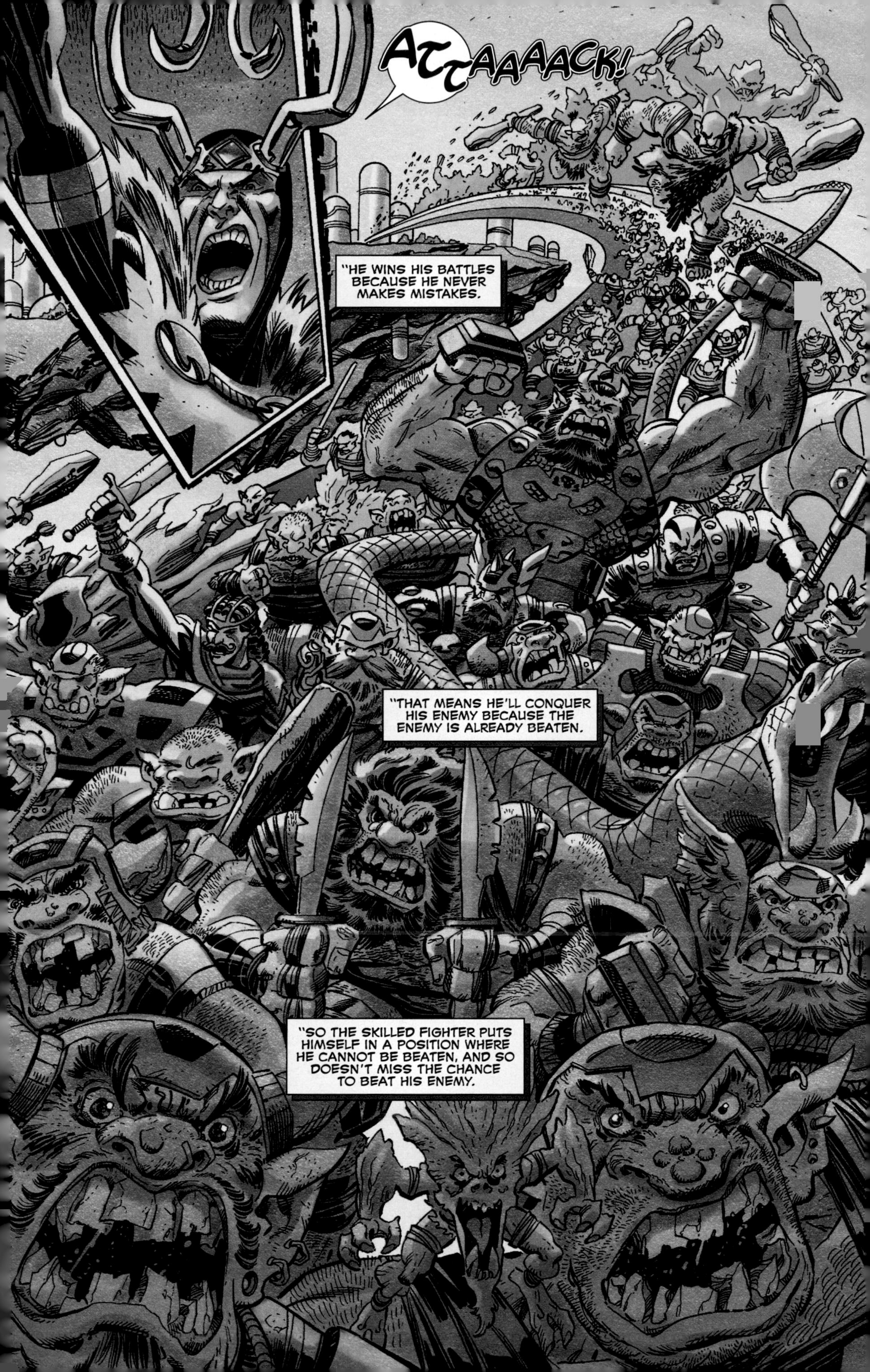
ATTAAAAACK!
"HE WINS HIS BATTLES BECAUSE HE NEVER MAKES MISTAKES.
"THAT MEANS HE'LL CONQUER HIS ENEMY BECAUSE THE ENEMY IS ALREADY BEATEN.
"SO THE SKILLED FIGHTER PUTS HIMSELF IN A POSITION WHERE HE CANNOT BE BEATEN, AND SO DOESN'T MISS THE CHANCE TO BEAT HIS ENEMY.

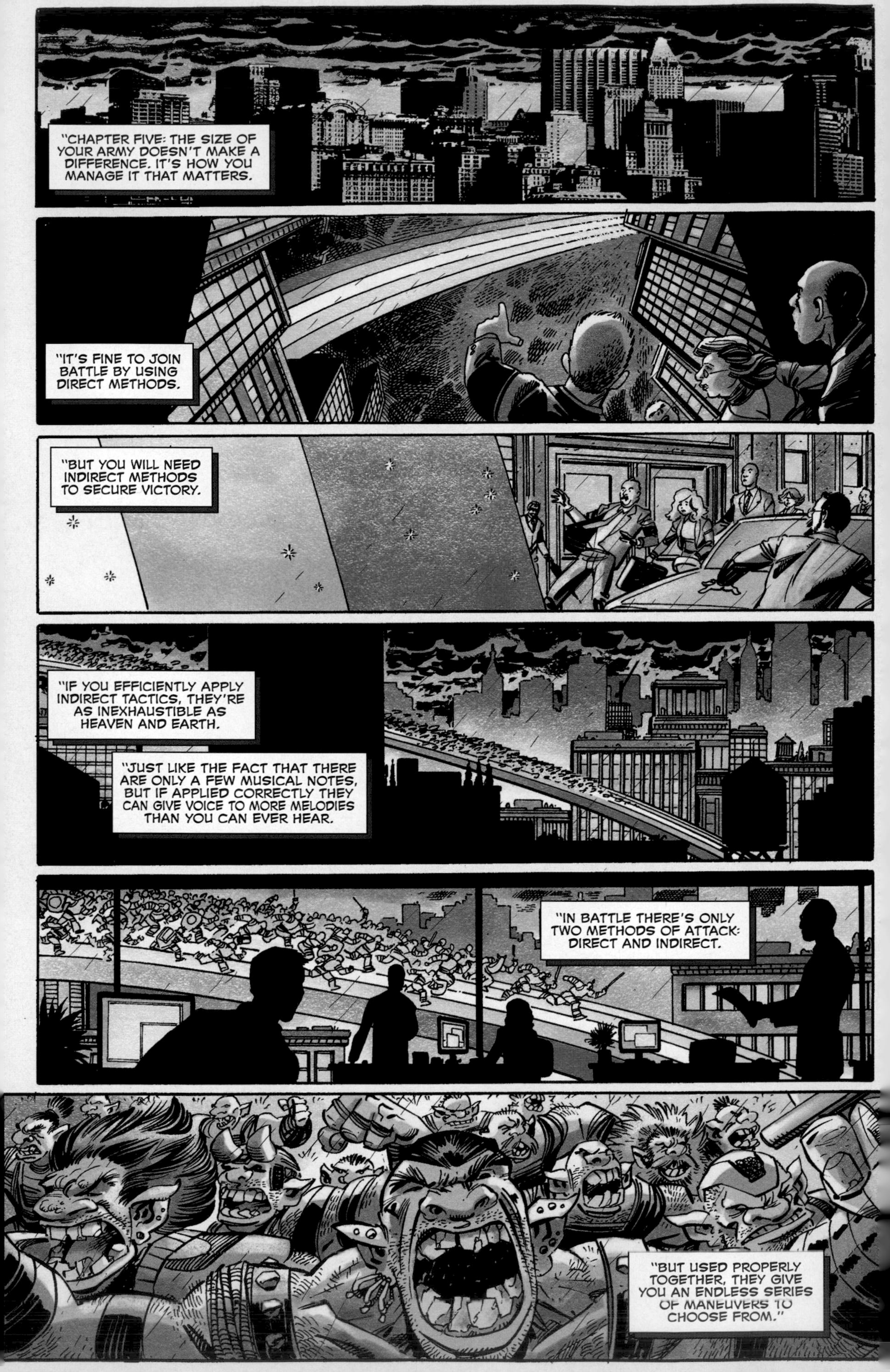
"CHAPTER FIVE: THE SIZE OF YOUR ARMY DOESN'T MAKE A DIFFERENCE. IT'S HOW YOU MANAGE IT THAT MATTERS.
"IT'S FINE TO JOIN BATTLE BY USING DIRECT METHODS.
"BUT YOU WILL NEED INDIRECT METHODS TO SECURE VICTORY.
"IF YOU EFFICIENTLY APPLY INDIRECT TACTICS, THEY'RE AS INEXHAUSTIBLE AS HEAVEN AND EARTH.
"JUST LIKE THE FACT THAT THERE ARE ONLY A FEW MUSICAL NOTES, BUT IF APPLIED CORRECTLY THEY CAN GIVE VOICE TO MORE MELODIES THAN YOU CAN EVER HEAR.
"IN BATTLE THERE'S ONLY TWO METHODS OF ATTACK: DIRECT AND INDIRECT.
"BUT USED PROPERLY TOGETHER, THEY GIVE YOU AN ENDLESS SERIES OF MANEUVERS TO CHOOSE FROM."

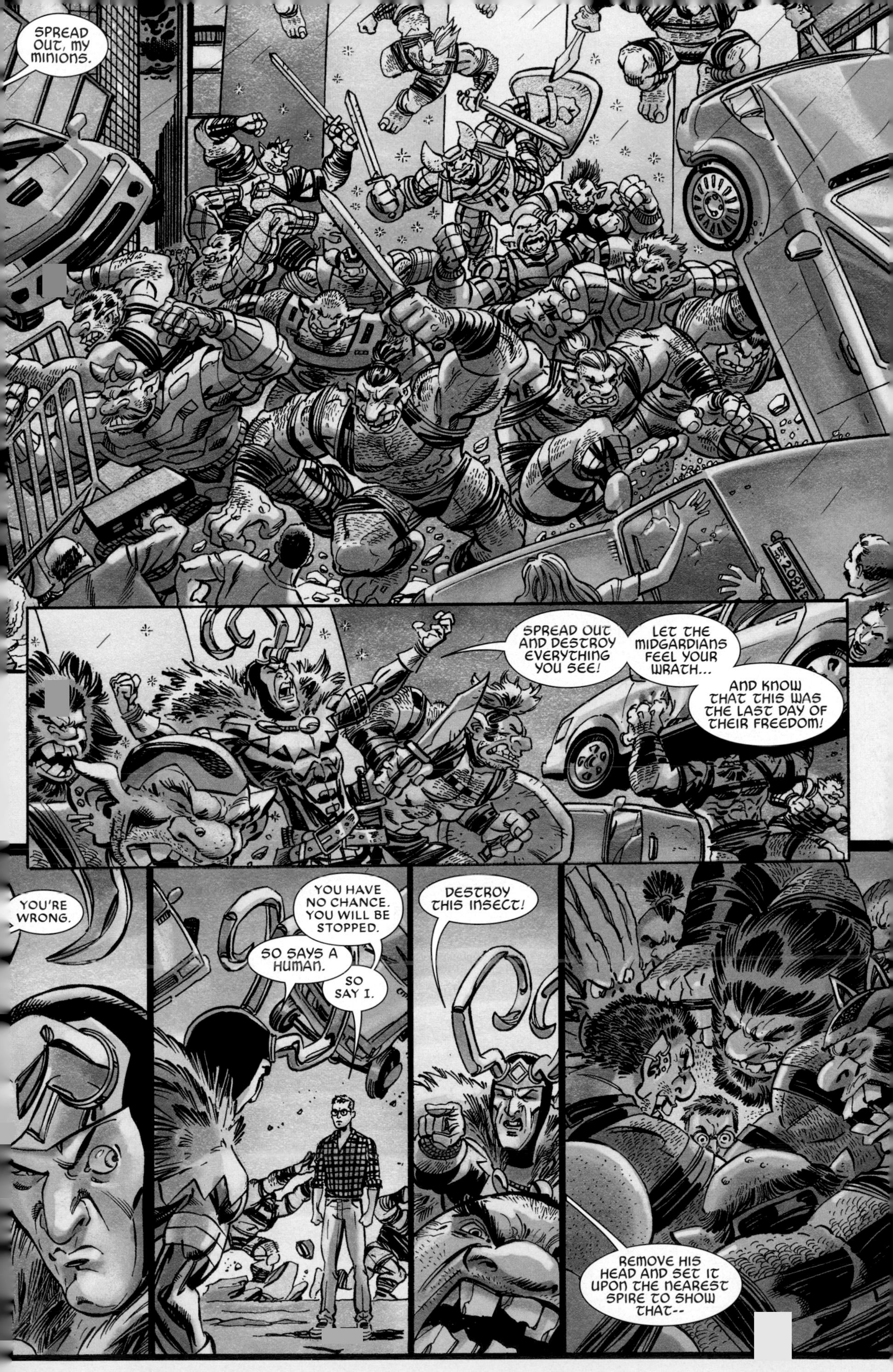
SPREAD OUT, MY MINIONS.
SPREAD OUT AND DESTROY EVERYTHING YOU SEE!
LET THE MIDGARDIANS FEEL YOUR WRATH...
AND KNOW THAT THIS WAS THE LAST DAY OF THEIR FREEDOM!
YOU'RE WRONG.
YOU HAVE NO CHANCE. YOU WILL BE STOPPED.
SO SAYS A HUMAN.
SO SAY I.
DESTROY THIS INSECT!
REMOVE HIS HEAD AND SET IT UPON THE NEAREST SPIRE TO SHOW THAT--

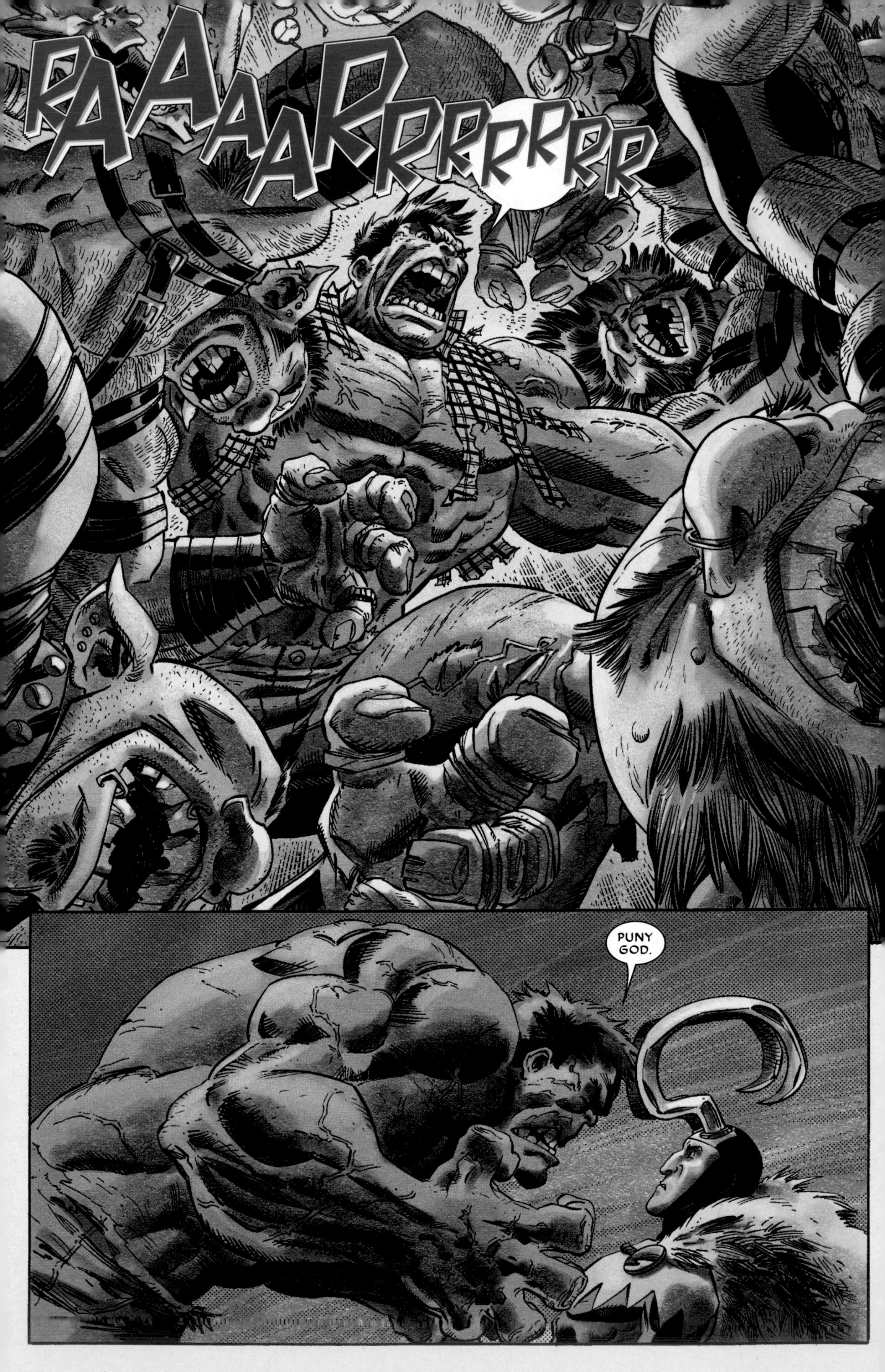
RAAAARRRRRRRR
PUNY GOD.

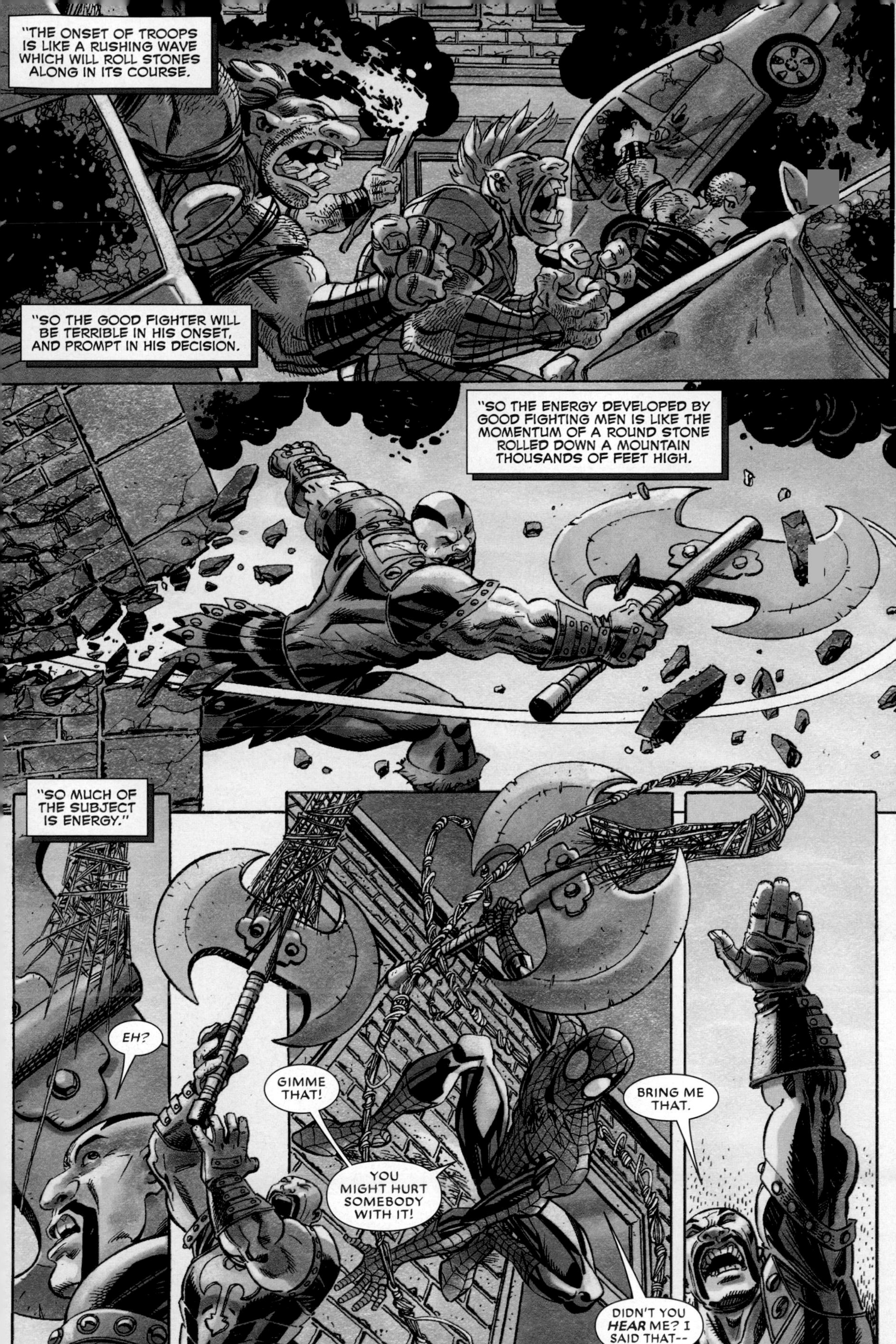
"THE ONSET OF TROOPS IS LIKE A RUSHING WAVE WHICH WILL ROLL STONES ALONG IN ITS COURSE.
"SO THE GOOD FIGHTER WILL BE TERRIBLE IN HIS ONSET, AND PROMPT IN HIS DECISION.
"SO THE ENERGY DEVELOPED BY GOOD FIGHTING MEN IS LIKE THE MOMENTUM OF A ROUND STONE ROLLED DOWN A MOUNTAIN THOUSANDS OF FEET HIGH.
"SO MUCH OF THE SUBJECT IS ENERGY."
EH?
GIMME THAT!
YOU MIGHT HURT SOMEBODY WITH IT!
BRING ME THAT.
DIDN'T YOU HEAR ME? I SAID THAT--

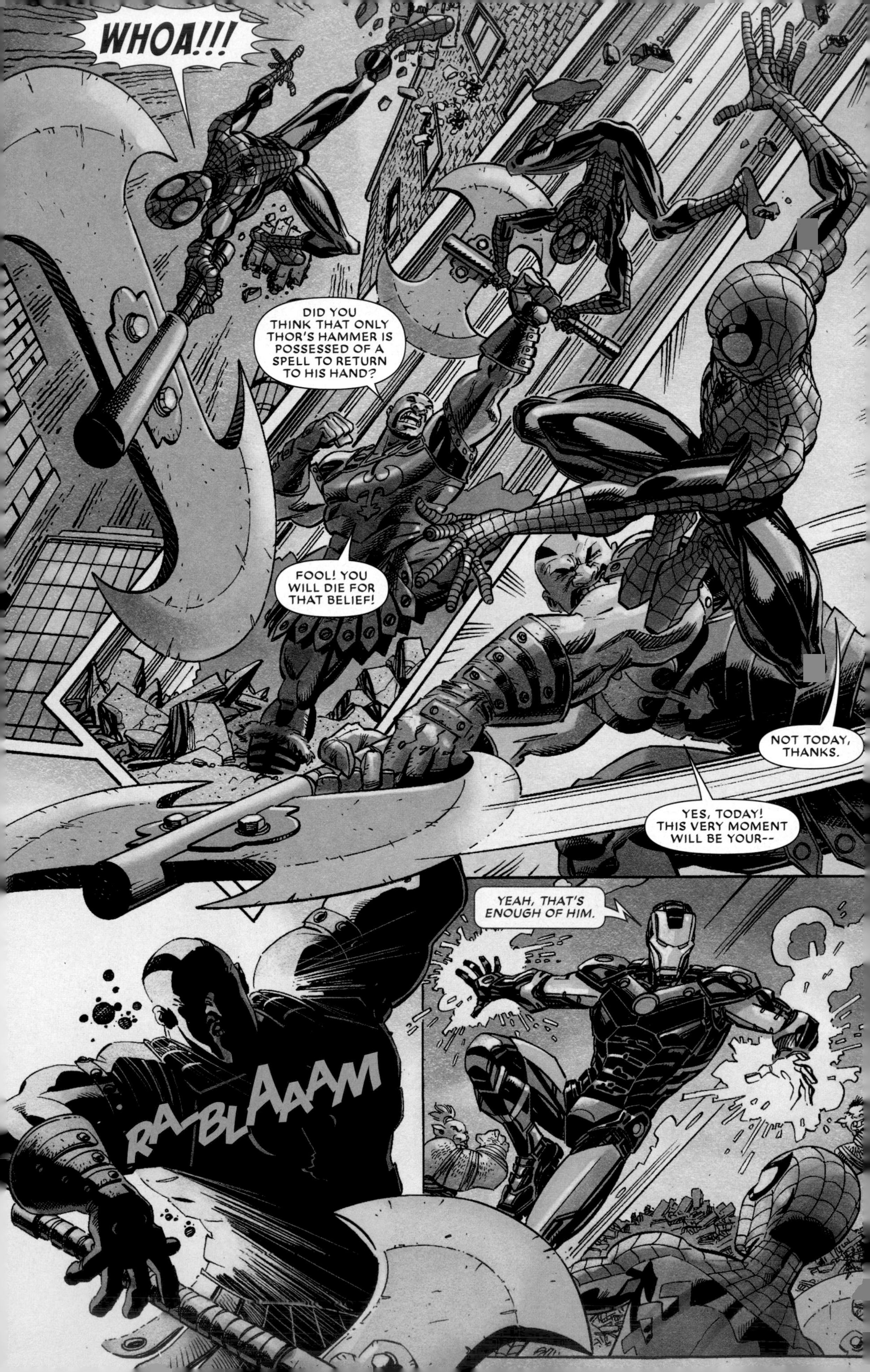
WHOA!!!
DID YOU THINK THAT ONLY THOR'S HAMMER IS POSSESSED OF A SPELL TO RETURN TO HIS HAND?
FOOL! YOU WILL DIE FOR THAT BELIEF!
NOT TODAY, THANKS.
YES, TODAY! THIS VERY MOMENT WILL BE YOUR--
YEAH, THAT'S ENOUGH OF HIM.
RA-BLAAAM

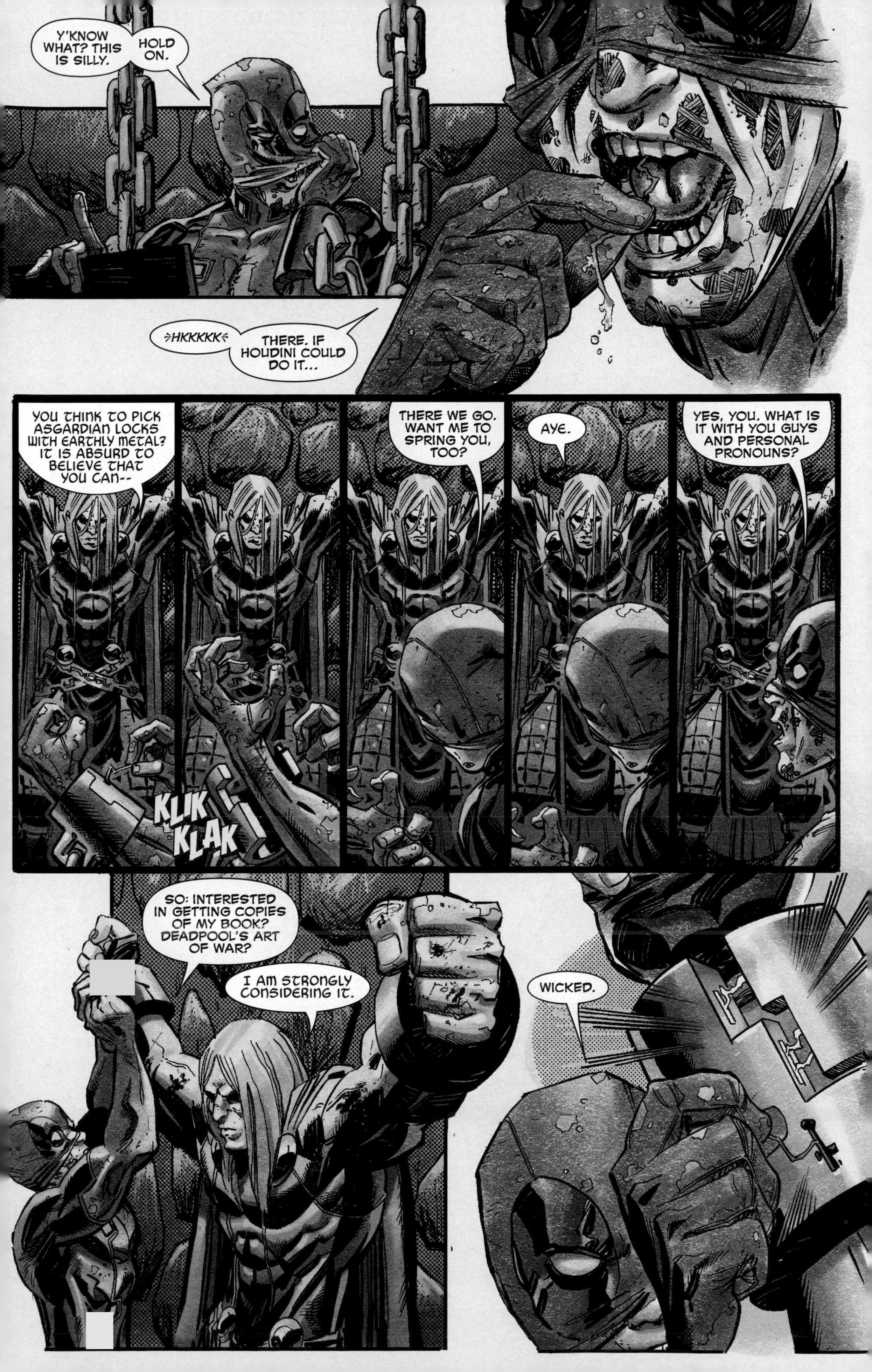
Y'KNOW WHAT? THIS IS SILLY.
HOLD ON.
HKKKKK
THERE. IF HOUDINI COULD DO IT...
YOU THINK TO PICK ASGARDIAN LOCKS WITH EARTHLY METAL? IT IS ABSURD TO BELIEVE THAT YOU CAN--
KLIK KLAK
THERE WE GO. WANT ME TO SPRING YOU, TOO?
AYE.
YES, YOU. WHAT IS IT WITH YOU GUYS AND PERSONAL PRONOUNS?
SO: INTERESTED IN GETTING COPIES OF MY BOOK? DEADPOOL'S ART OF WAR?
I AM STRONGLY CONSIDERING IT.
WICKED.

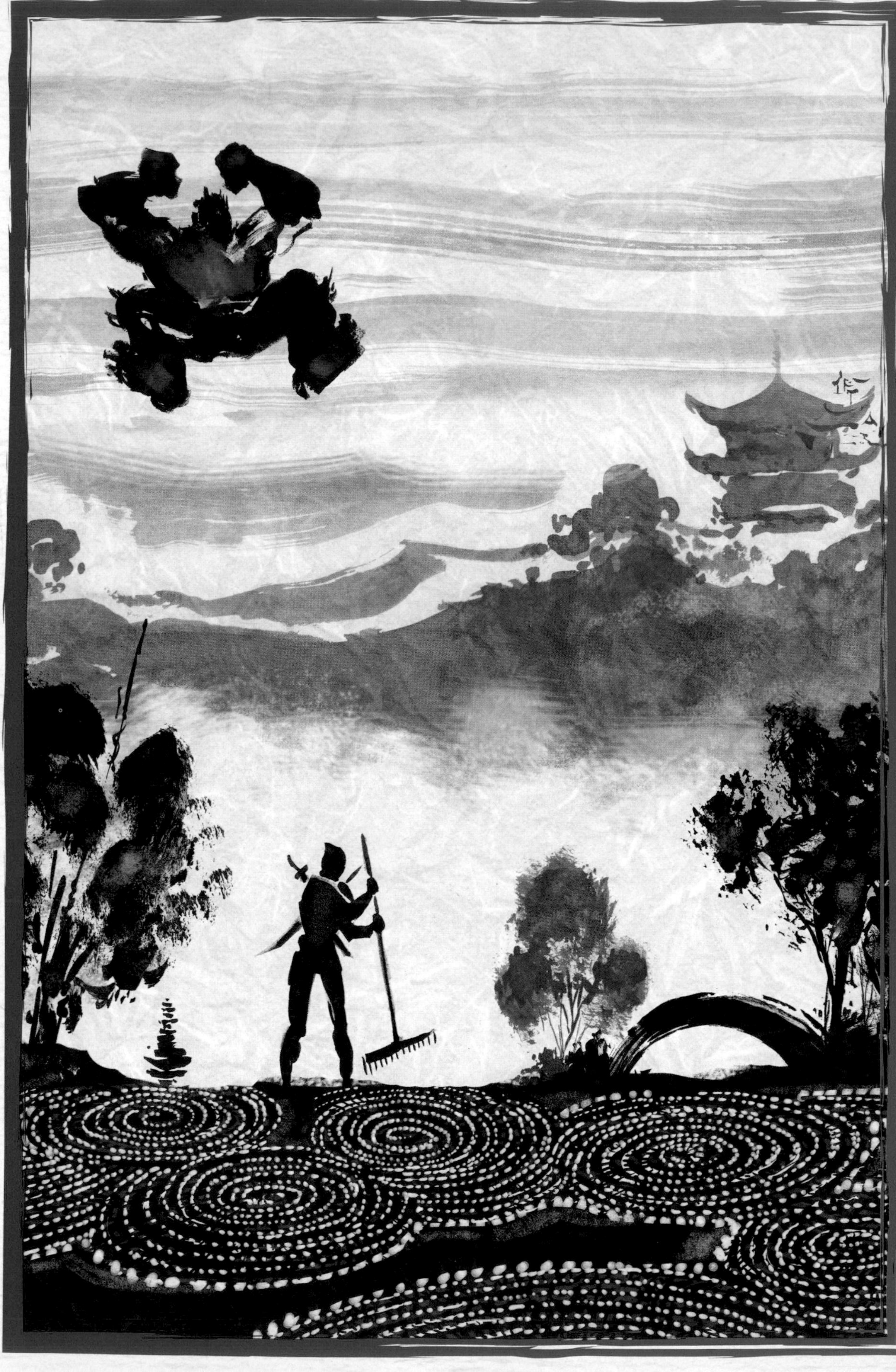

CHAPTER *THREE*

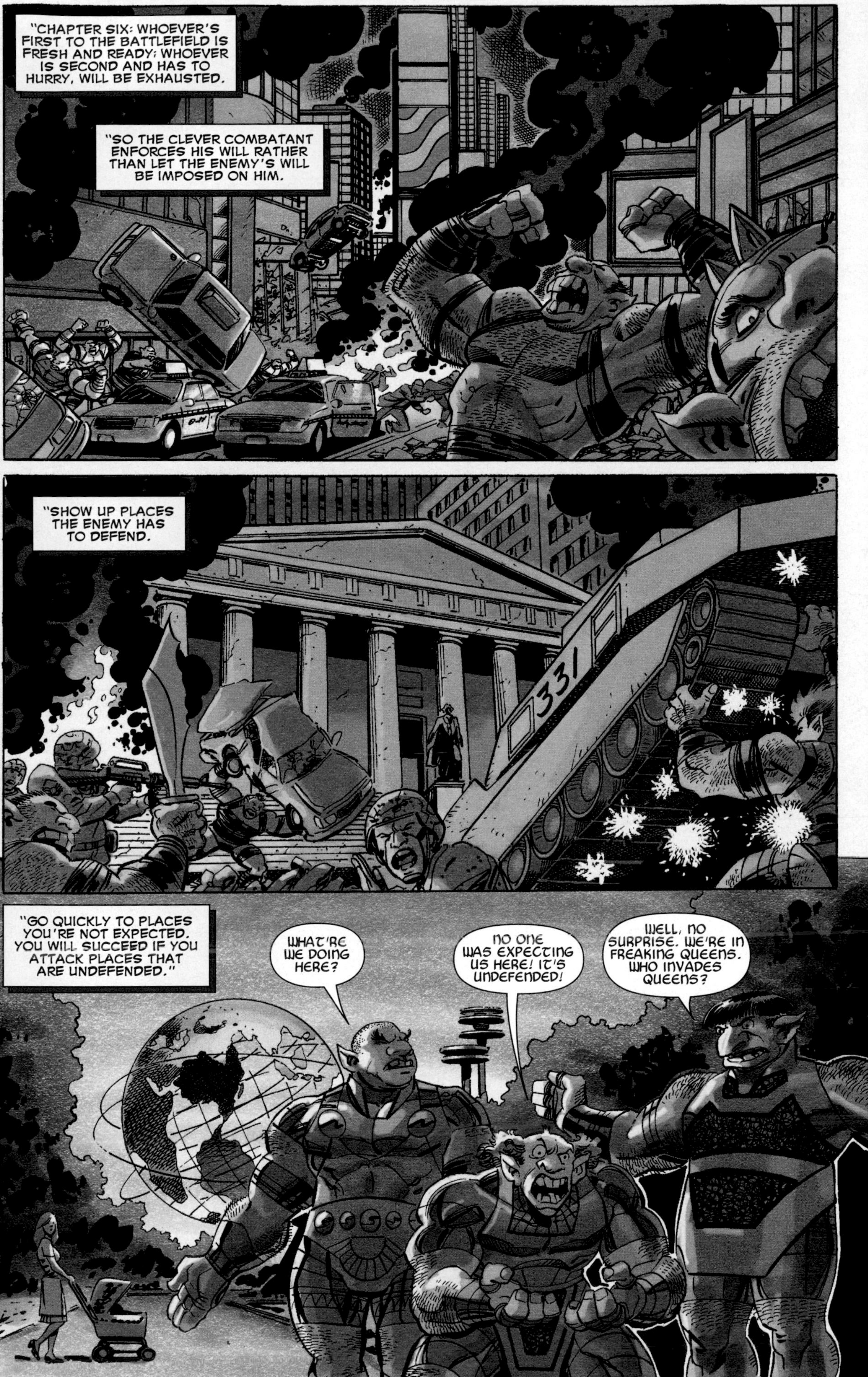
"CHAPTER SIX: WHOEVER'S FIRST TO THE BATTLEFIELD IS FRESH AND READY; WHOEVER IS SECOND AND HAS TO HURRY, WILL BE EXHAUSTED.
"SO THE CLEVER COMBATANT ENFORCES HIS WILL RATHER THAN LET THE ENEMY'S WILL BE IMPOSED ON HIM.
"SHOW UP PLACES THE ENEMY HAS TO DEFEND.
331
"GO QUICKLY TO PLACES YOU'RE NOT EXPECTED. YOU WILL SUCCEED IF YOU ATTACK PLACES THAT ARE UNDEFENDED."
WHAT'RE WE DOING HERE?
NO ONE WAS EXPECTING US HERE! IT'S UNDEFENDED!
WELL, NO SURPRISE. WE'RE IN FREAKING QUEENS. WHO INVADES QUEENS?

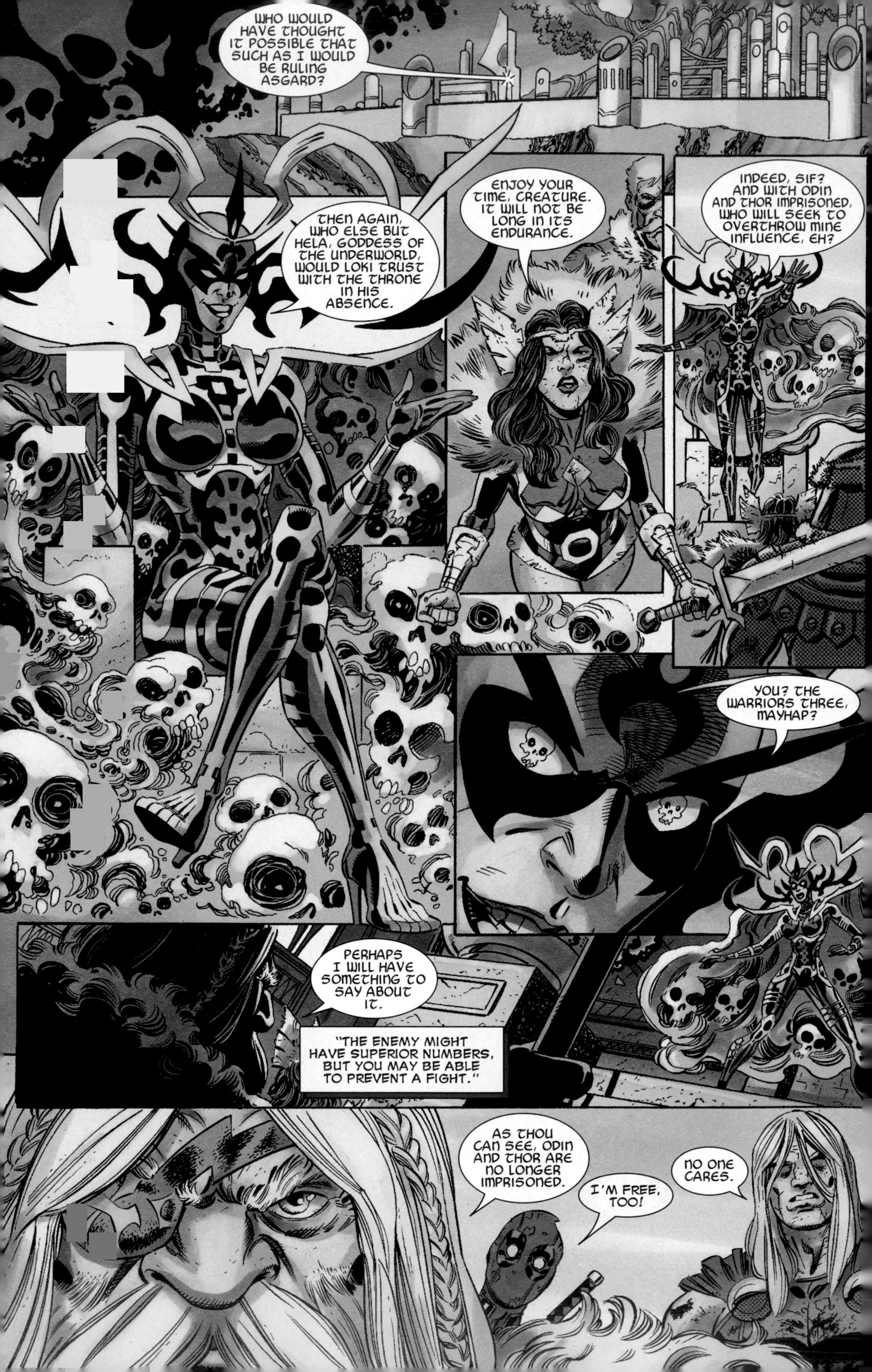
WHO WOULD HAVE THOUGHT IT POSSIBLE THAT SUCH AS I WOULD BE RULING ASGARD?
THEN AGAIN, WHO ELSE BUT HELA, GODDESS OF THE UNDERWORLD, WOULD LOKI TRUST WITH THE THRONE IN HIS ABSENCE.
ENJOY YOUR TIME, CREATURE. IT WILL NOT BE LONG IN ITS ENDURANCE.
INDEED, SIF? AND WITH ODIN AND THOR IMPRISONED, WHO WILL SEEK TO OVERTHROW MINE INFLUENCE, EH?
YOU? THE WARRIORS THREE, MAYHAP?
PERHAPS I WILL HAVE SOMETHING TO SAY ABOUT IT.
"THE ENEMY MIGHT HAVE SUPERIOR NUMBERS, BUT YOU MAY BE ABLE TO PREVENT A FIGHT."
AS THOU CAN SEE, ODIN AND THOR ARE NO LONGER IMPRISONED.
I'M FREE, TOO!
NO ONE CARES.

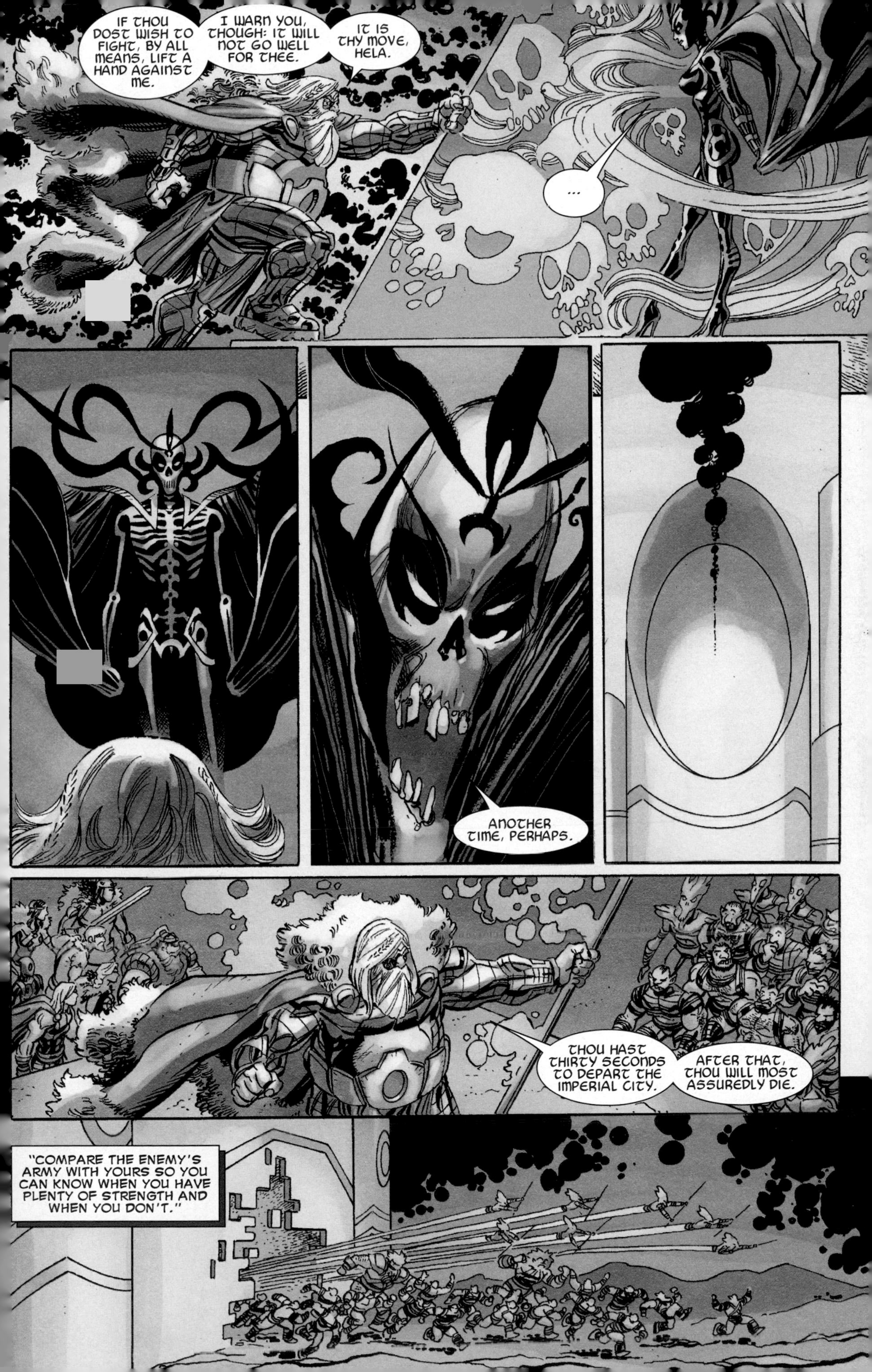
IF THOU DOST WISH TO FIGHT, BY ALL MEANS, LIFT A HAND AGAINST ME.
I WARN YOU, THOUGH: IT WILL NOT GO WELL FOR THEE.
IT IS THY MOVE, HELA.
...
ANOTHER TIME, PERHAPS.
THOU HAST THIRTY SECONDS TO DEPART THE IMPERIAL CITY.
AFTER THAT, THOU WILL MOST ASSUREDLY DIE.
"COMPARE THE ENEMY'S ARMY WITH YOURS SO YOU CAN KNOW WHEN YOU HAVE PLENTY OF STRENGTH AND WHEN YOU DON'T."

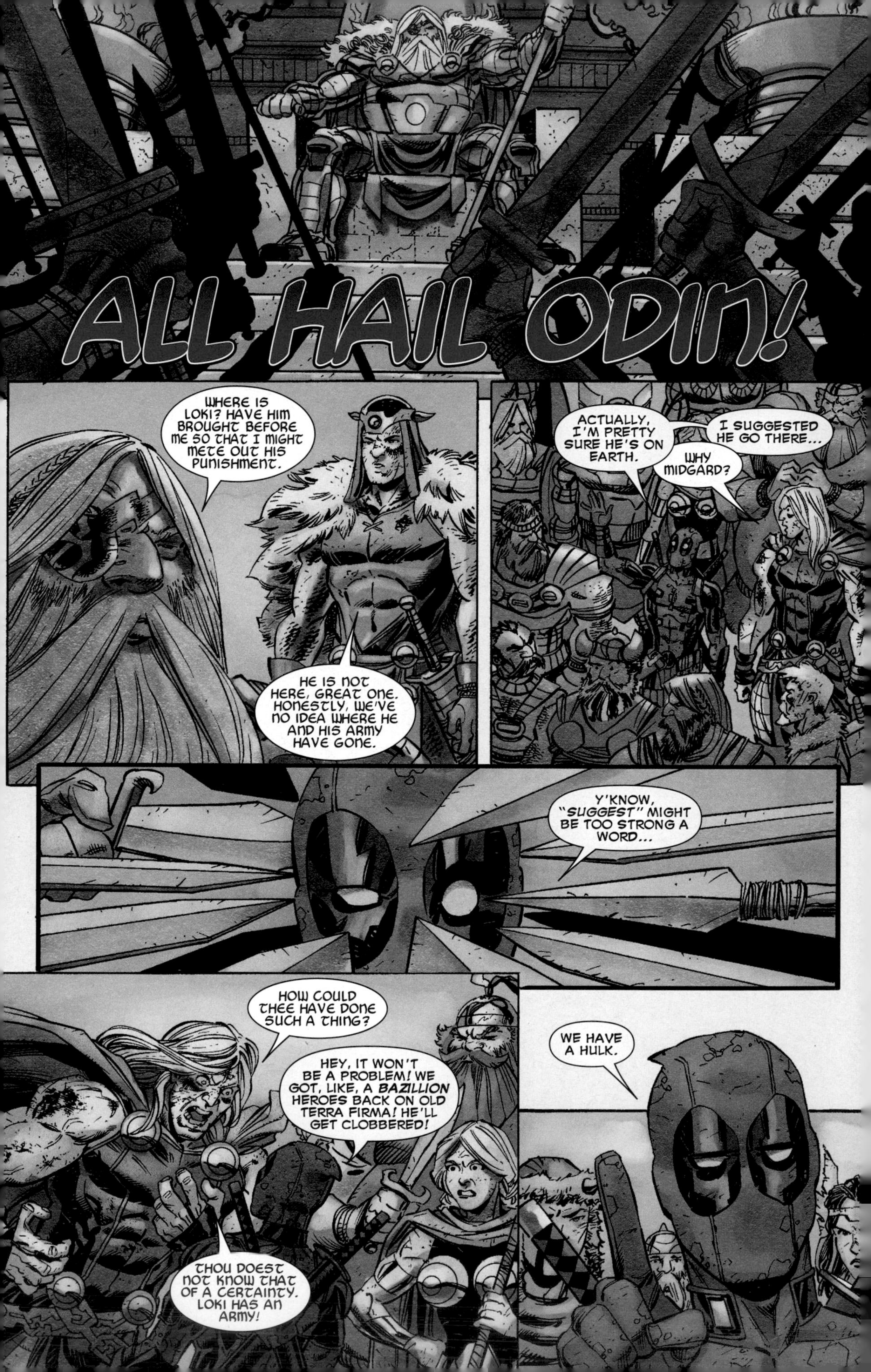
ALL HAIL ODIN!
WHERE IS LOKI? HAVE HIM BROUGHT BEFORE ME SO THAT I MIGHT METE OUT HIS PUNISHMENT.
HE IS NOT HERE, GREAT ONE. HONESTLY, WE'VE NO IDEA WHERE HE AND HIS ARMY HAVE GONE.
ACTUALLY, I'M PRETTY SURE HE'S ON EARTH.
I SUGGESTED HE GO THERE...
WHY MIDGARD?
Y'KNOW, "SUGGEST" MIGHT BE TOO STRONG A WORD...
HOW COULD THEE HAVE DONE SUCH A THING?
HEY, IT WON'T BE A PROBLEM! WE GOT, LIKE, A BAZILLION HEROES BACK ON OLD TERRA FIRMA! HE'LL GET CLOBBERED!
THOU DOEST NOT KNOW THAT OF A CERTAINTY. LOKI HAS AN ARMY!
WE HAVE A HULK.

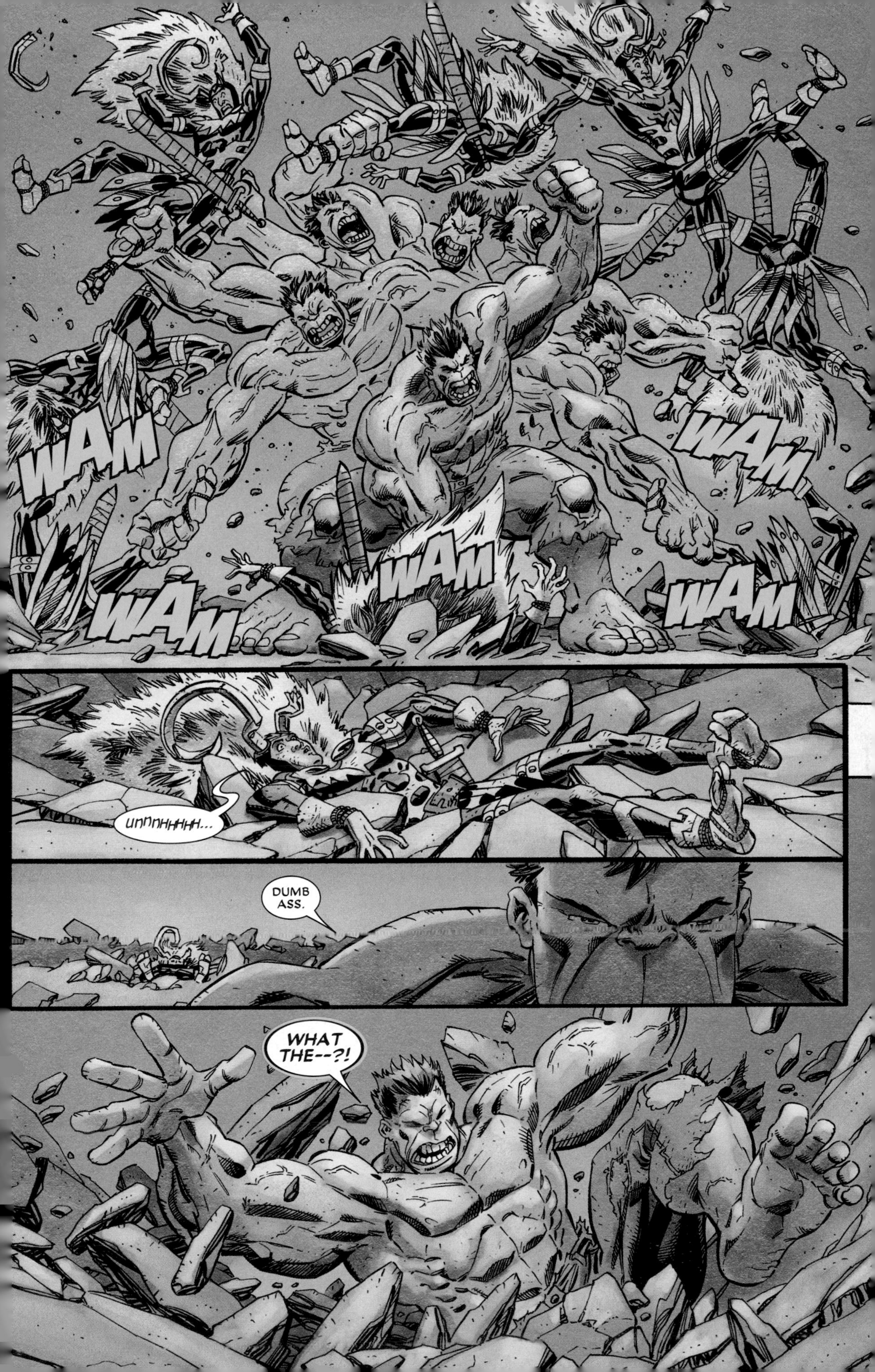

WAM
WAM
WAM
WAM
WAM
UNNNHHHHH...
DUMB ASS.
WHAT THE--?!

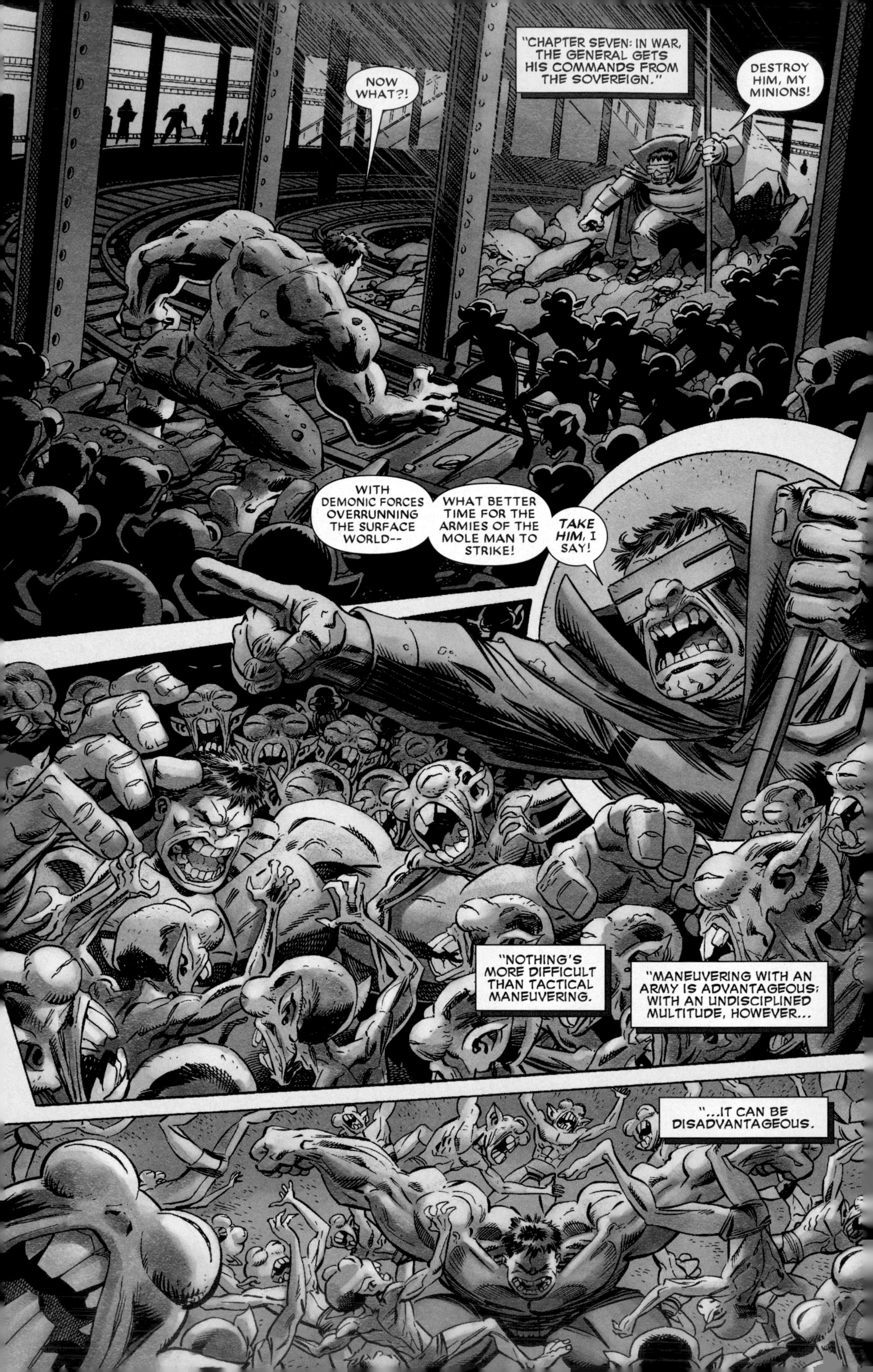
"CHAPTER SEVEN: IN WAR, THE GENERAL GETS HIS COMMANDS FROM THE SOVEREIGN."
NOW WHAT?!
DESTROY HIM, MY MINIONS!
WITH DEMONIC FORCES OVERRUNNING THE SURFACE WORLD--
WHAT BETTER TIME FOR THE ARMIES OF THE MOLE MAN TO STRIKE!
TAKE HIM, I SAY!
"NOTHING'S MORE DIFFICULT THAN TACTICAL MANEUVERING.
"MANEUVERING WITH AN ARMY IS ADVANTAGEOUS; WITH AN UNDISCIPLINED MULTITUDE, HOWEVER...
"...IT CAN BE DISADVANTAGEOUS.

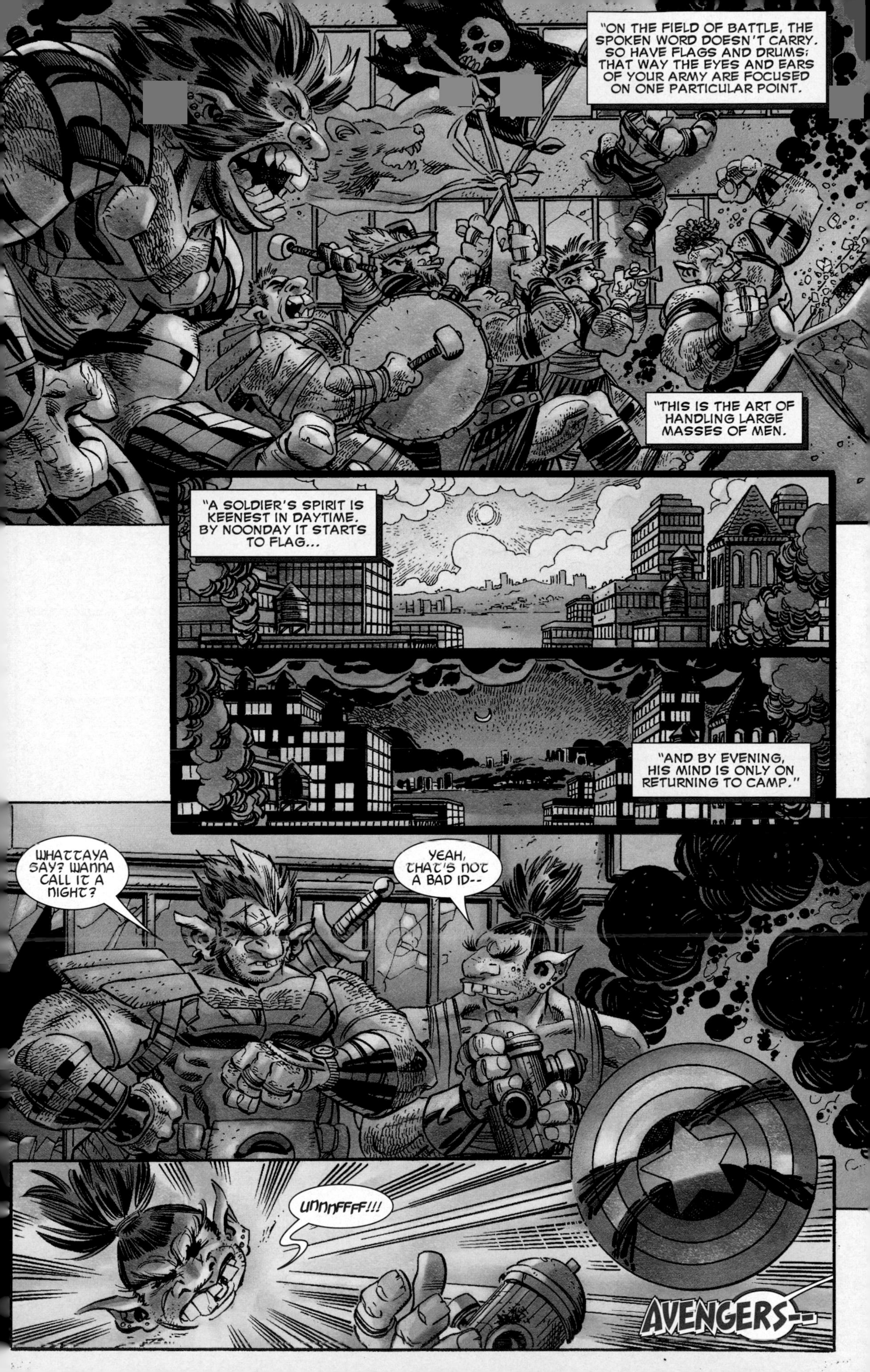
"ON THE FIELD OF BATTLE, THE SPOKEN WORD DOESN'T CARRY. SO HAVE FLAGS AND DRUMS; THAT WAY THE EYES AND EARS OF YOUR ARMY ARE FOCUSED ON ONE PARTICULAR POINT.
"THIS IS THE ART OF HANDLING LARGE MASSES OF MEN.
"A SOLDIER'S SPIRIT IS KEENEST IN DAYTIME. BY NOONDAY IT STARTS TO FLAG...
"AND BY EVENING, HIS MIND IS ONLY ON RETURNING TO CAMP."
WHATTAYA SAY? WANNA CALL IT A NIGHT?
YEAH, THAT'S NOT A BAD ID--
UNNNFFFF!!!
AVENGERS--

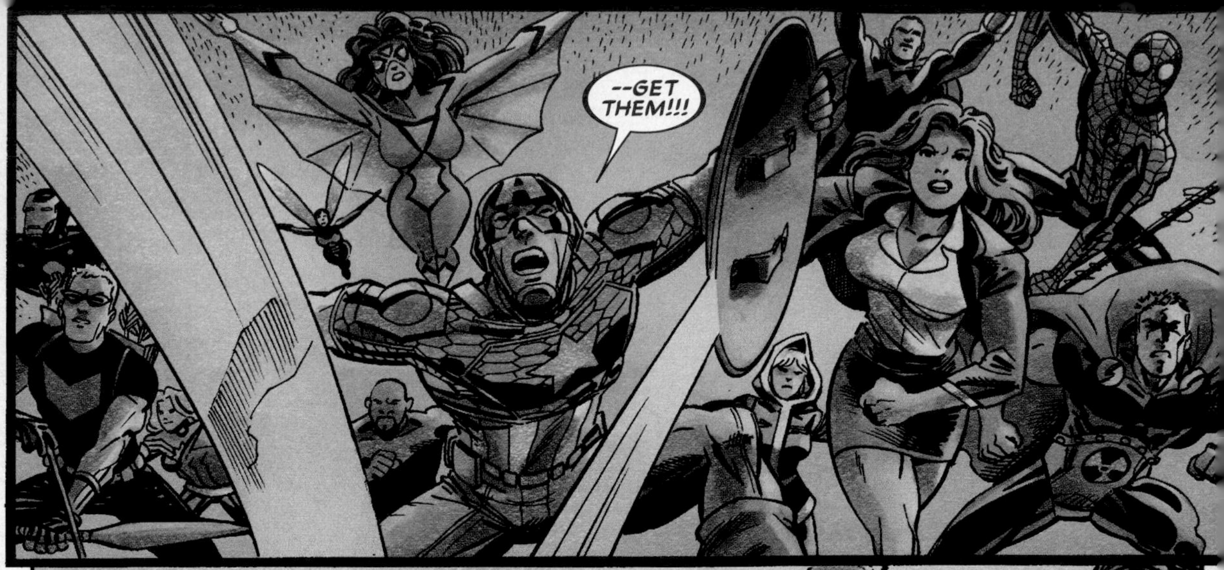
--GET THEM!!!

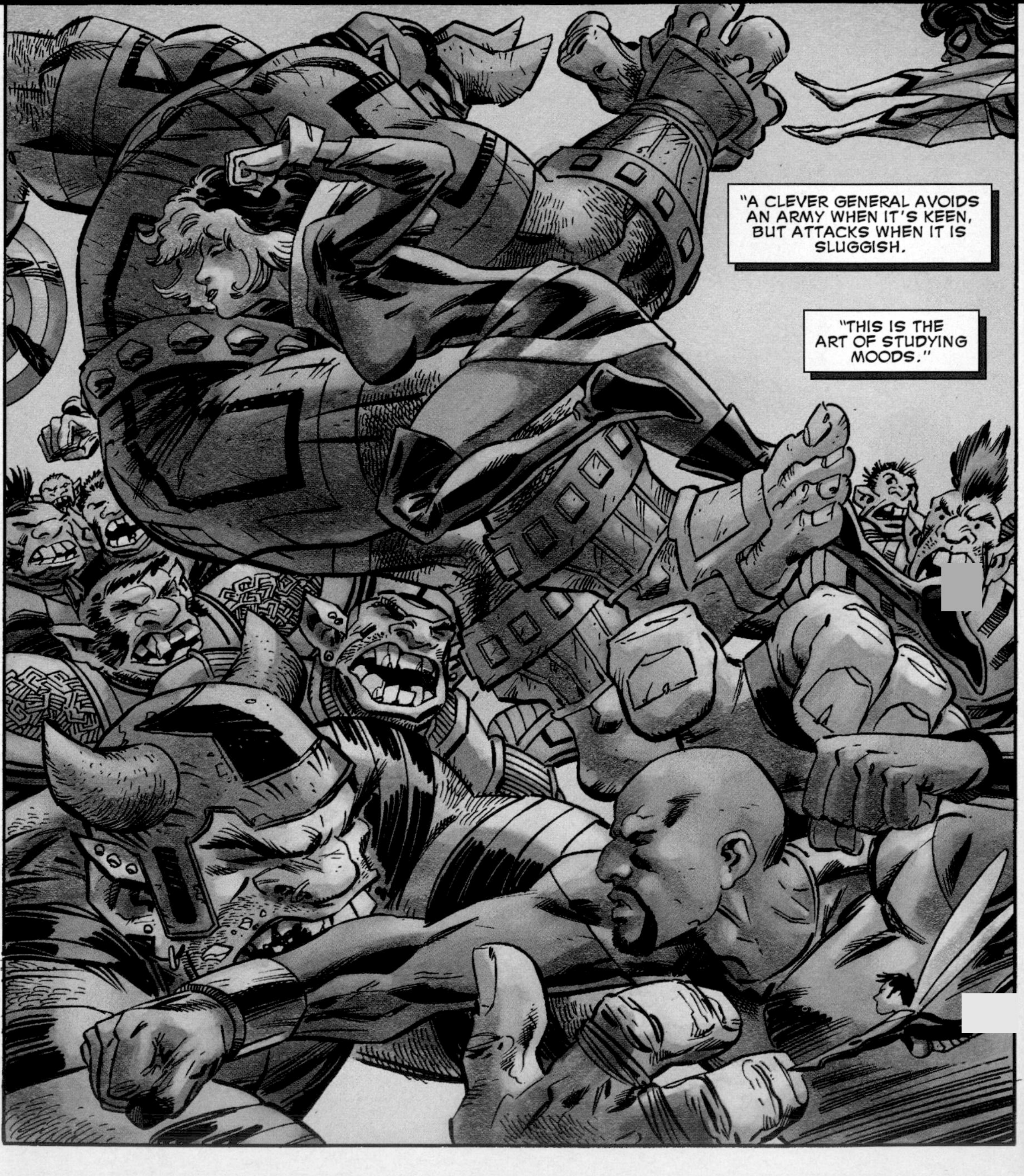
"A CLEVER GENERAL AVOIDS AN ARMY WHEN IT'S KEEN, BUT ATTACKS WHEN IT IS SLUGGISH.
"THIS IS THE ART OF STUDYING MOODS."

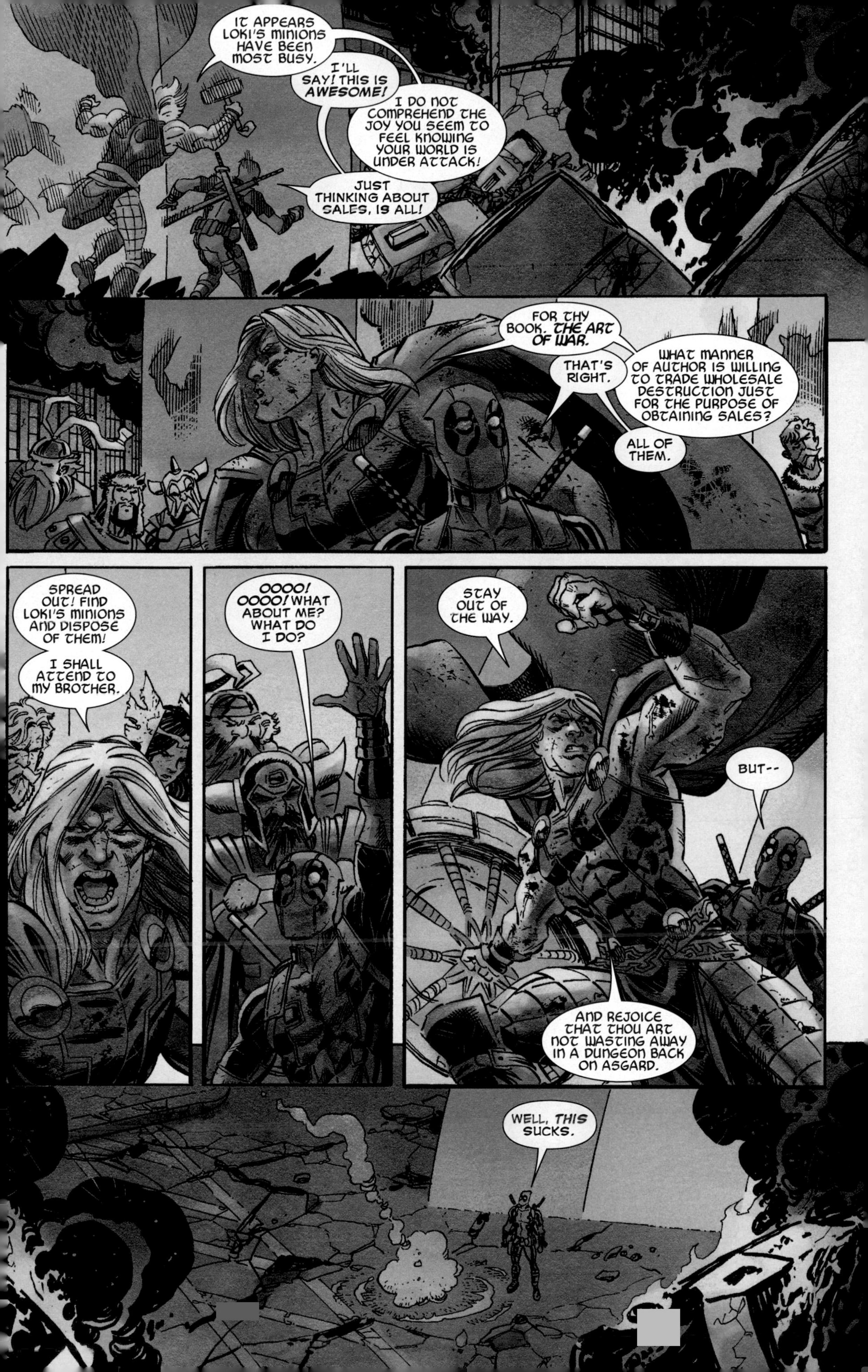
IT APPEARS LOKI'S MINIONS HAVE BEEN MOST BUSY.
I'LL SAY! THIS IS *AWESOME!*
I DO NOT COMPREHEND THE JOY YOU SEEM TO FEEL KNOWING YOUR WORLD IS UNDER ATTACK!
JUST THINKING ABOUT SALES, IS ALL!
FOR THY BOOK. *THE ART OF WAR.*
THAT'S RIGHT.
WHAT MANNER OF AUTHOR IS WILLING TO TRADE WHOLESALE DESTRUCTION JUST FOR THE PURPOSE OF OBTAINING SALES?
ALL OF THEM.
SPREAD OUT! FIND LOKI'S MINIONS AND DISPOSE OF THEM!
I SHALL ATTEND TO MY BROTHER.
OOOO! OOOO! WHAT ABOUT ME? WHAT DO I DO?
STAY OUT OF THE WAY.
BUT--
AND REJOICE THAT THOU ART NOT WASTING AWAY IN A DUNGEON BACK ON ASGARD.
WELL, *THIS* SUCKS.

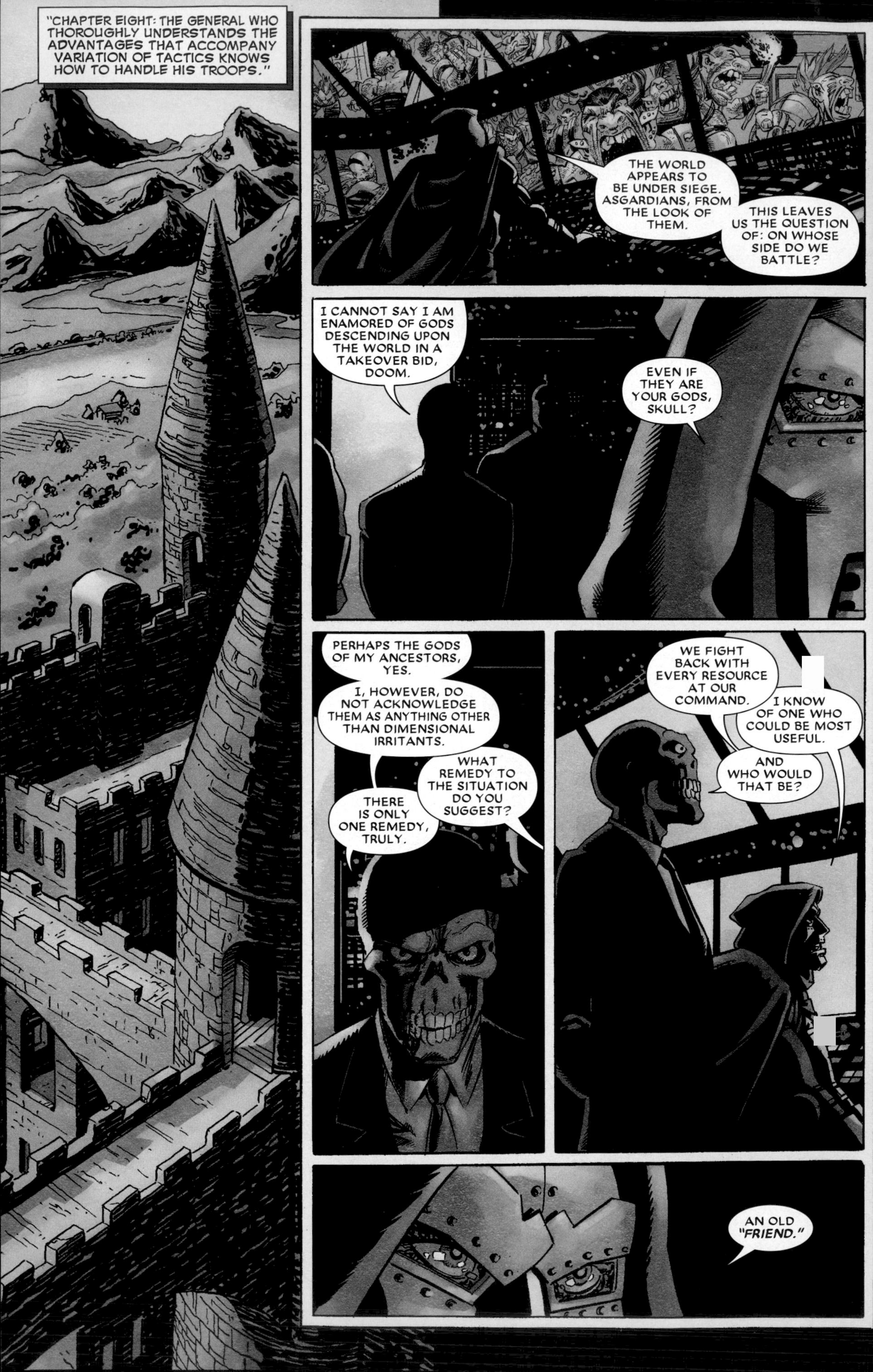
"CHAPTER EIGHT: THE GENERAL WHO THOROUGHLY UNDERSTANDS THE ADVANTAGES THAT ACCOMPANY VARIATION OF TACTICS KNOWS HOW TO HANDLE HIS TROOPS."
THE WORLD APPEARS TO BE UNDER SIEGE. ASGARDIANS, FROM THE LOOK OF THEM.
THIS LEAVES US THE QUESTION OF: ON WHOSE SIDE DO WE BATTLE?
I CANNOT SAY I AM ENAMORED OF GODS DESCENDING UPON THE WORLD IN A TAKEOVER BID, DOOM.
EVEN IF THEY ARE YOUR GODS, SKULL?
PERHAPS THE GODS OF MY ANCESTORS, YES.
I, HOWEVER, DO NOT ACKNOWLEDGE THEM AS ANYTHING OTHER THAN DIMENSIONAL IRRITANTS.
WHAT REMEDY TO THE SITUATION DO YOU SUGGEST?
THERE IS ONLY ONE REMEDY, TRULY.
WE FIGHT BACK WITH EVERY RESOURCE AT OUR COMMAND.
I KNOW OF ONE WHO COULD BE MOST USEFUL.
AND WHO WOULD THAT BE?
AN OLD "FRIEND."

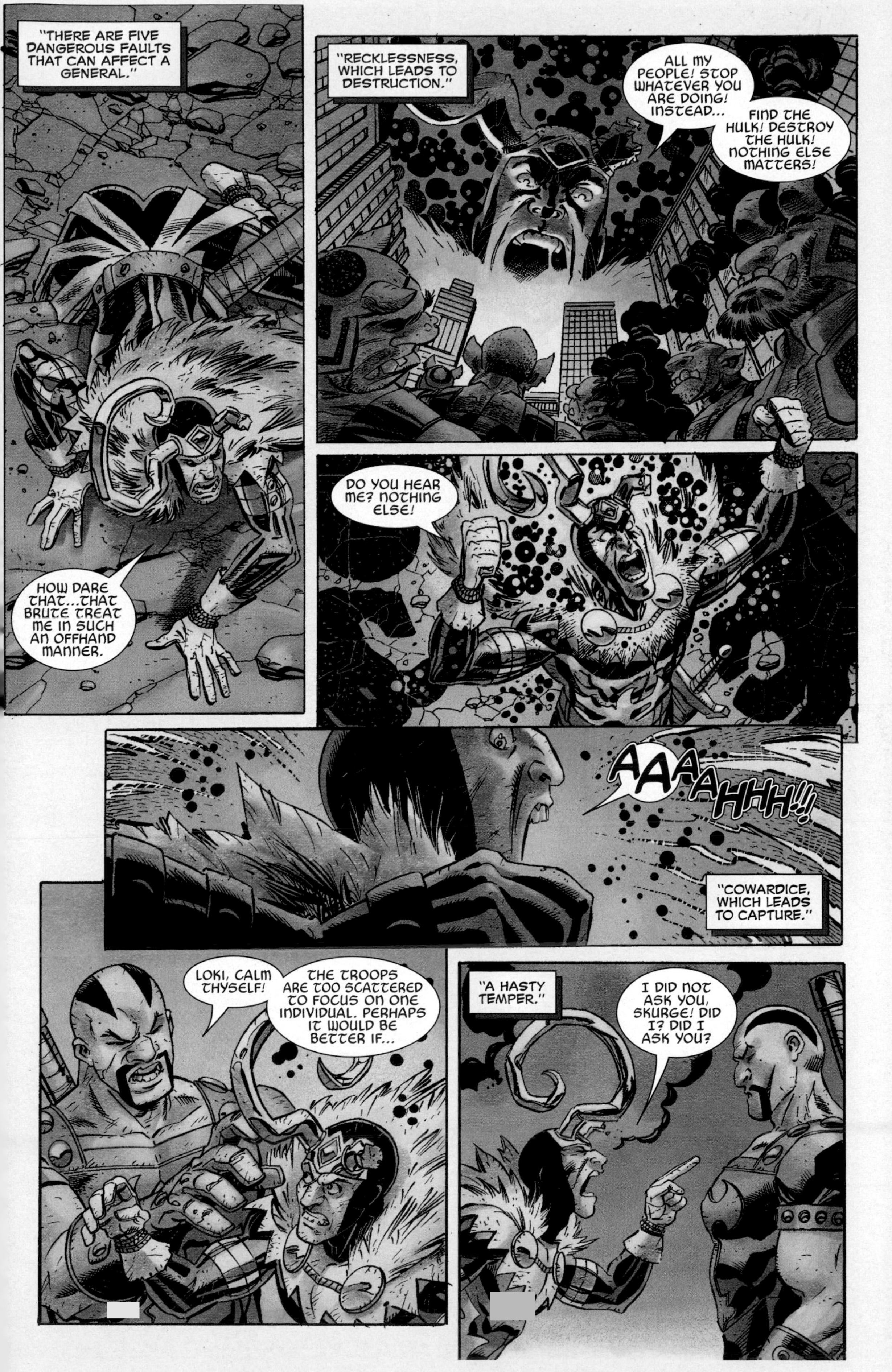
"THERE ARE FIVE DANGEROUS FAULTS THAT CAN AFFECT A GENERAL."
HOW DARE THAT...THAT BRUTE TREAT ME IN SUCH AN OFFHAND MANNER.
"RECKLESSNESS, WHICH LEADS TO DESTRUCTION."
ALL MY PEOPLE! STOP WHATEVER YOU ARE DOING! INSTEAD...
FIND THE HULK! DESTROY THE HULK! NOTHING ELSE MATTERS!
DO YOU HEAR ME? NOTHING ELSE!
AAAAHHH!!!
"COWARDICE, WHICH LEADS TO CAPTURE."
LOKI, CALM THYSELF!
THE TROOPS ARE TOO SCATTERED TO FOCUS ON ONE INDIVIDUAL. PERHAPS IT WOULD BE BETTER IF...
"A HASTY TEMPER."
I DID NOT ASK YOU, SKURGE! DID I? DID I ASK YOU?

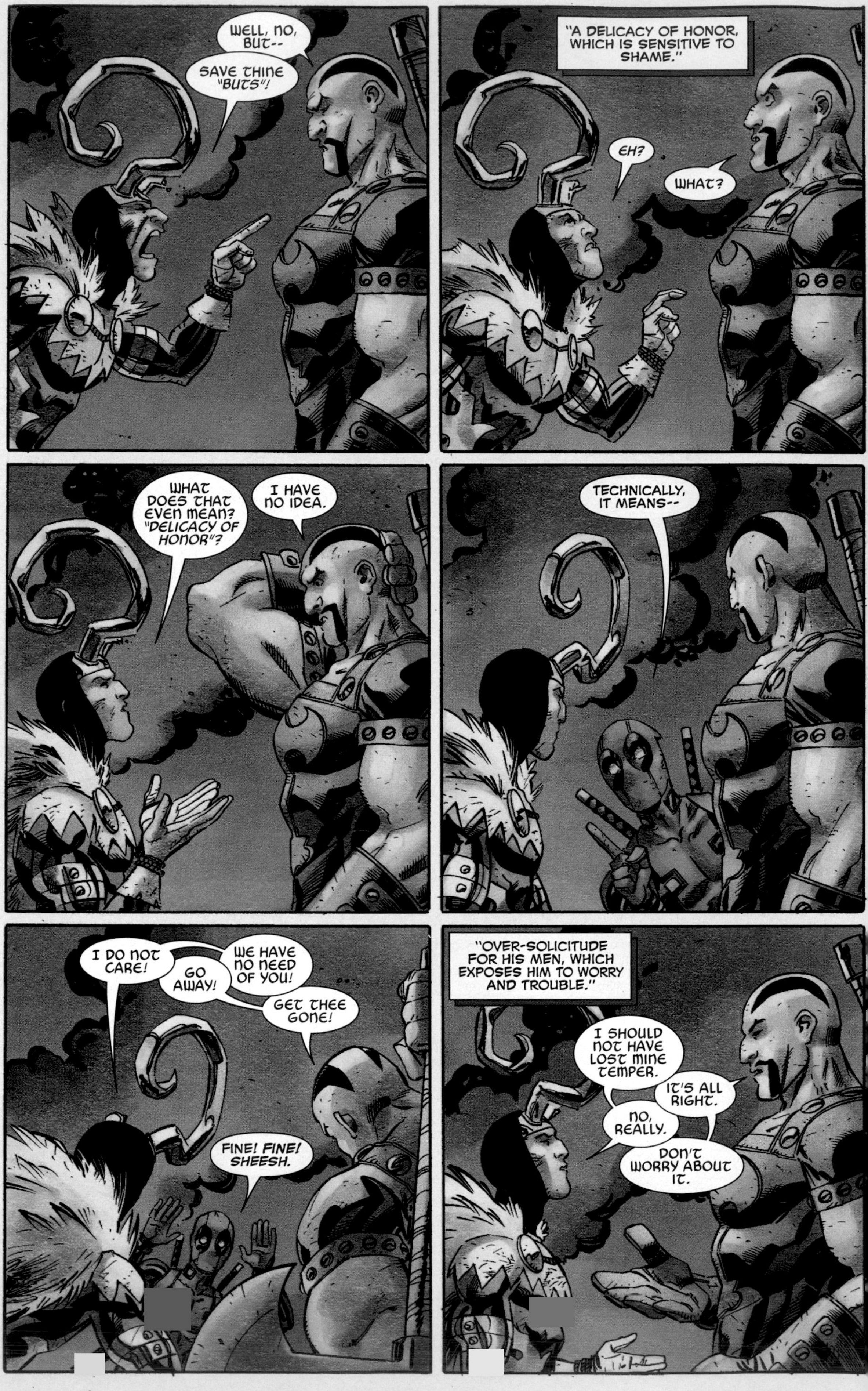
WELL, NO, BUT--
SAVE THINE "BUTS"!
"A DELICACY OF HONOR, WHICH IS SENSITIVE TO SHAME."
EH?
WHAT?
WHAT DOES THAT EVEN MEAN? "DELICACY OF HONOR"?
I HAVE NO IDEA.
TECHNICALLY, IT MEANS--
I DO NOT CARE!
GO AWAY!
WE HAVE NO NEED OF YOU!
GET THEE GONE!
FINE! FINE! SHEESH.
"OVER-SOLICITUDE FOR HIS MEN, WHICH EXPOSES HIM TO WORRY AND TROUBLE."
I SHOULD NOT HAVE LOST MINE TEMPER.
IT'S ALL RIGHT.
NO, REALLY.
DON'T WORRY ABOUT IT.

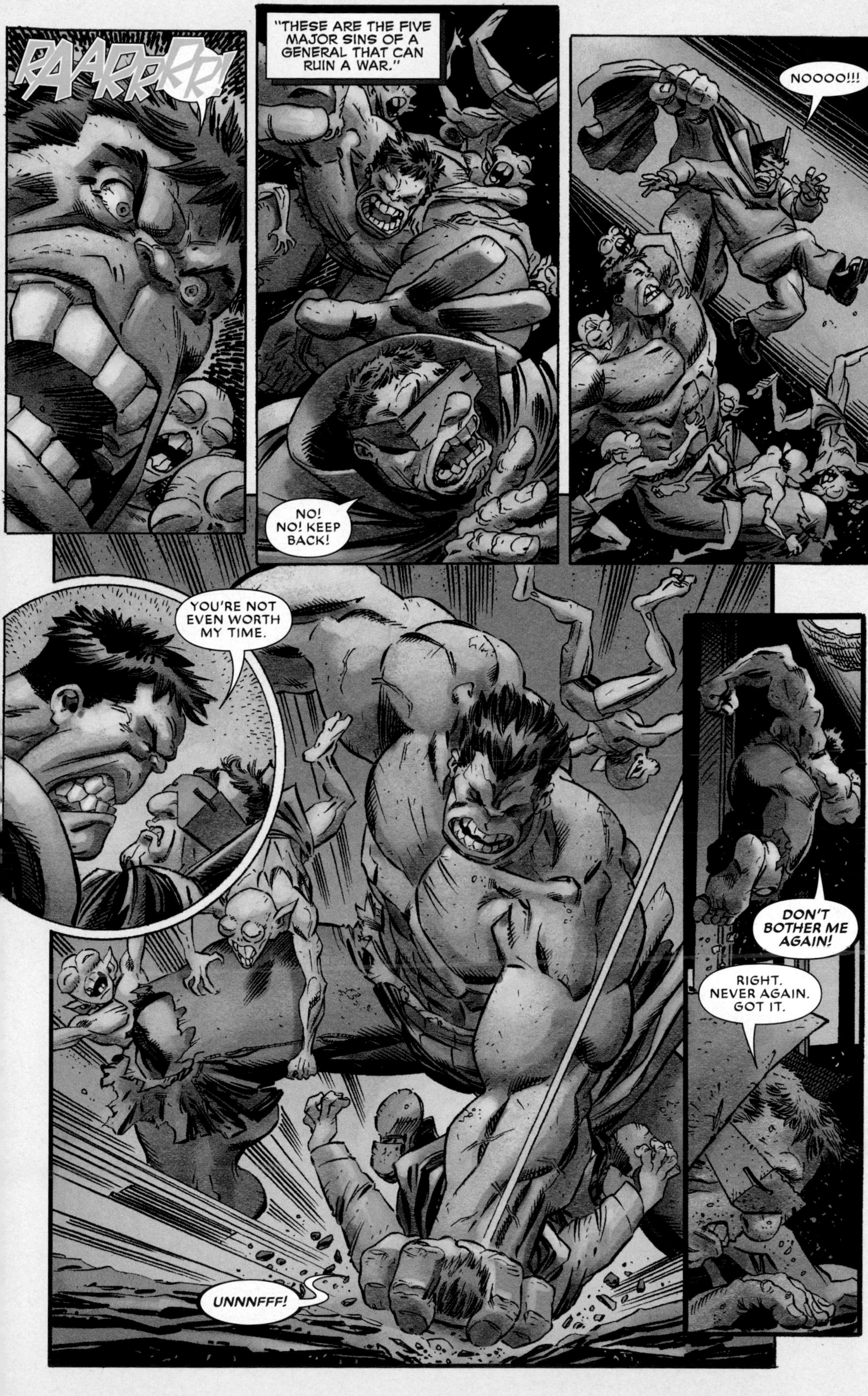
RAARRRRR!
"THESE ARE THE FIVE MAJOR SINS OF A GENERAL THAT CAN RUIN A WAR."
NO! NO! KEEP BACK!
NOOOO!!!
YOU'RE NOT EVEN WORTH MY TIME.
UNNNFFF!
DON'T BOTHER ME AGAIN!
RIGHT. NEVER AGAIN. GOT IT.

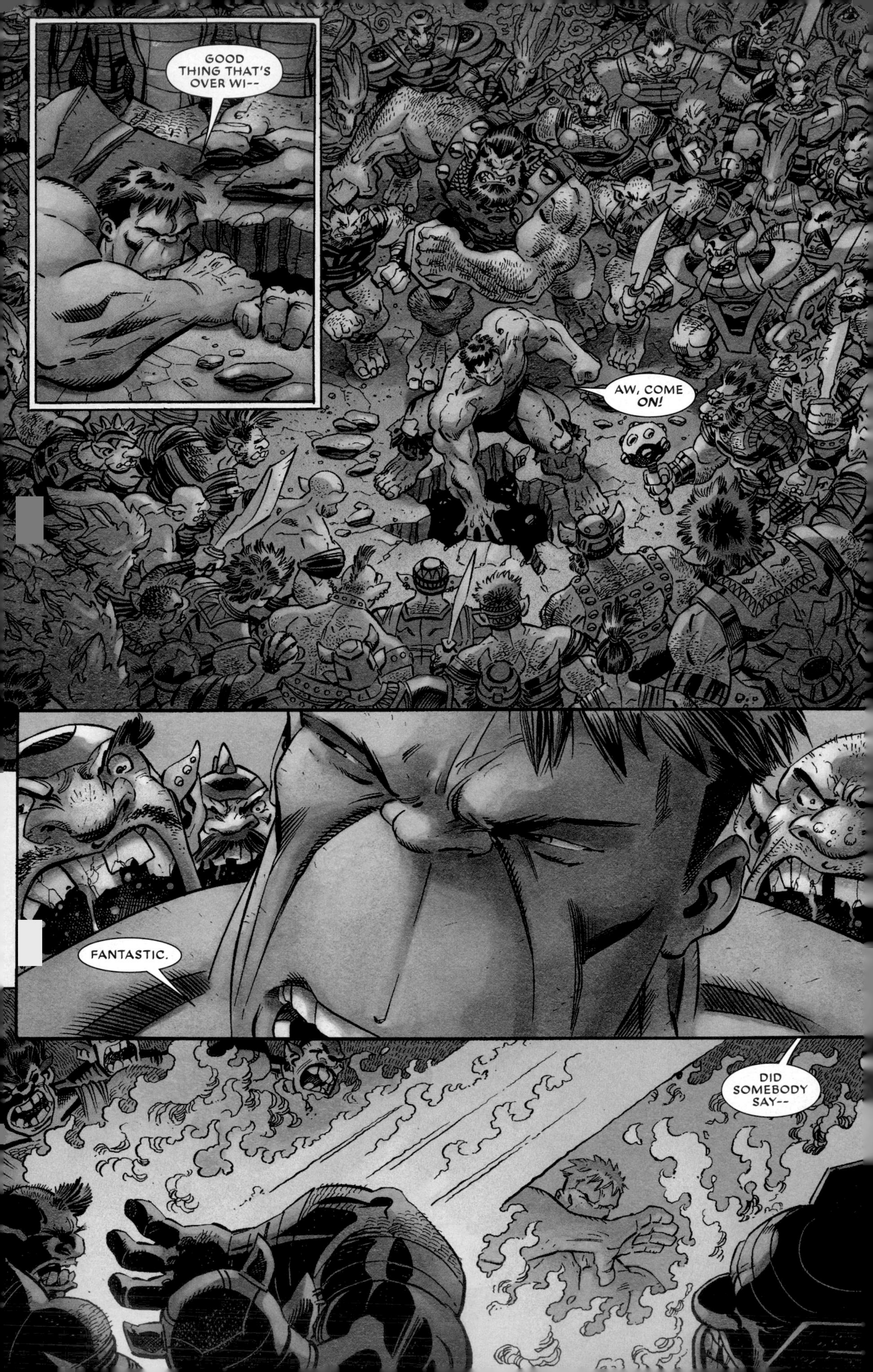
GOOD THING THAT'S OVER WI--
AW, COME ON!
FANTASTIC.
DID SOMEBODY SAY--

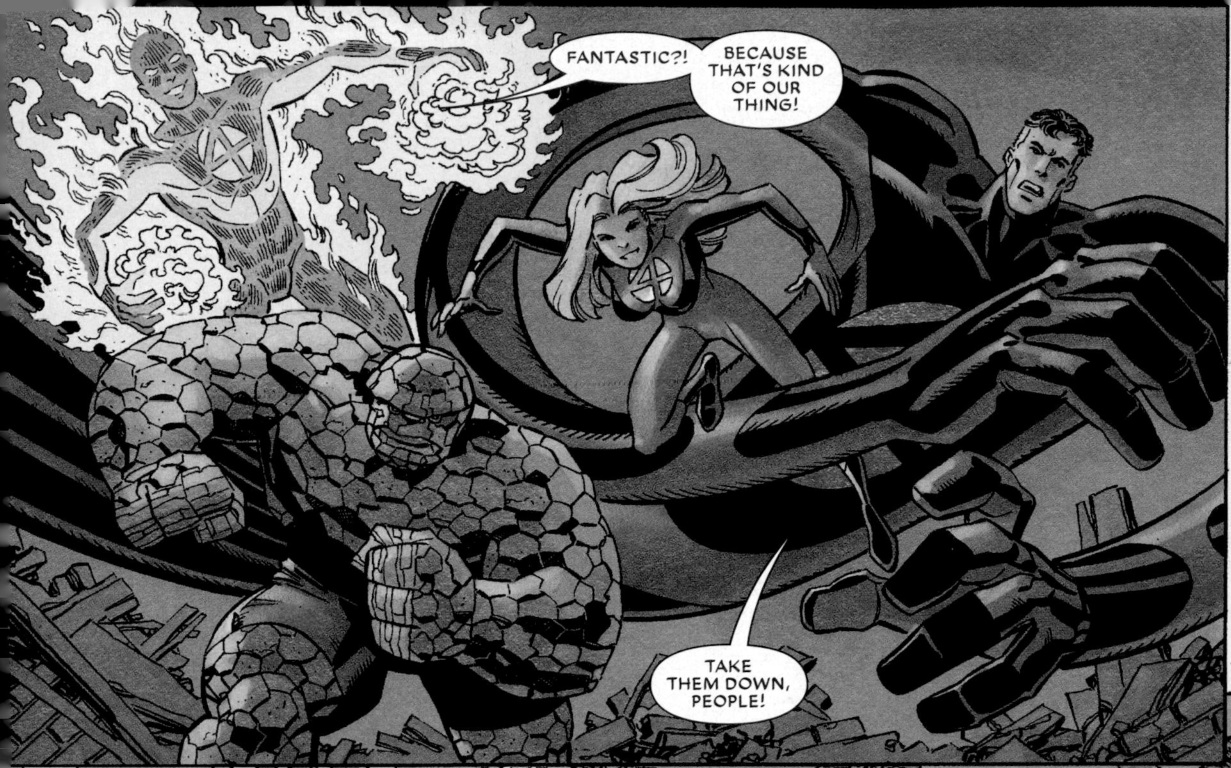
FANTASTIC?!
BECAUSE THAT'S KIND OF OUR THING!
TAKE THEM DOWN, PEOPLE!

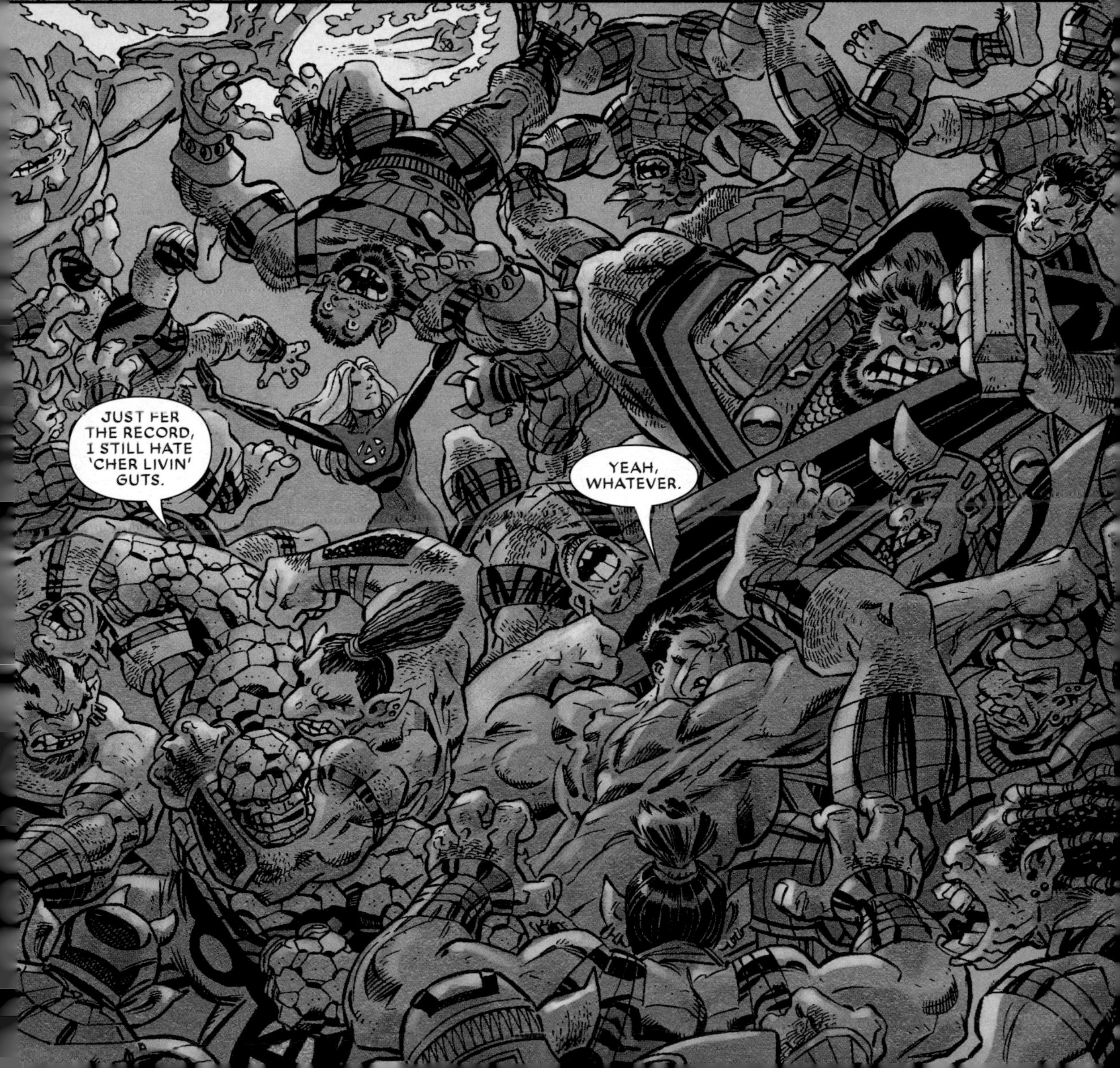
JUST FER THE RECORD, I STILL HATE 'CHER LIVIN' GUTS.
YEAH, WHATEVER.

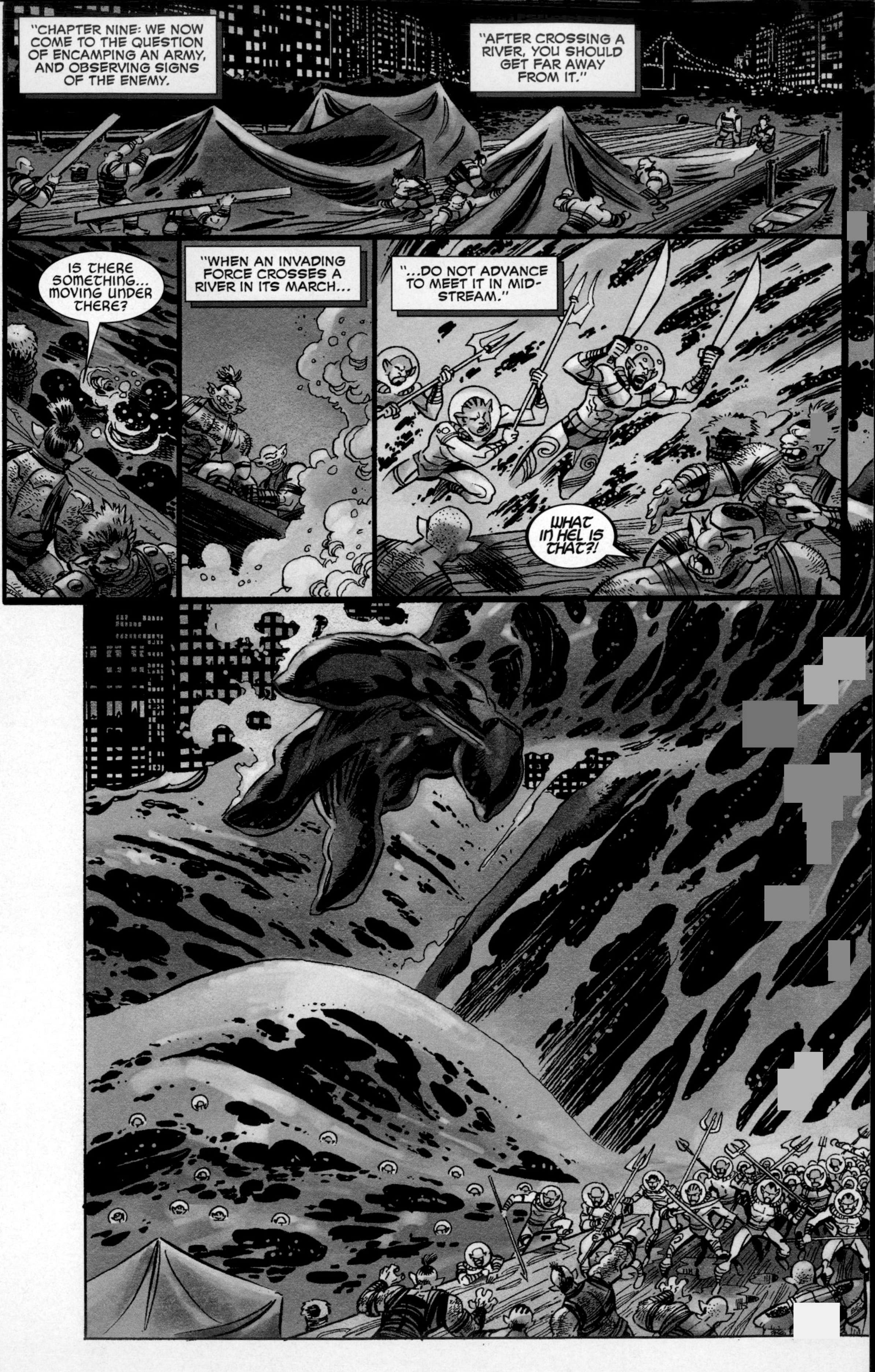
"CHAPTER NINE: WE NOW COME TO THE QUESTION OF ENCAMPING AN ARMY, AND OBSERVING SIGNS OF THE ENEMY.
"AFTER CROSSING A RIVER, YOU SHOULD GET FAR AWAY FROM IT."
IS THERE SOMETHING... MOVING UNDER THERE?
"WHEN AN INVADING FORCE CROSSES A RIVER IN ITS MARCH...
"...DO NOT ADVANCE TO MEET IT IN MID-STREAM."
WHAT IN HEL IS THAT?!

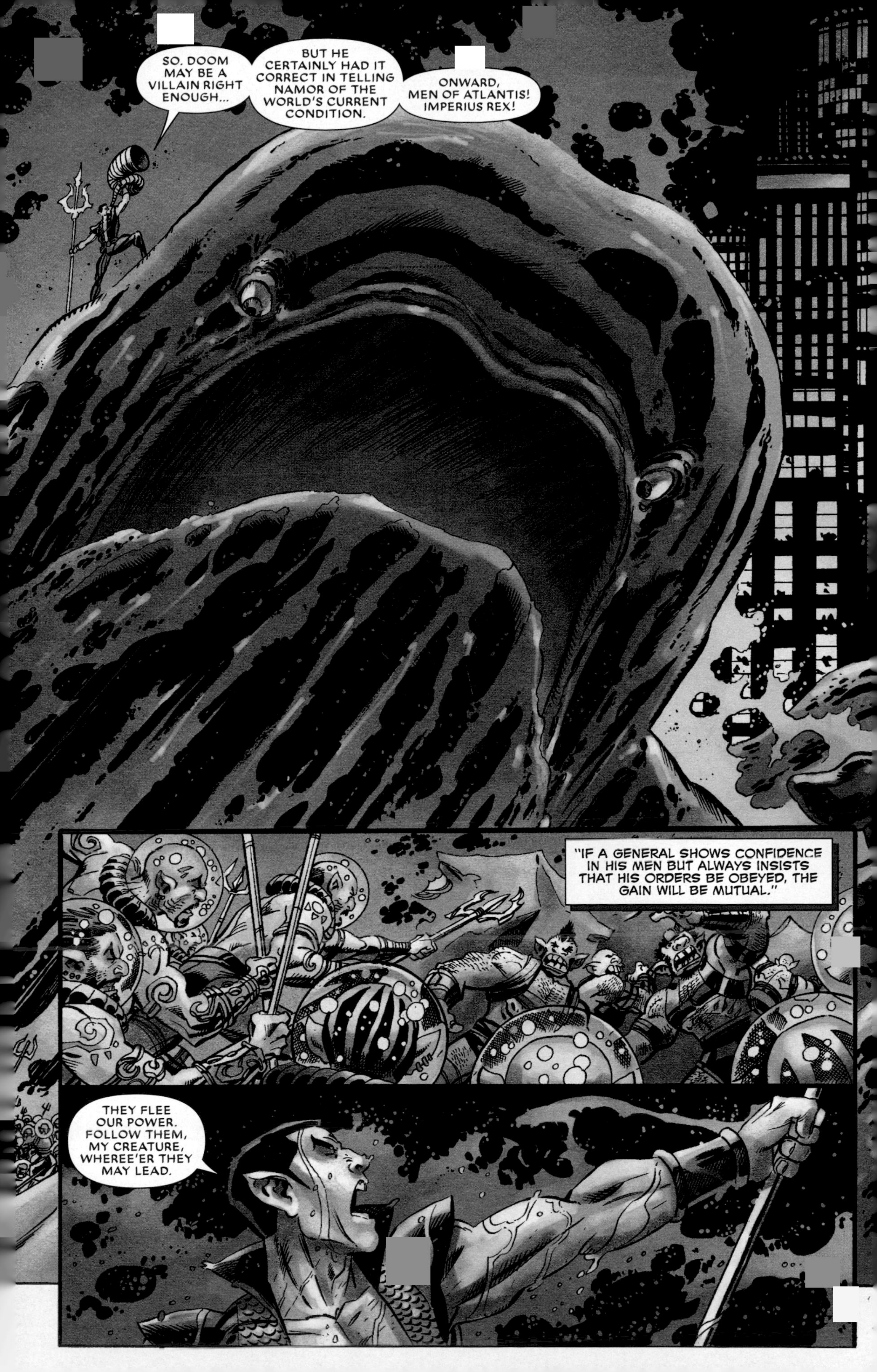
SO. DOOM MAY BE A VILLAIN RIGHT ENOUGH...
BUT HE CERTAINLY HAD IT CORRECT IN TELLING NAMOR OF THE WORLD'S CURRENT CONDITION.
ONWARD, MEN OF ATLANTIS! IMPERIUS REX!
"IF A GENERAL SHOWS CONFIDENCE IN HIS MEN BUT ALWAYS INSISTS THAT HIS ORDERS BE OBEYED, THE GAIN WILL BE MUTUAL."
THEY FLEE OUR POWER. FOLLOW THEM, MY CREATURE, WHEREE'ER THEY MAY LEAD.

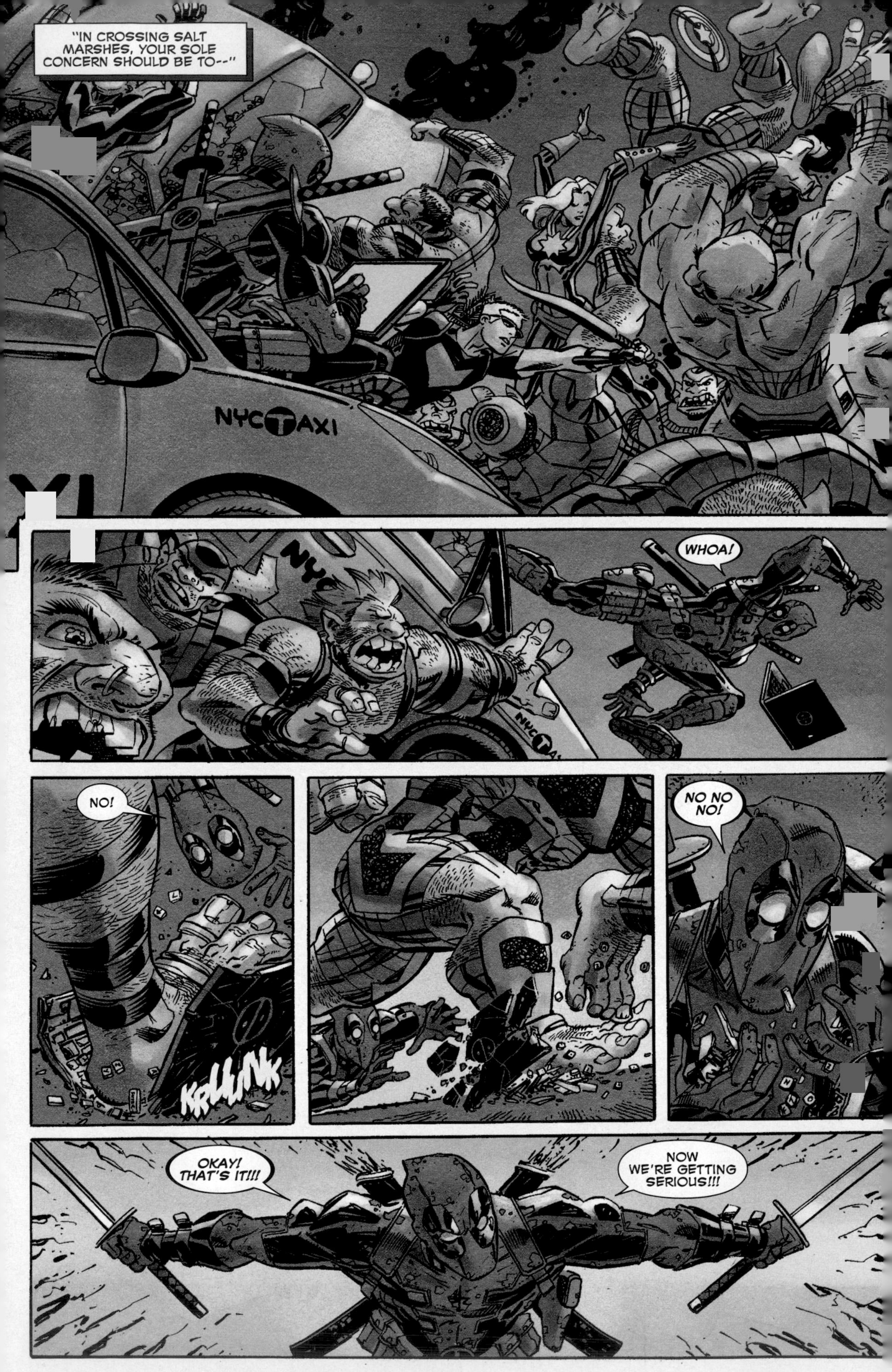

"IN CROSSING SALT MARSHES, YOUR SOLE CONCERN SHOULD BE TO--"
NYC TAXI
WHOA!
NO!
KRUUNK
NO NO NO!
OKAY! THAT'S IT!!!
NOW WE'RE GETTING SERIOUS!!!

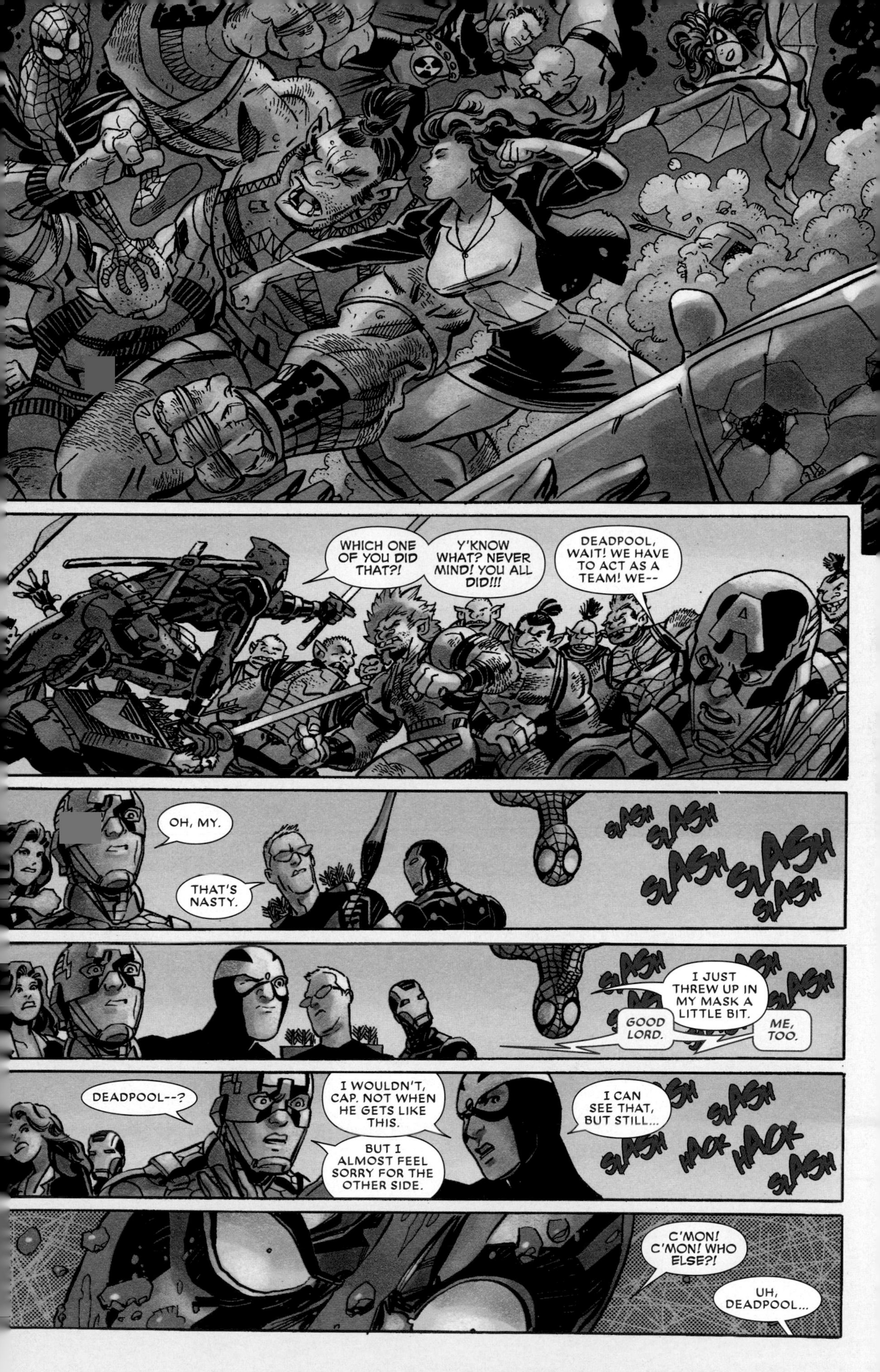
WHICH ONE OF YOU DID THAT?!
Y'KNOW WHAT? NEVER MIND! YOU ALL DID!!!
DEADPOOL, WAIT! WE HAVE TO ACT AS A TEAM! WE--
OH, MY.
THAT'S NASTY.
SLASH SLASH SLASH SLASH SLASH
I JUST THREW UP IN MY MASK A LITTLE BIT.
GOOD LORD.
ME, TOO.
DEADPOOL--?
I WOULDN'T, CAP. NOT WHEN HE GETS LIKE THIS.
BUT I ALMOST FEEL SORRY FOR THE OTHER SIDE.
I CAN SEE THAT, BUT STILL...
SLASH HACK HACK SLASH SLASH
C'MON! C'MON! WHO ELSE?!
UH, DEADPOOL...

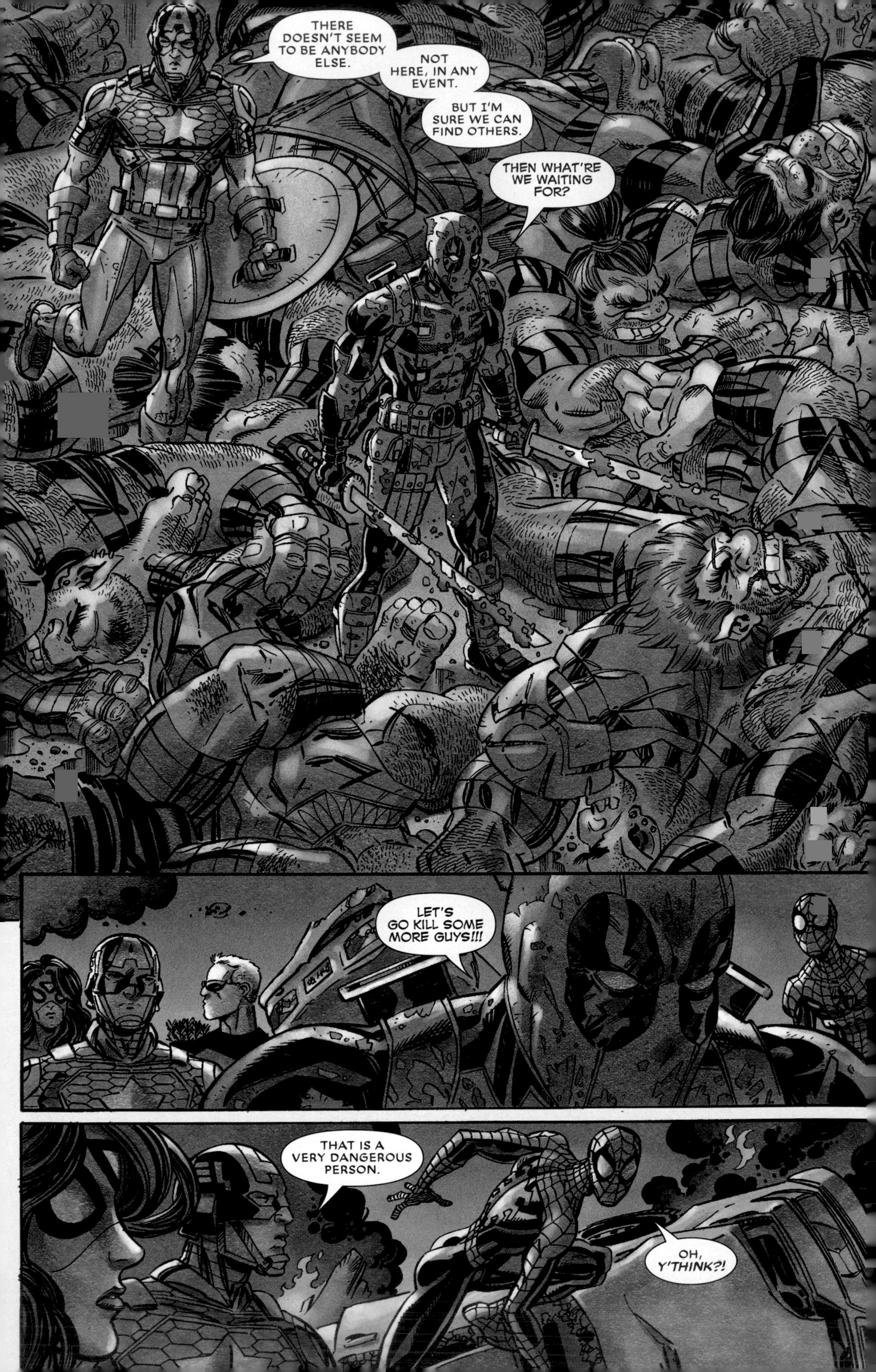
THERE DOESN'T SEEM TO BE ANYBODY ELSE.
NOT HERE, IN ANY EVENT.
BUT I'M SURE WE CAN FIND OTHERS.
THEN WHAT'RE WE WAITING FOR?
LET'S GO KILL SOME MORE GUYS!!!
THAT IS A VERY DANGEROUS PERSON.
OH, Y'THINK?!

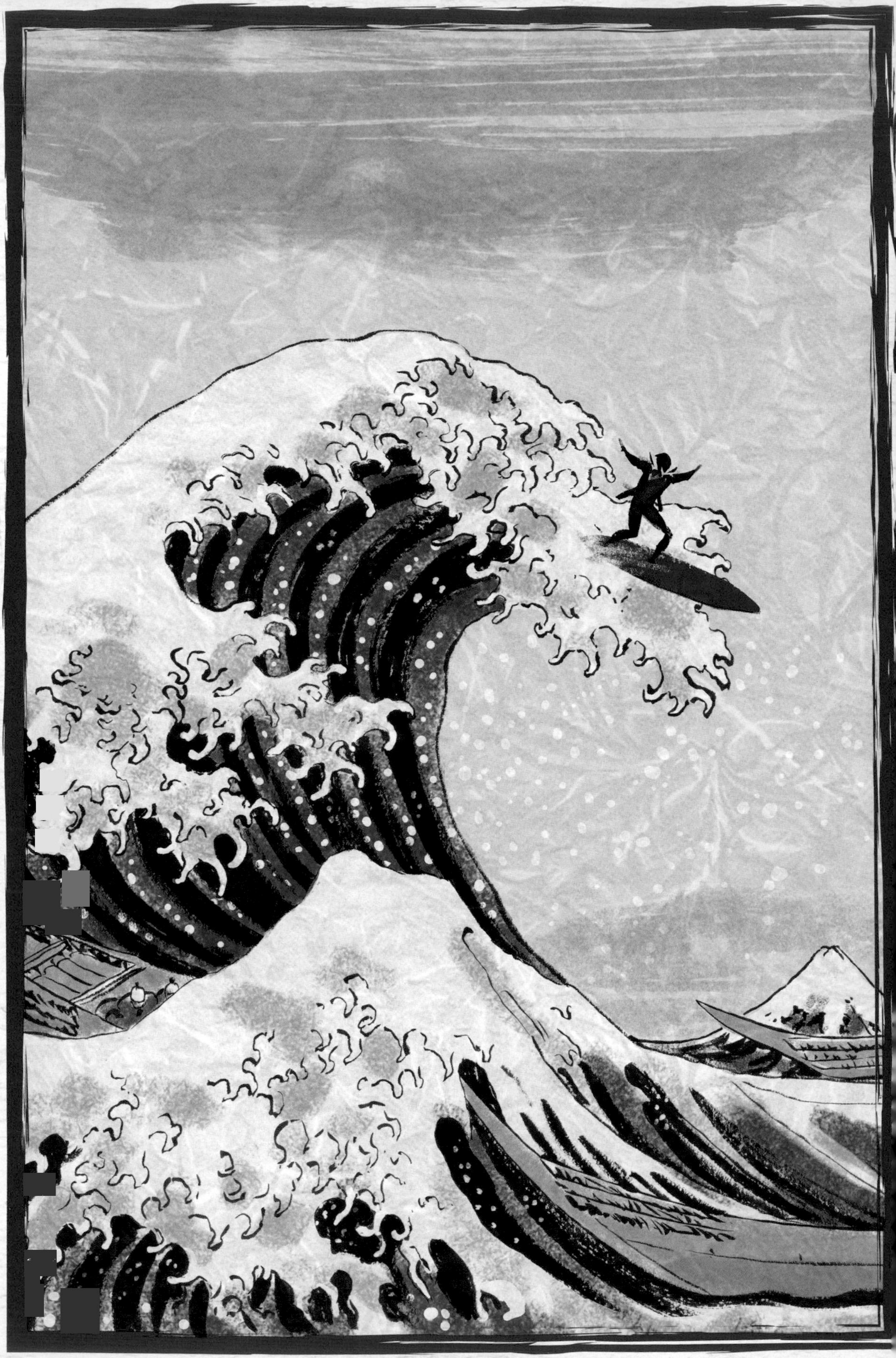

CHAPTER FOUR

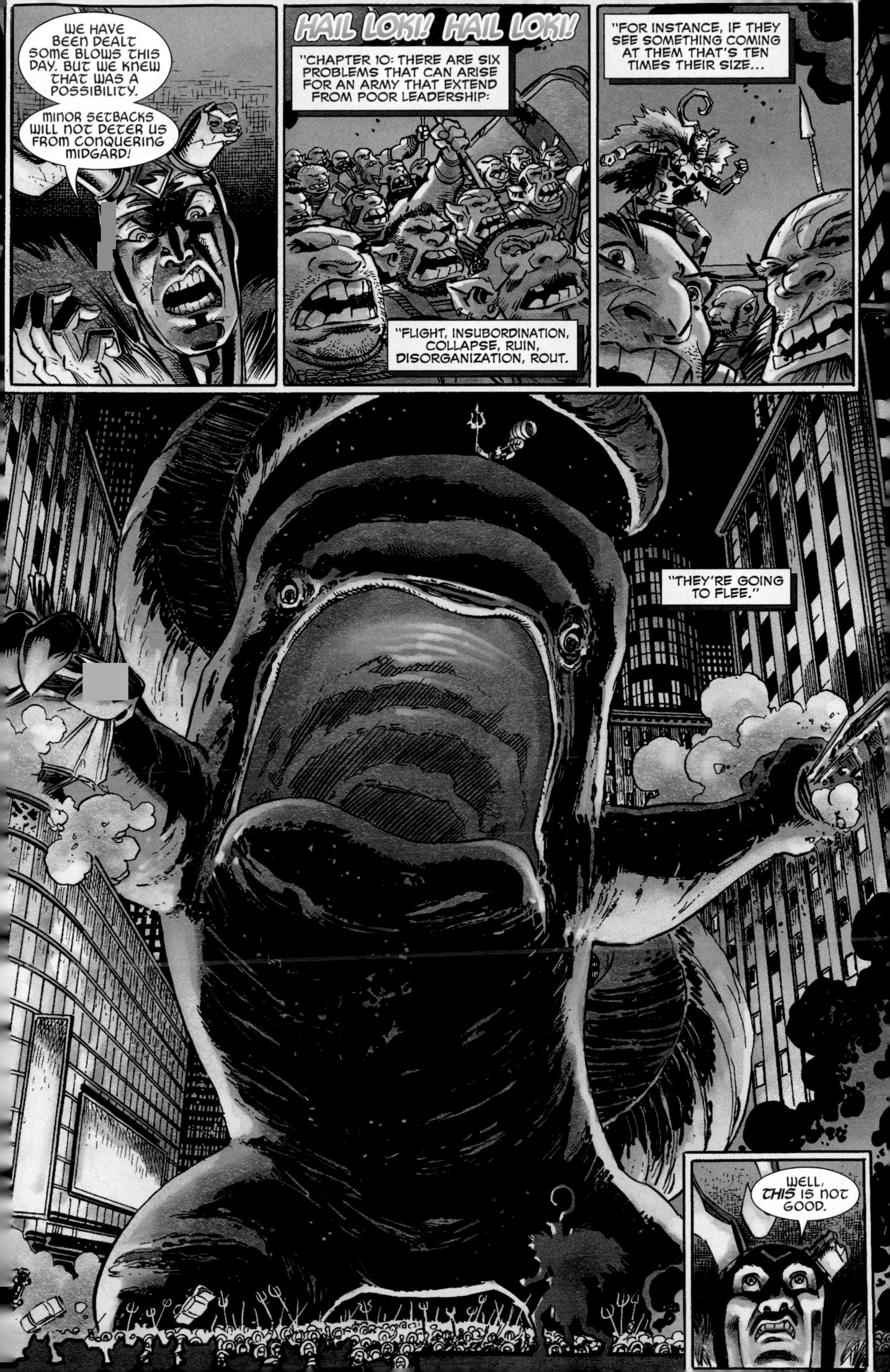
WE HAVE BEEN DEALT SOME BLOWS THIS DAY. BUT WE KNEW THAT WAS A POSSIBILITY.
MINOR SETBACKS WILL NOT DETER US FROM CONQUERING MIDGARD!
HAIL LOKI! HAIL LOKI!
"CHAPTER 10: THERE ARE SIX PROBLEMS THAT CAN ARISE FOR AN ARMY THAT EXTEND FROM POOR LEADERSHIP:
"FLIGHT, INSUBORDINATION, COLLAPSE, RUIN, DISORGANIZATION, ROUT.
"FOR INSTANCE, IF THEY SEE SOMETHING COMING AT THEM THAT'S TEN TIMES THEIR SIZE...
"THEY'RE GOING TO FLEE."
WELL, *THIS* IS NOT GOOD.

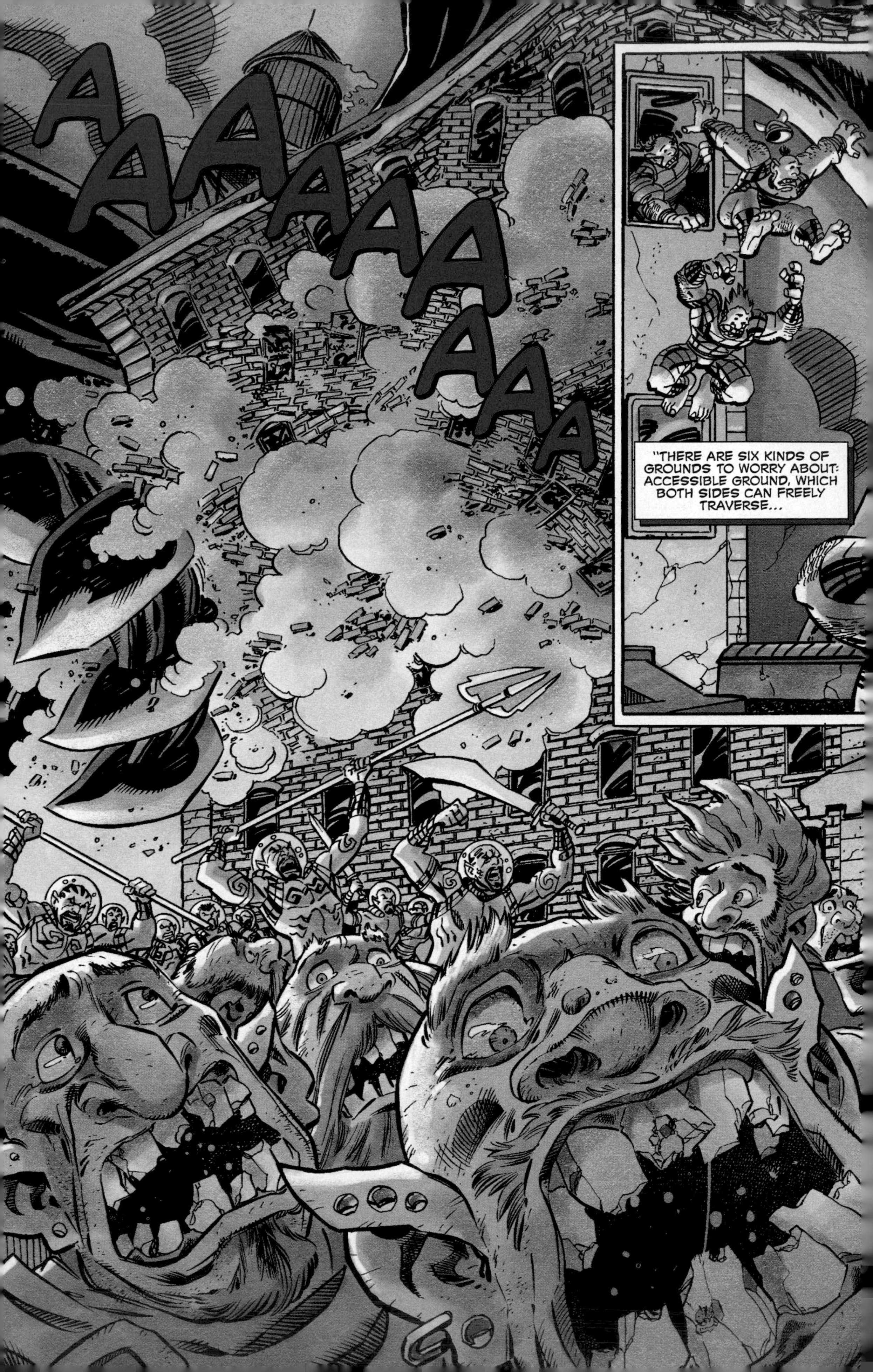
AAAAAAAAAAAA
"THERE ARE SIX KINDS OF GROUNDS TO WORRY ABOUT: ACCESSIBLE GROUND, WHICH BOTH SIDES CAN FREELY TRAVERSE...

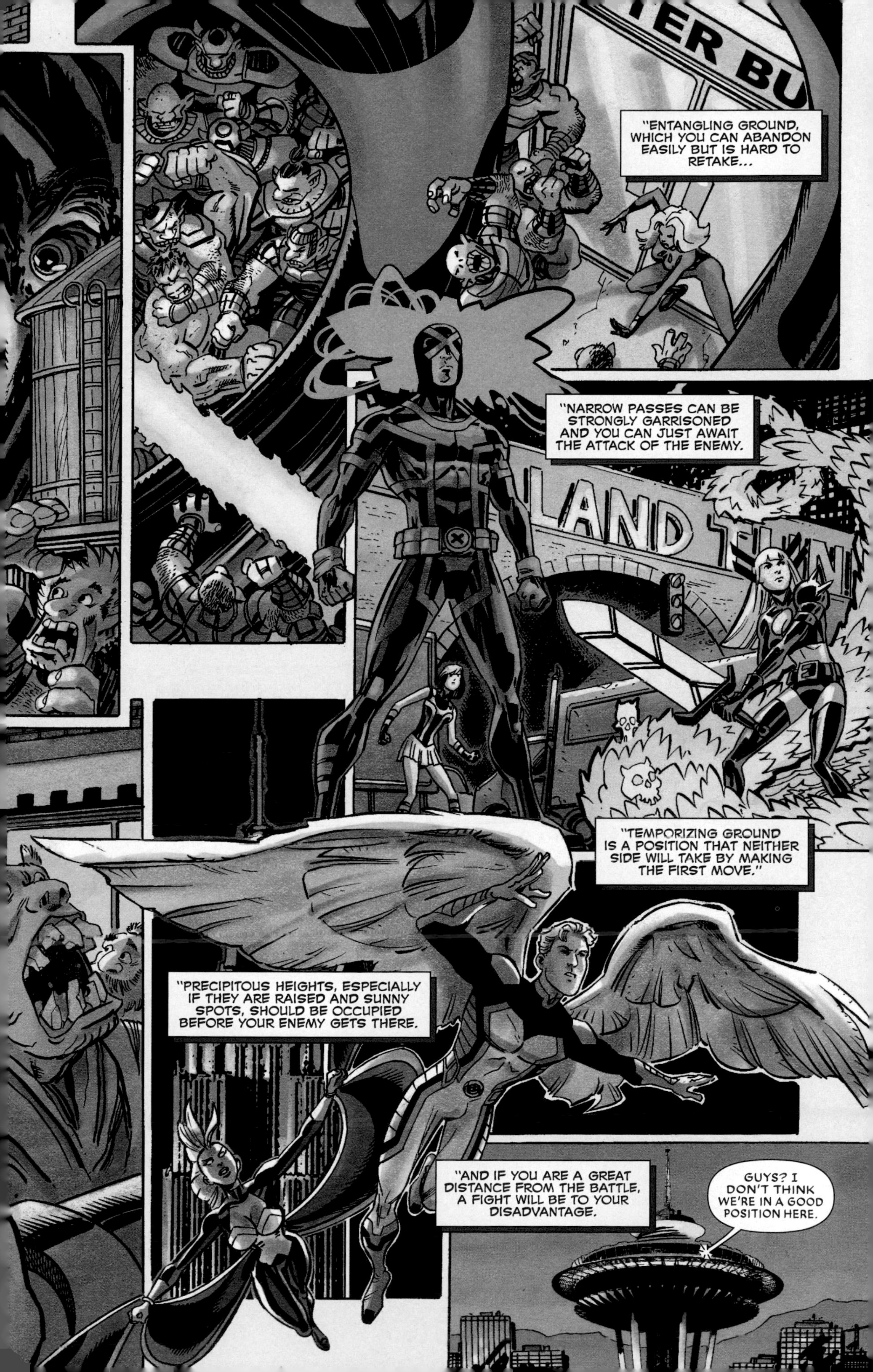

TER BU
"ENTANGLING GROUND, WHICH YOU CAN ABANDON EASILY BUT IS HARD TO RETAKE...
"NARROW PASSES CAN BE STRONGLY GARRISONED AND YOU CAN JUST AWAIT THE ATTACK OF THE ENEMY.
LAND
"TEMPORIZING GROUND IS A POSITION THAT NEITHER SIDE WILL TAKE BY MAKING THE FIRST MOVE."
"PRECIPITOUS HEIGHTS, ESPECIALLY IF THEY ARE RAISED AND SUNNY SPOTS, SHOULD BE OCCUPIED BEFORE YOUR ENEMY GETS THERE.
"AND IF YOU ARE A GREAT DISTANCE FROM THE BATTLE, A FIGHT WILL BE TO YOUR DISADVANTAGE.
GUYS? I DON'T THINK WE'RE IN A GOOD POSITION HERE.

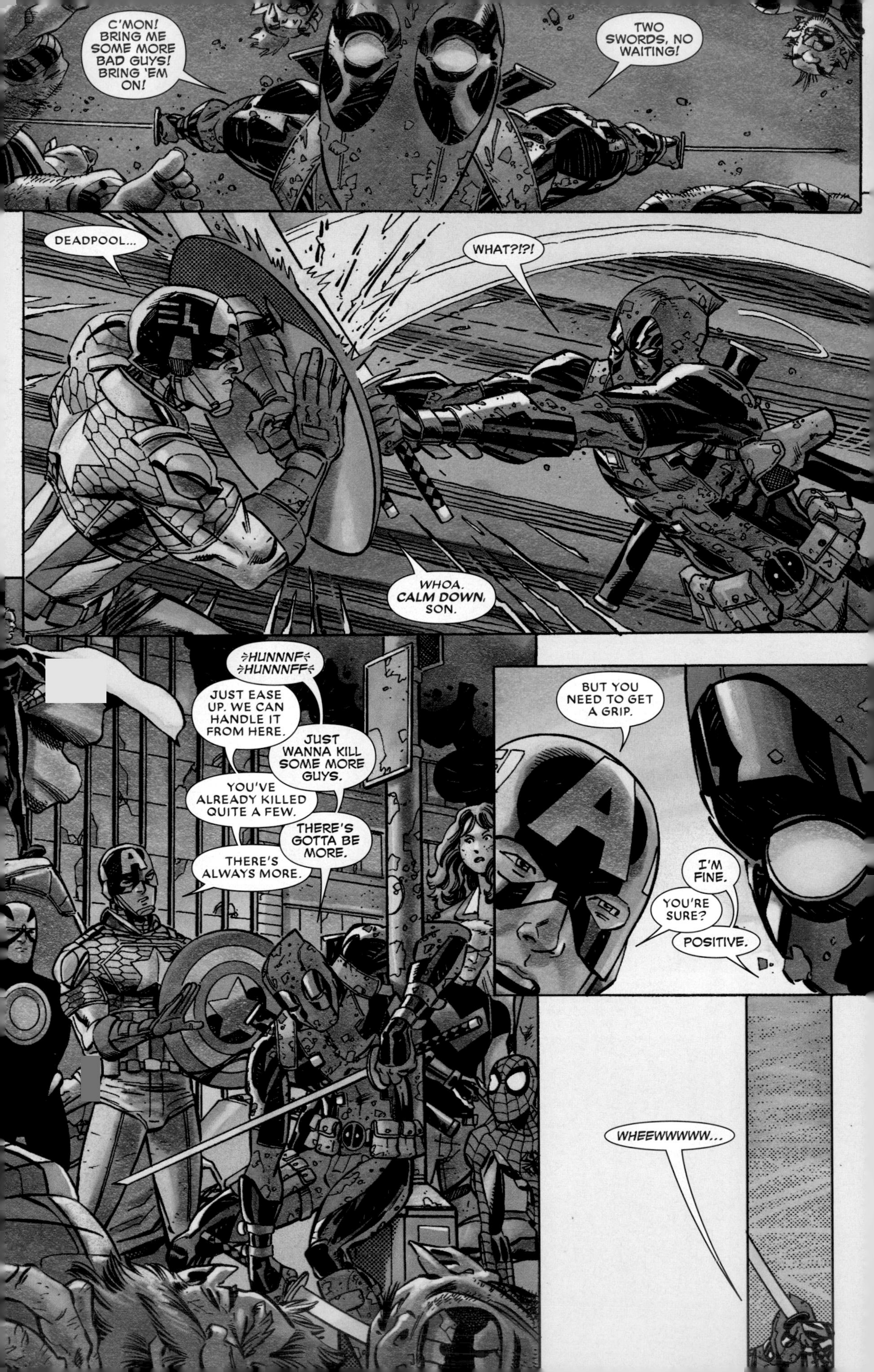
C'MON! BRING ME SOME MORE BAD GUYS! BRING 'EM ON!
TWO SWORDS, NO WAITING!
DEADPOOL...
WHAT?!?!
WHOA. CALM DOWN, SON.
HUNNNF HUNNNFF
JUST EASE UP. WE CAN HANDLE IT FROM HERE.
JUST WANNA KILL SOME MORE GUYS.
YOU'VE ALREADY KILLED QUITE A FEW.
THERE'S GOTTA BE MORE.
THERE'S ALWAYS MORE.
BUT YOU NEED TO GET A GRIP.
I'M FINE.
YOU'RE SURE?
POSITIVE.
WHEEWWWWW...

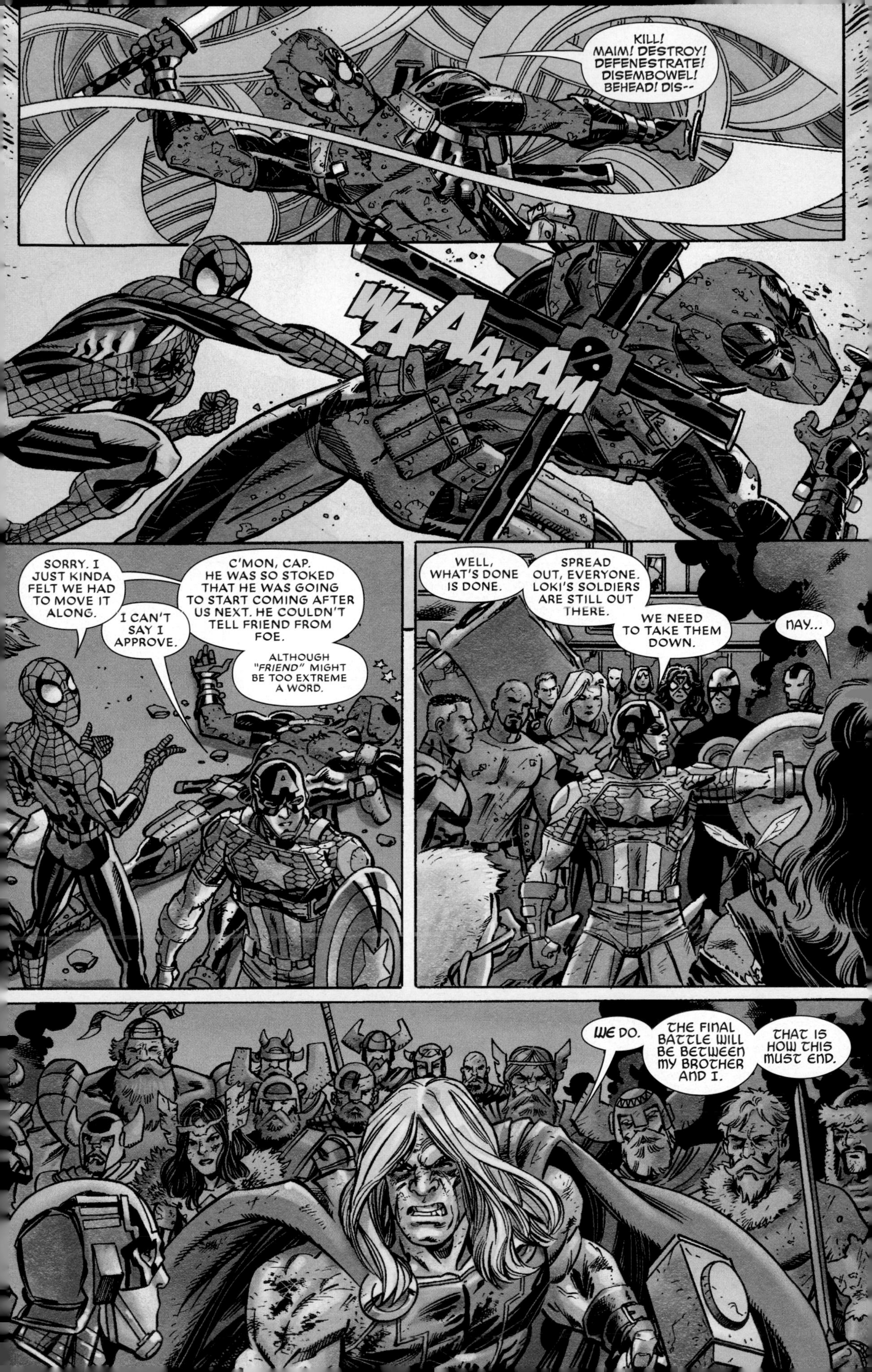
KILL! MAIM! DESTROY! DEFENESTRATE! DISEMBOWEL! BEHEAD! DIS--
WAAAAAAAM
SORRY. I JUST KINDA FELT WE HAD TO MOVE IT ALONG.
I CAN'T SAY I APPROVE.
C'MON, CAP. HE WAS SO STOKED THAT HE WAS GOING TO START COMING AFTER US NEXT. HE COULDN'T TELL FRIEND FROM FOE.
ALTHOUGH "FRIEND" MIGHT BE TOO EXTREME A WORD.
WELL, WHAT'S DONE IS DONE.
SPREAD OUT, EVERYONE. LOKI'S SOLDIERS ARE STILL OUT THERE.
WE NEED TO TAKE THEM DOWN.
NAY...
WE DO.
THE FINAL BATTLE WILL BE BETWEEN MY BROTHER AND I.
THAT IS HOW THIS MUST END.

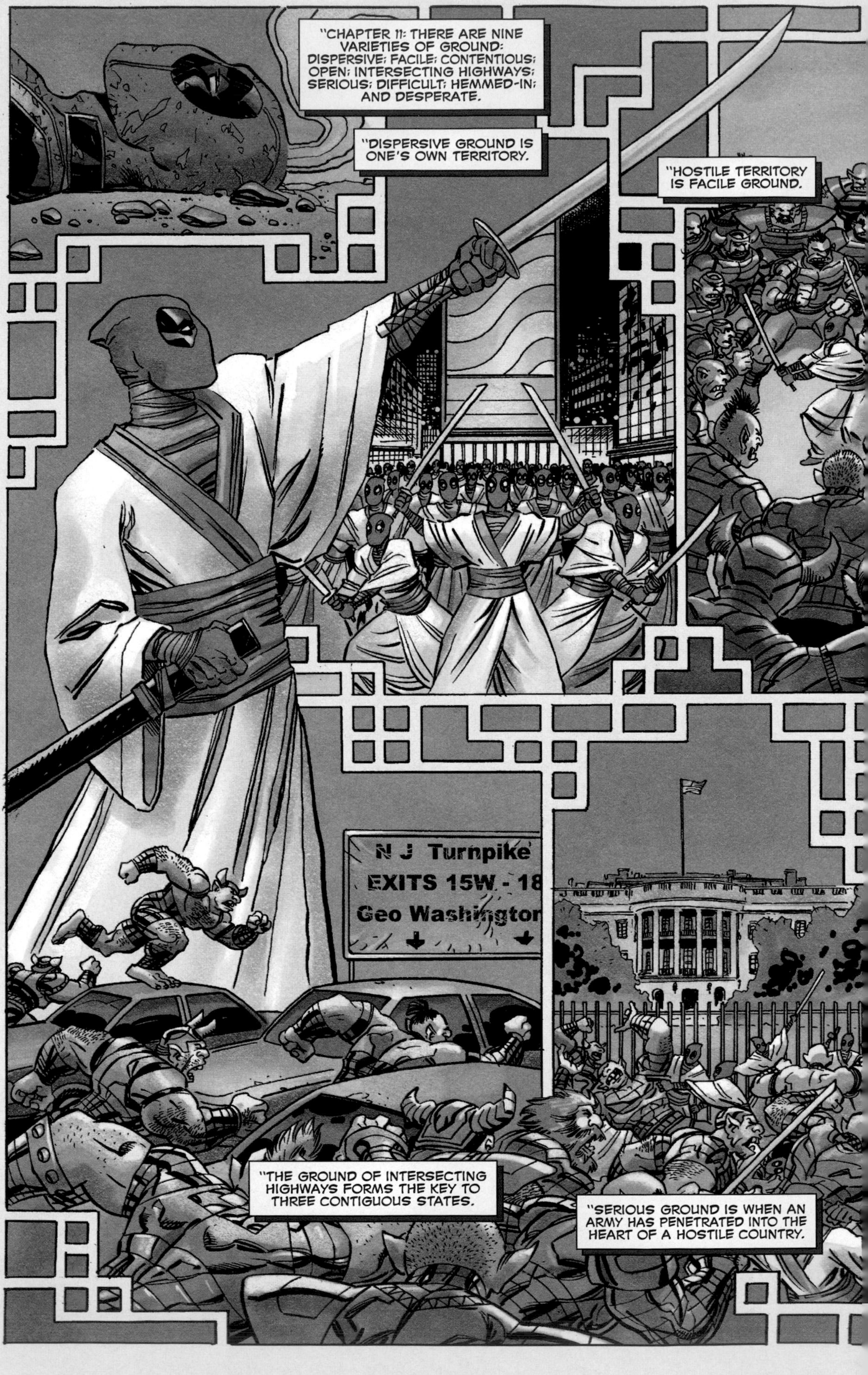
"CHAPTER 11: THERE ARE NINE VARIETIES OF GROUND: DISPERSIVE; FACILE; CONTENTIOUS; OPEN; INTERSECTING HIGHWAYS; SERIOUS; DIFFICULT; HEMMED-IN; AND DESPERATE.
"DISPERSIVE GROUND IS ONE'S OWN TERRITORY.
"HOSTILE TERRITORY IS FACILE GROUND.
N J Turnpike
EXITS 15W - 18
Geo Washington
"THE GROUND OF INTERSECTING HIGHWAYS FORMS THE KEY TO THREE CONTIGUOUS STATES.
"SERIOUS GROUND IS WHEN AN ARMY HAS PENETRATED INTO THE HEART OF A HOSTILE COUNTRY.

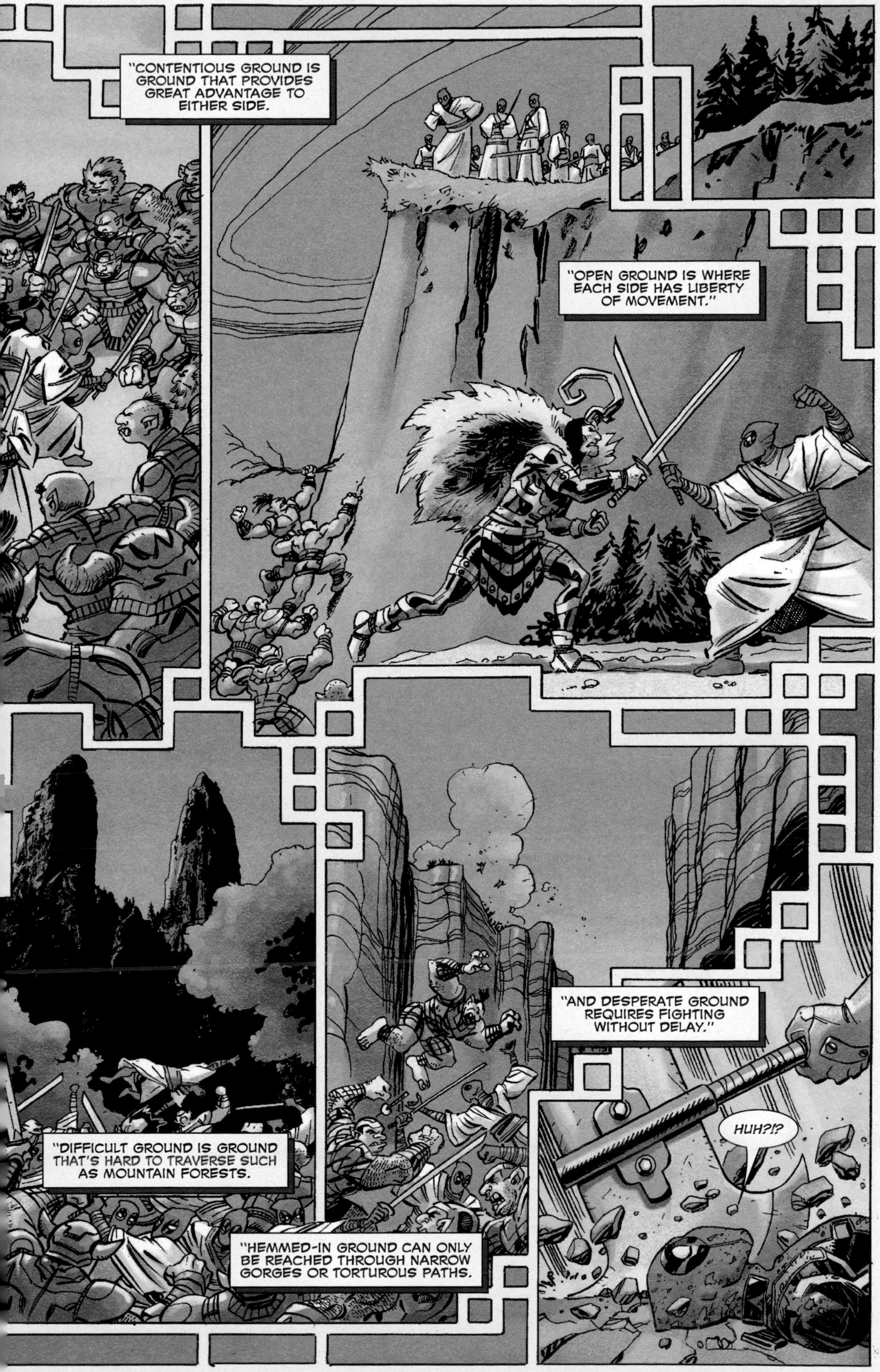
"CONTENTIOUS GROUND IS GROUND THAT PROVIDES GREAT ADVANTAGE TO EITHER SIDE.
"OPEN GROUND IS WHERE EACH SIDE HAS LIBERTY OF MOVEMENT."
"DIFFICULT GROUND IS GROUND THAT'S HARD TO TRAVERSE SUCH AS MOUNTAIN FORESTS.
"HEMMED-IN GROUND CAN ONLY BE REACHED THROUGH NARROW GORGES OR TORTUROUS PATHS.
"AND DESPERATE GROUND REQUIRES FIGHTING WITHOUT DELAY."
HUH?!?

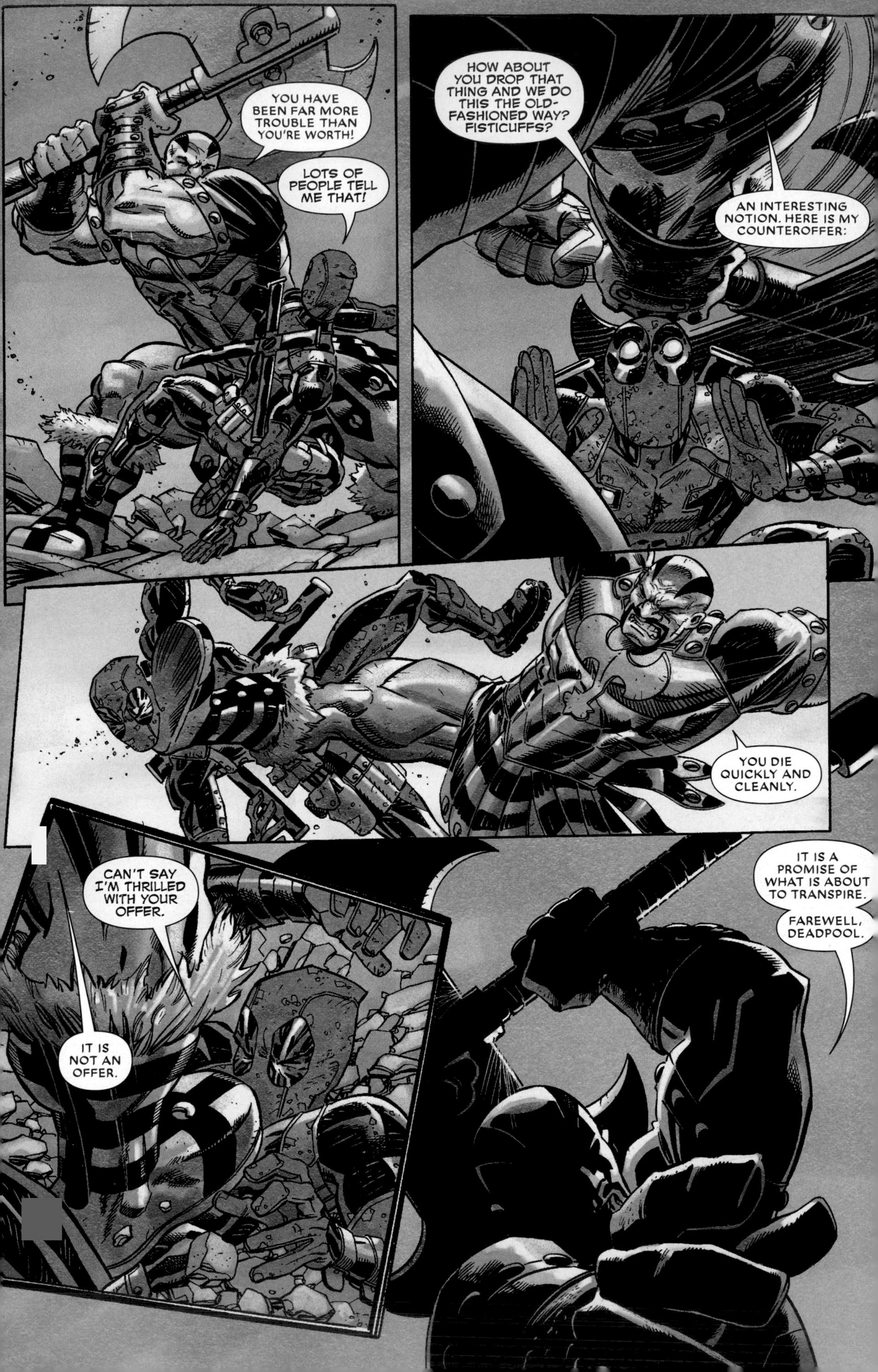
YOU HAVE BEEN FAR MORE TROUBLE THAN YOU'RE WORTH!
LOTS OF PEOPLE TELL ME THAT!
HOW ABOUT YOU DROP THAT THING AND WE DO THIS THE OLD-FASHIONED WAY? FISTICUFFS?
AN INTERESTING NOTION. HERE IS MY COUNTEROFFER:
YOU DIE QUICKLY AND CLEANLY.
CAN'T SAY I'M THRILLED WITH YOUR OFFER.
IT IS NOT AN OFFER.
IT IS A PROMISE OF WHAT IS ABOUT TO TRANSPIRE.
FAREWELL, DEADPOOL.

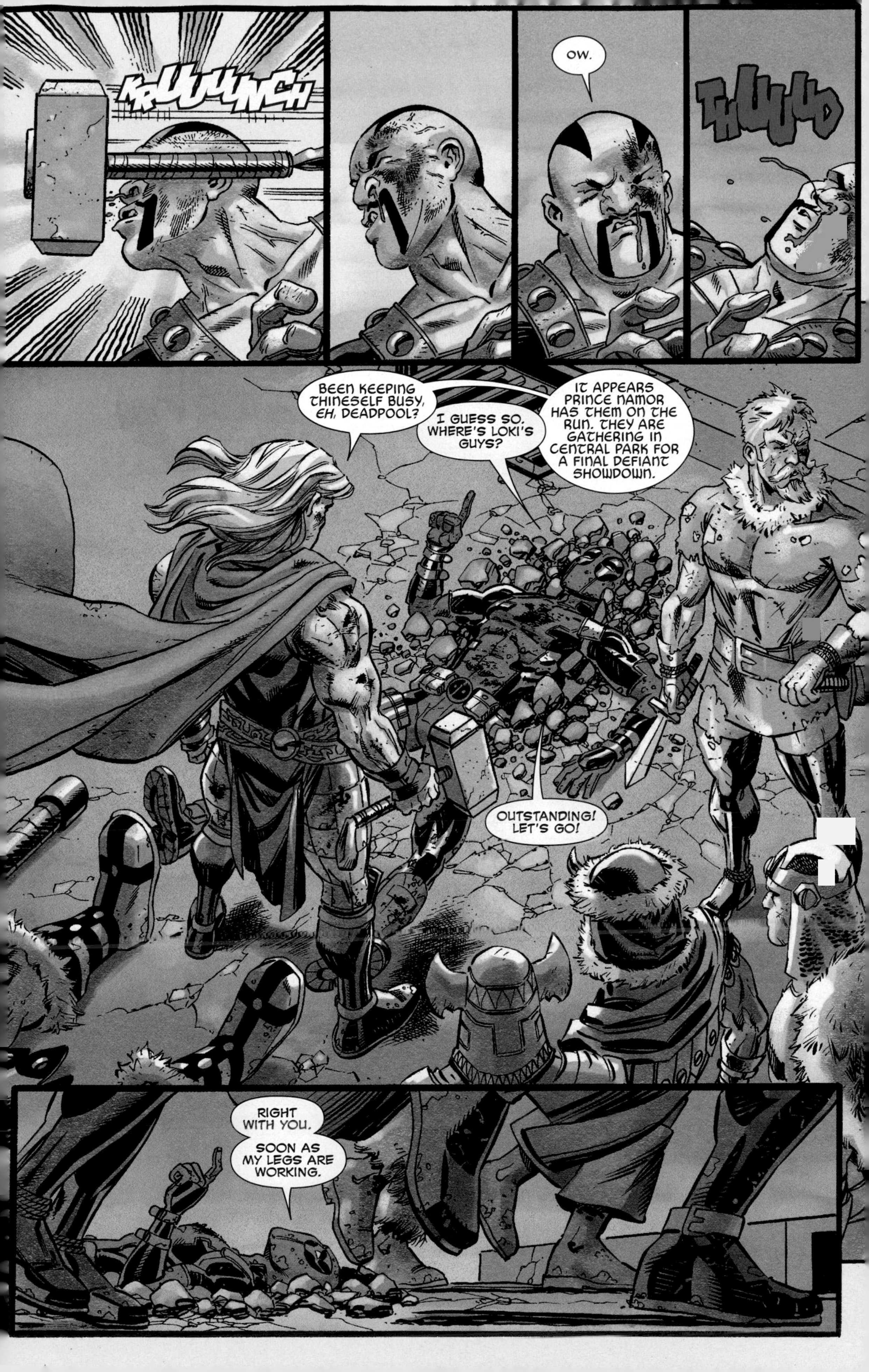
KRUUUUNCH
OW.
THUUUD
BEEN KEEPING THINESELF BUSY, EH, DEADPOOL?
I GUESS SO. WHERE'S LOKI'S GUYS?
IT APPEARS PRINCE NAMOR HAS THEM ON THE RUN. THEY ARE GATHERING IN CENTRAL PARK FOR A FINAL DEFIANT SHOWDOWN.
OUTSTANDING! LET'S GO!
RIGHT WITH YOU.
SOON AS MY LEGS ARE WORKING.

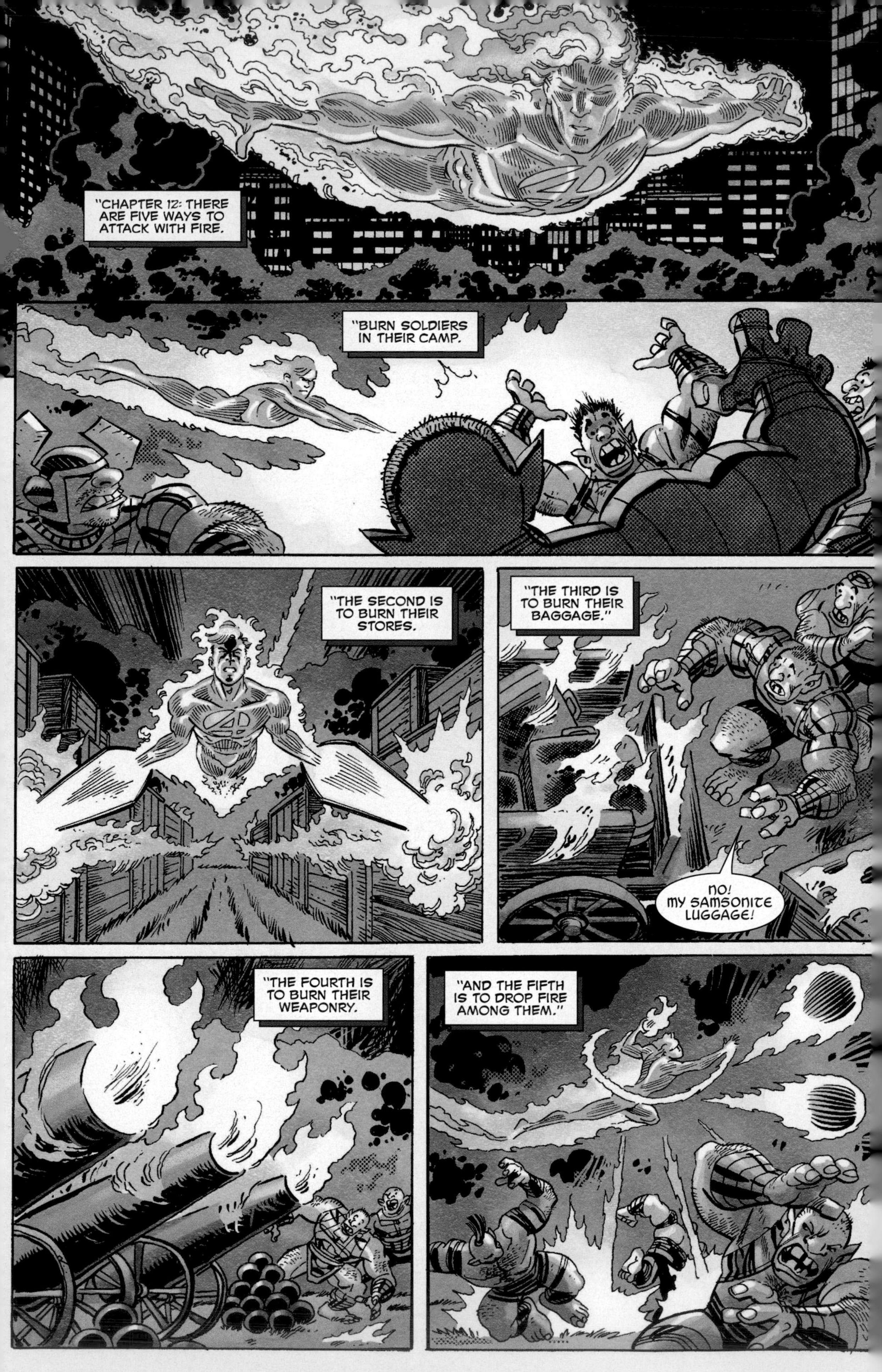
"CHAPTER 12: THERE ARE FIVE WAYS TO ATTACK WITH FIRE.
"BURN SOLDIERS IN THEIR CAMP.
"THE SECOND IS TO BURN THEIR STORES.
"THE THIRD IS TO BURN THEIR BAGGAGE."
NO! MY SAMSONITE LUGGAGE!
"THE FOURTH IS TO BURN THEIR WEAPONRY.
"AND THE FIFTH IS TO DROP FIRE AMONG THEM."

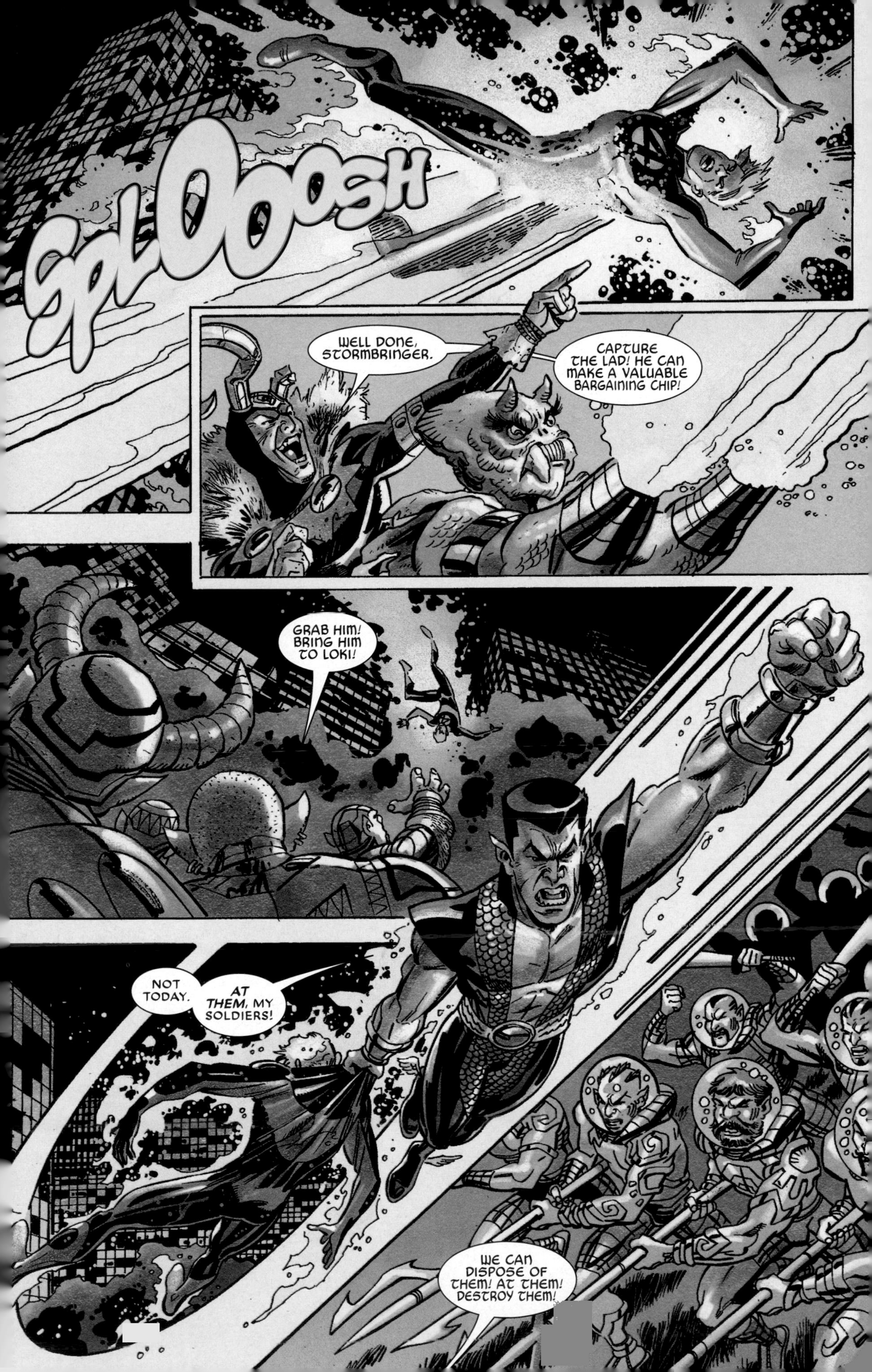
SPLOOOSH
WELL DONE, STORMBRINGER.
CAPTURE THE LAD! HE CAN MAKE A VALUABLE BARGAINING CHIP!
GRAB HIM! BRING HIM TO LOKI!
NOT TODAY.
AT THEM, MY SOLDIERS!
WE CAN DISPOSE OF THEM! AT THEM! DESTROY THEM!

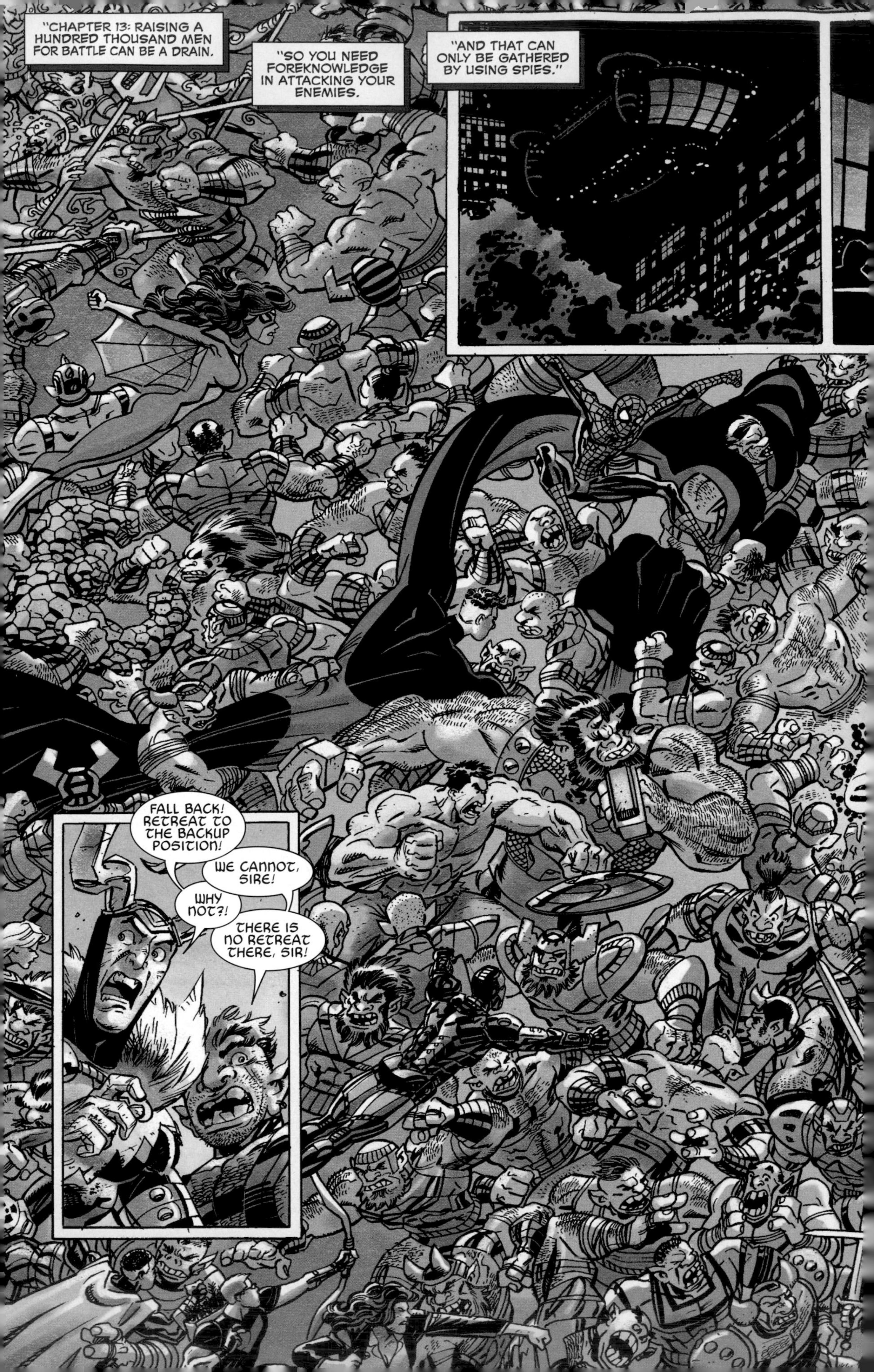
"CHAPTER 13: RAISING A HUNDRED THOUSAND MEN FOR BATTLE CAN BE A DRAIN.
"SO YOU NEED FOREKNOWLEDGE IN ATTACKING YOUR ENEMIES.
"AND THAT CAN ONLY BE GATHERED BY USING SPIES."
FALL BACK! RETREAT TO THE BACKUP POSITION!
WE CANNOT, SIRE!
WHY NOT?!
THERE IS NO RETREAT THERE, SIR!

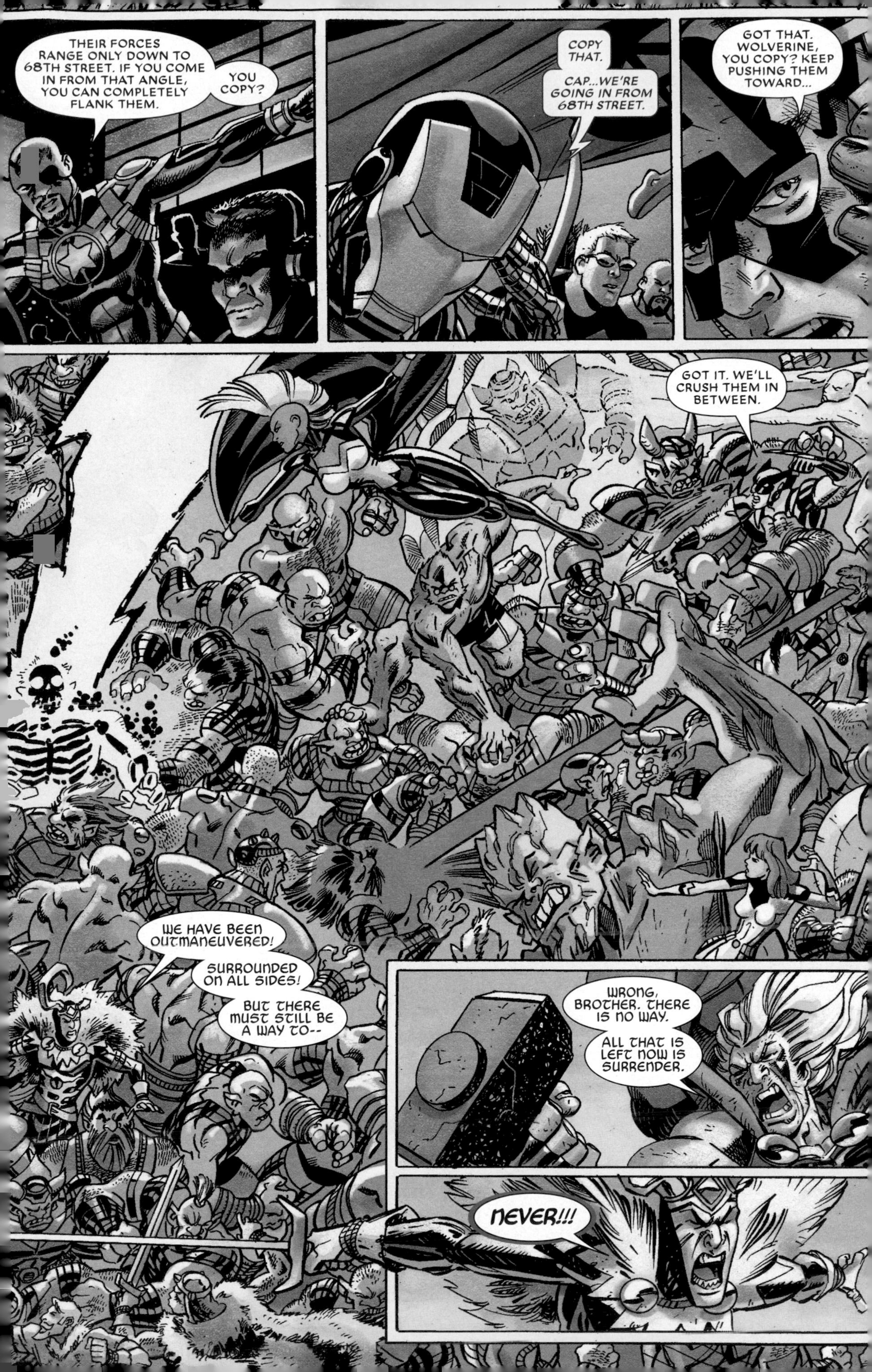
THEIR FORCES RANGE ONLY DOWN TO 68TH STREET. IF YOU COME IN FROM THAT ANGLE, YOU CAN COMPLETELY FLANK THEM.
YOU COPY?
COPY THAT.
CAP...WE'RE GOING IN FROM 68TH STREET.
GOT THAT. WOLVERINE, YOU COPY? KEEP PUSHING THEM TOWARD...
GOT IT. WE'LL CRUSH THEM IN BETWEEN.
WE HAVE BEEN OUTMANEUVERED!
SURROUNDED ON ALL SIDES!
BUT THERE MUST STILL BE A WAY TO--
WRONG, BROTHER. THERE IS NO WAY.
ALL THAT IS LEFT NOW IS SURRENDER.
NEVER!!!

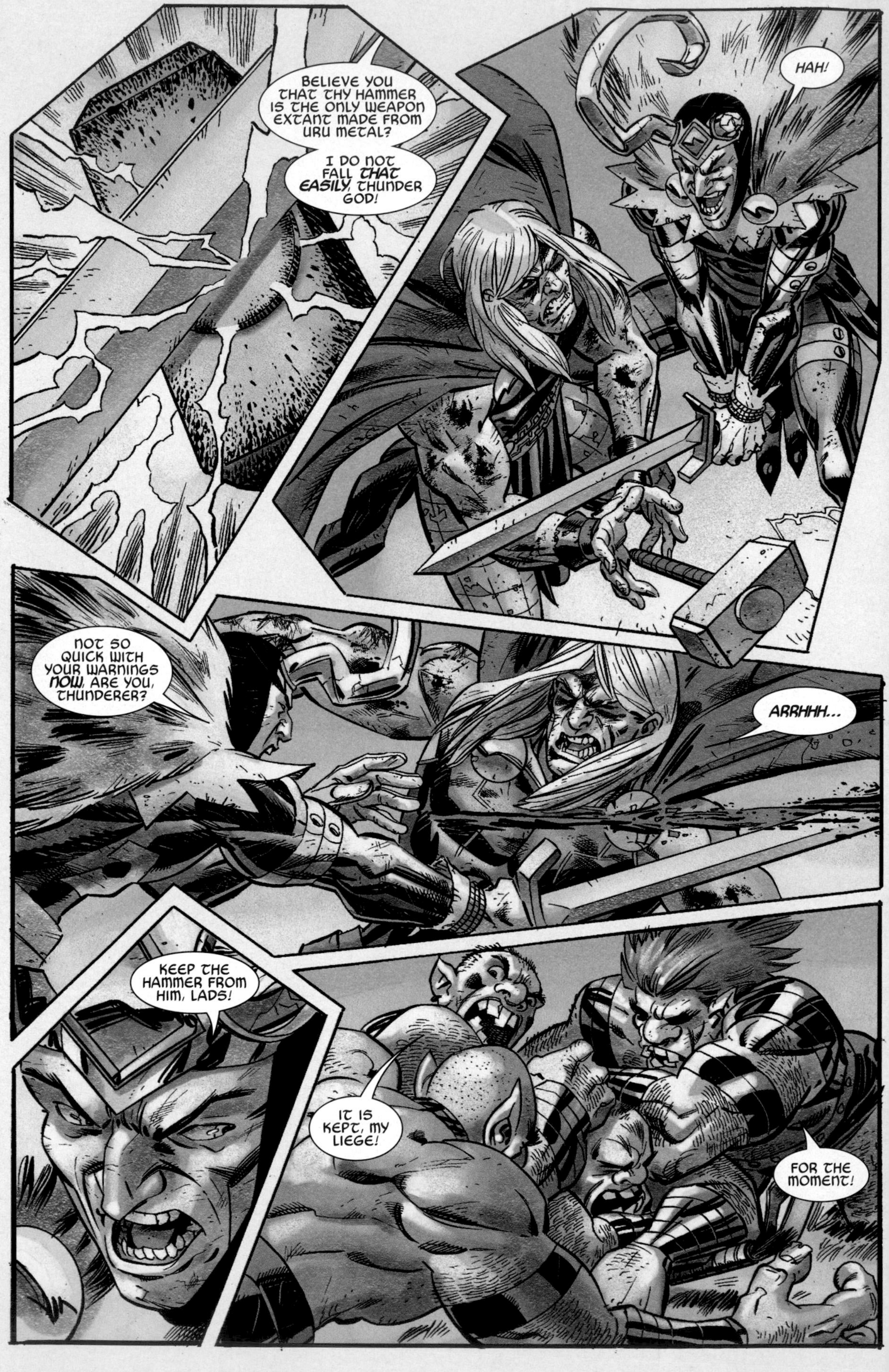
BELIEVE YOU THAT THY HAMMER IS THE ONLY WEAPON EXTANT MADE FROM URU METAL?
I DO NOT FALL *THAT EASILY*, THUNDER GOD!
HAH!
NOT SO QUICK WITH YOUR WARNINGS *NOW*, ARE YOU, THUNDERER?
ARRHHH...
KEEP THE HAMMER FROM HIM, LADS!
IT IS KEPT, MY LIEGE!
FOR THE MOMENT!

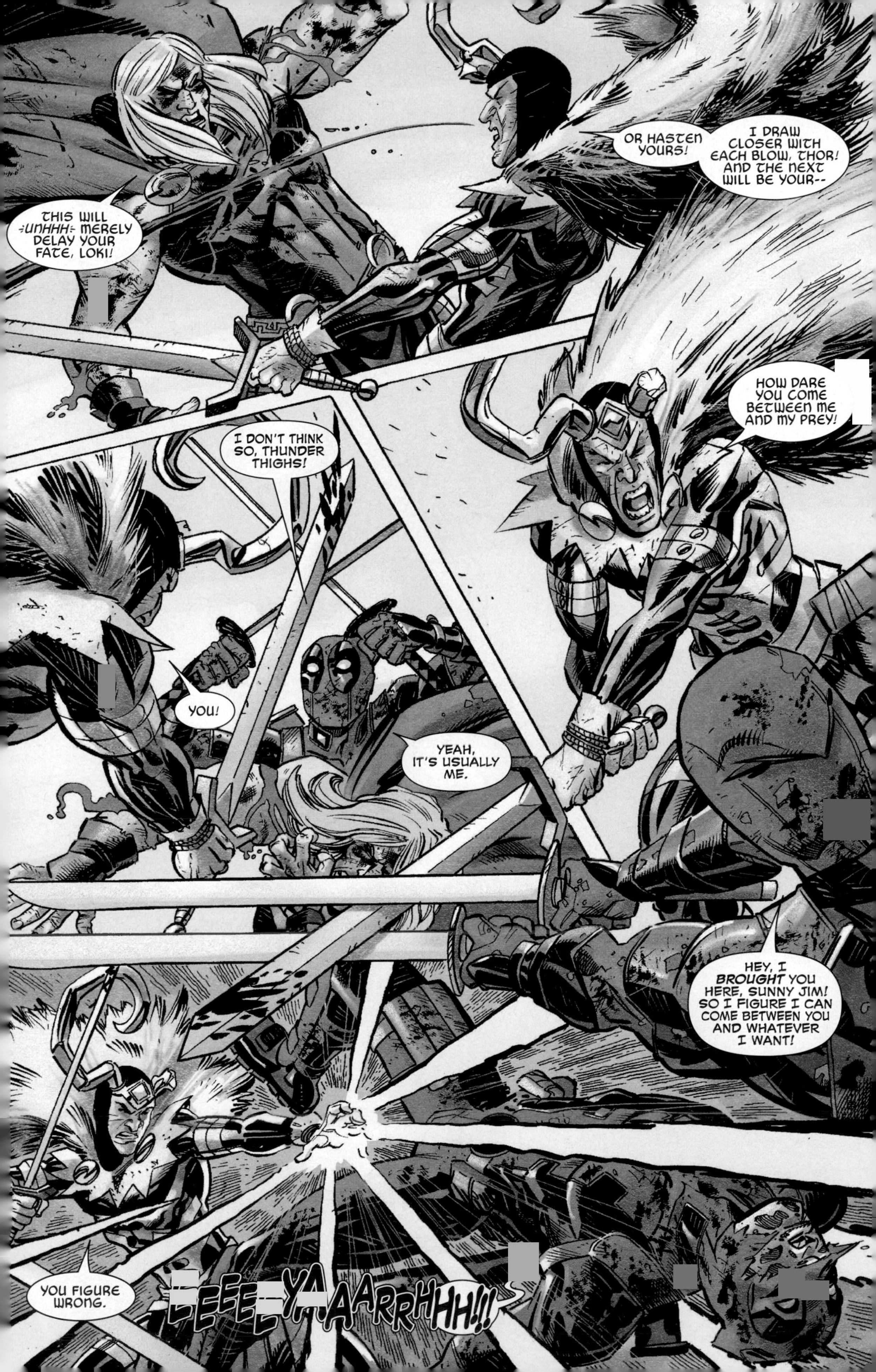
THIS WILL -UNHHH- MERELY DELAY YOUR FATE, LOKI!
OR HASTEN YOURS!
I DRAW CLOSER WITH EACH BLOW, THOR! AND THE NEXT WILL BE YOUR--
HOW DARE YOU COME BETWEEN ME AND MY PREY!
I DON'T THINK SO, THUNDER THIGHS!
YOU!
YEAH, IT'S USUALLY ME.
HEY, I *BROUGHT* YOU HERE, SUNNY JIM! SO I FIGURE I CAN COME BETWEEN YOU AND WHATEVER I WANT!
YOU FIGURE WRONG.
EEEEE-YAAARRHHH!!!

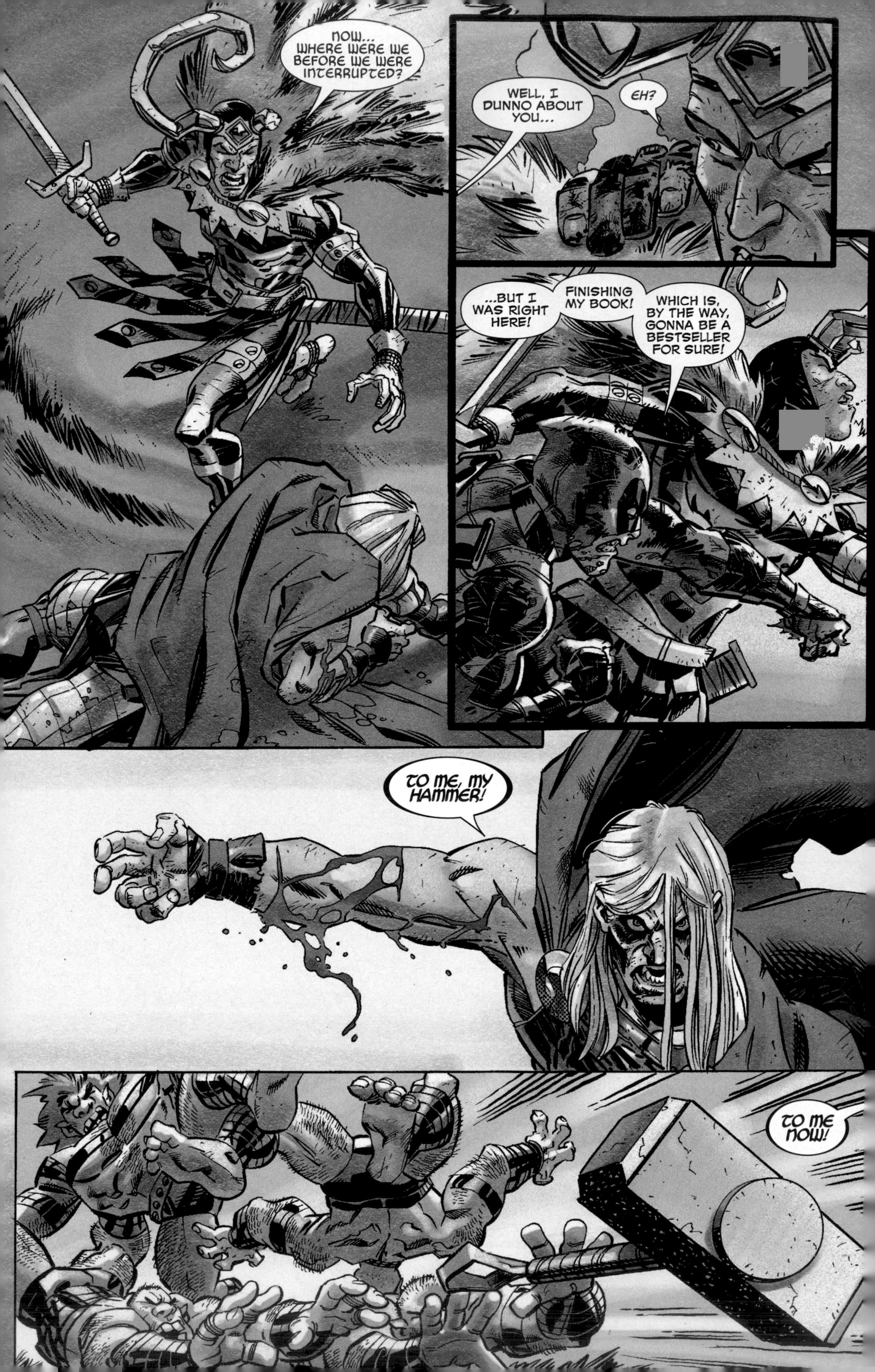
NOW... WHERE WERE WE BEFORE WE WERE INTERRUPTED?
WELL, I DUNNO ABOUT YOU...
EH?
...BUT I WAS RIGHT HERE!
FINISHING MY BOOK!
WHICH IS, BY THE WAY, GONNA BE A BESTSELLER FOR SURE!
TO ME, MY HAMMER!
TO ME NOW!

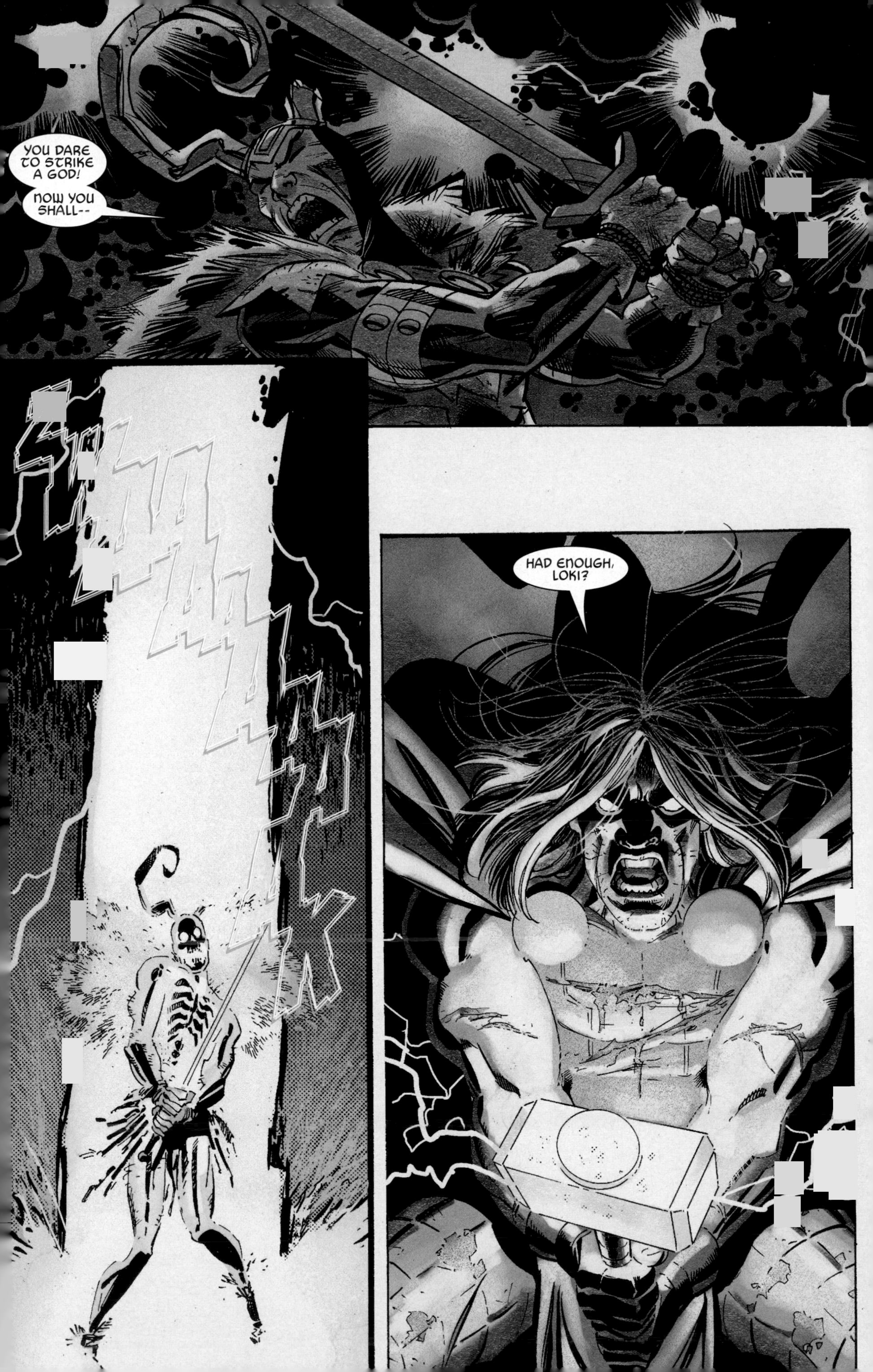
YOU DARE TO STRIKE A GOD!
NOW YOU SHALL--
HAD ENOUGH, LOKI?

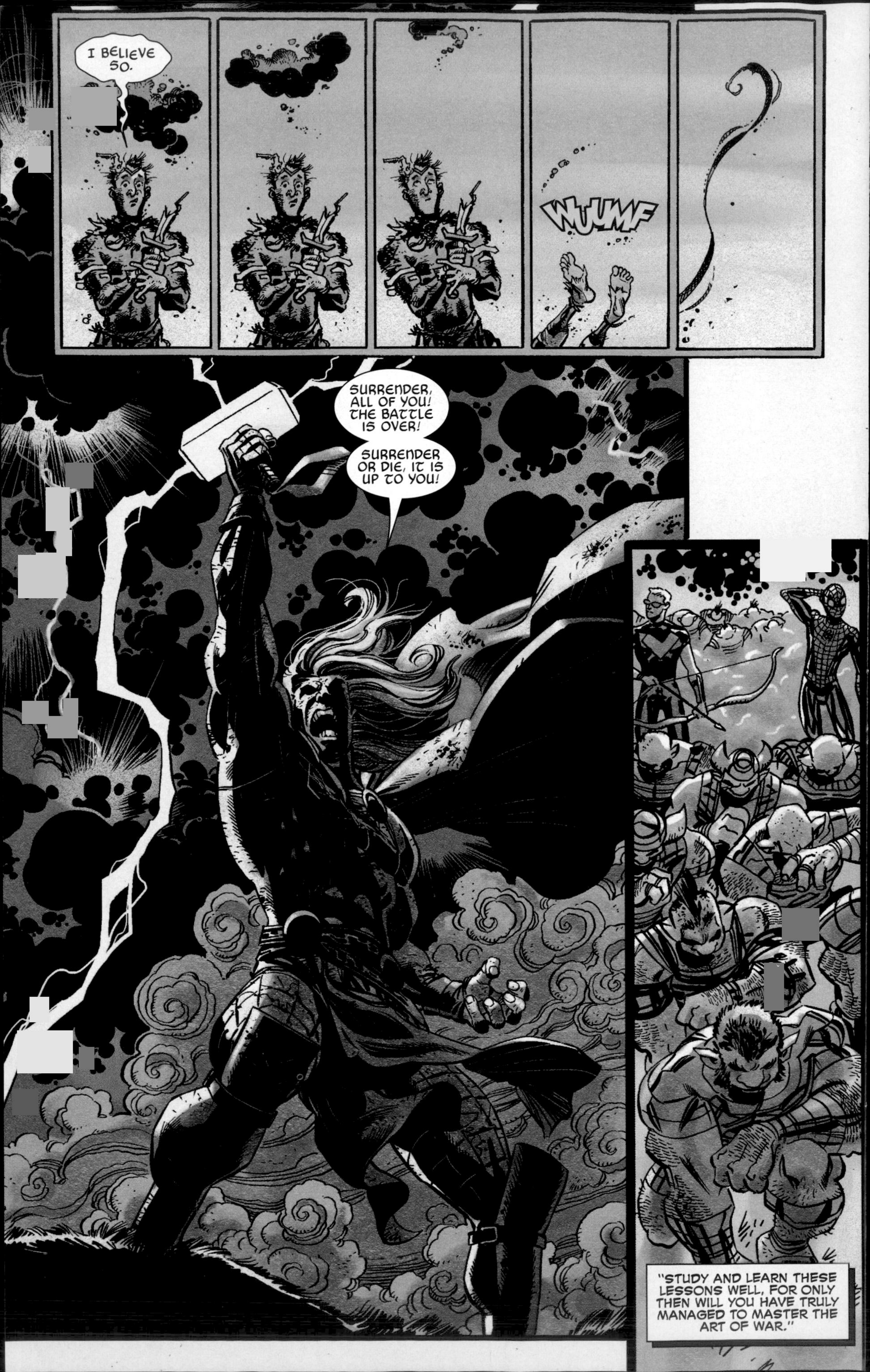
I BELIEVE SO.
WUUMF
SURRENDER, ALL OF YOU! THE BATTLE IS OVER!
SURRENDER OR DIE, IT IS UP TO YOU!
"STUDY AND LEARN THESE LESSONS WELL, FOR ONLY THEN WILL YOU HAVE TRULY MANAGED TO MASTER THE ART OF WAR."

MOST IMPRESSIVE, MR. POOL.

I LIKE THE REAL WORLD APPLICATIONS. THE WAY YOU COMBINED IT WITH THE MASSIVE WAR THAT WENT ON HERE IN NEW YORK.

AND HOW ARE YOU DOING?

THANKS.

OHHHH FINE. HEALING UP.

SO THIS WAS A RESULT OF LOKI BURNING YOU?

THIS? OH, NO. THIS WAS AFTER THE HEROES FOUND OUT I WAS RESPONSIBLE FOR LOKI COMING HERE.

"THEY FELT THE NEED TO, UH...MAKE CLEAR EXACTLY HOW THEY FELT ABOUT THAT."

"BUT DON'T WORRY. I'M HEALING. I'LL BE FINE IN NO TIME. LIKE A MONTH."

WELL, THE GOOD NEWS IS THAT WE ARE HAPPY TO PUBLISH YOUR BOOK.

GREAT. HOW MUCH WILL YOU PAY ME?

PAY YOU?

BWWA HAHA AHAHA

NO, MR. POOL: YOU PAY US. I HAVE A LIST OF EXPENSES RIGHT HERE.

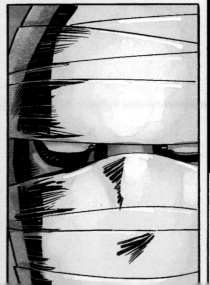

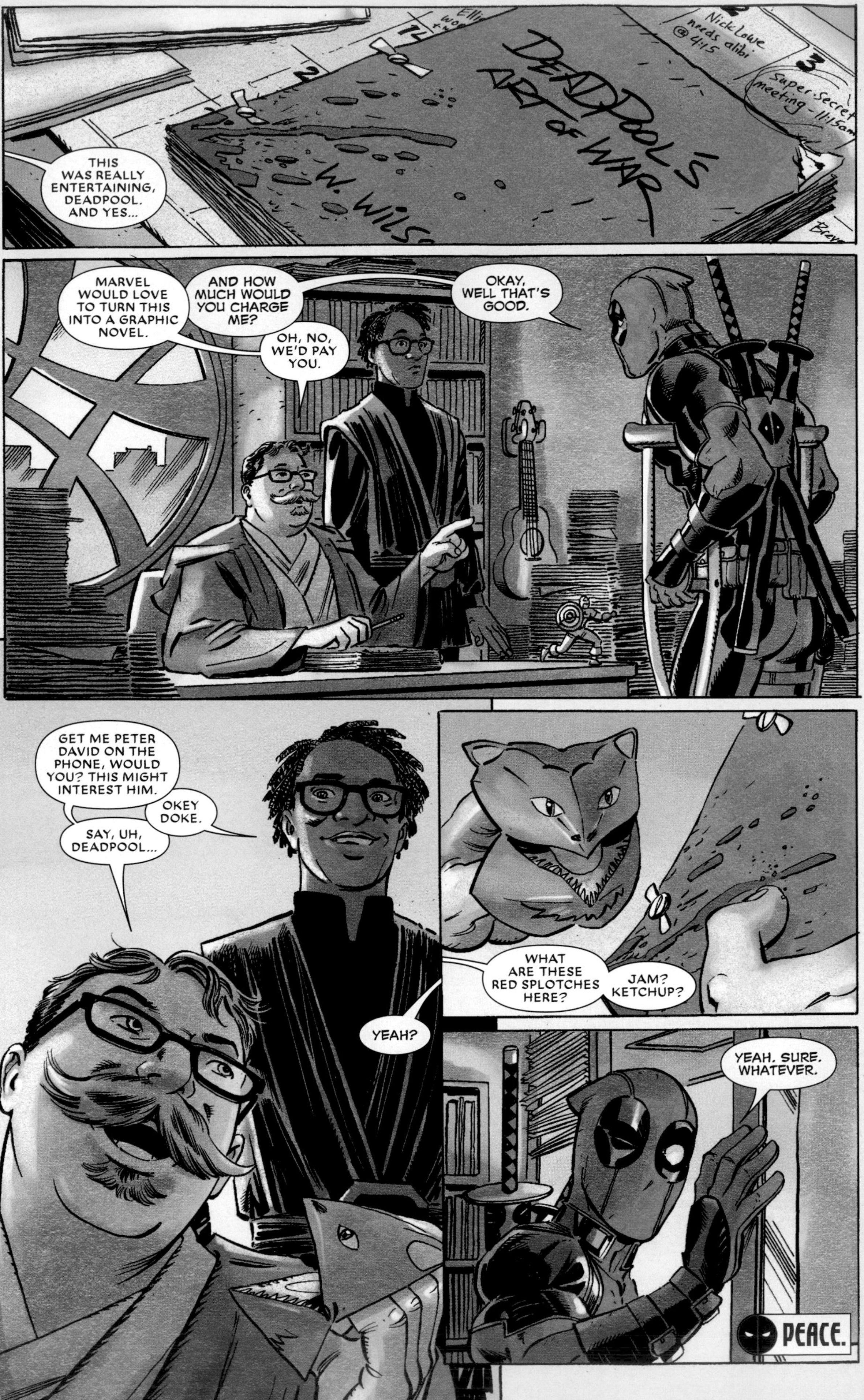
DEADPOOL'S ART OF WAR
Nick Lowe needs alibi @4:15
Super-Secret meeting - 11:15am
THIS WAS REALLY ENTERTAINING, DEADPOOL. AND YES...
MARVEL WOULD LOVE TO TURN THIS INTO A GRAPHIC NOVEL.
AND HOW MUCH WOULD YOU CHARGE ME?
OH, NO, WE'D PAY YOU.
OKAY, WELL THAT'S GOOD.
GET ME PETER DAVID ON THE PHONE, WOULD YOU? THIS MIGHT INTEREST HIM.
OKEY DOKE.
SAY, UH, DEADPOOL...
YEAH?
WHAT ARE THESE RED SPLOTCHES HERE?
JAM? KETCHUP?
YEAH. SURE. WHATEVER.
PEACE.

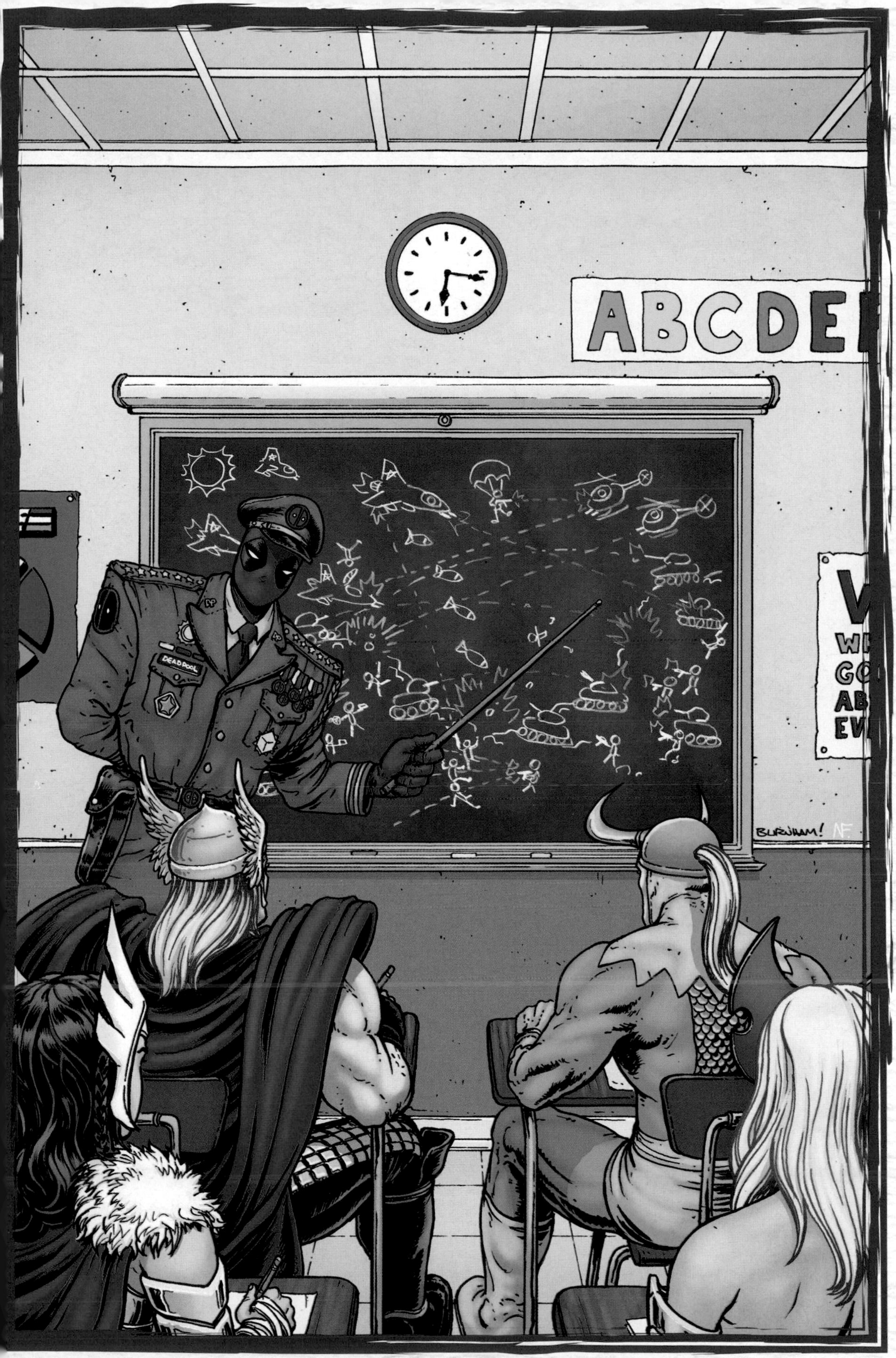
ABCDE
DEADPOOL
BURNHAM!
NF.

#*1* VARIANT BY **CHRIS BURNHAM & NATHAN FAIRBAIRN**

UNUSED COVER SKETCHES BY **SCOTT KOBLISH**

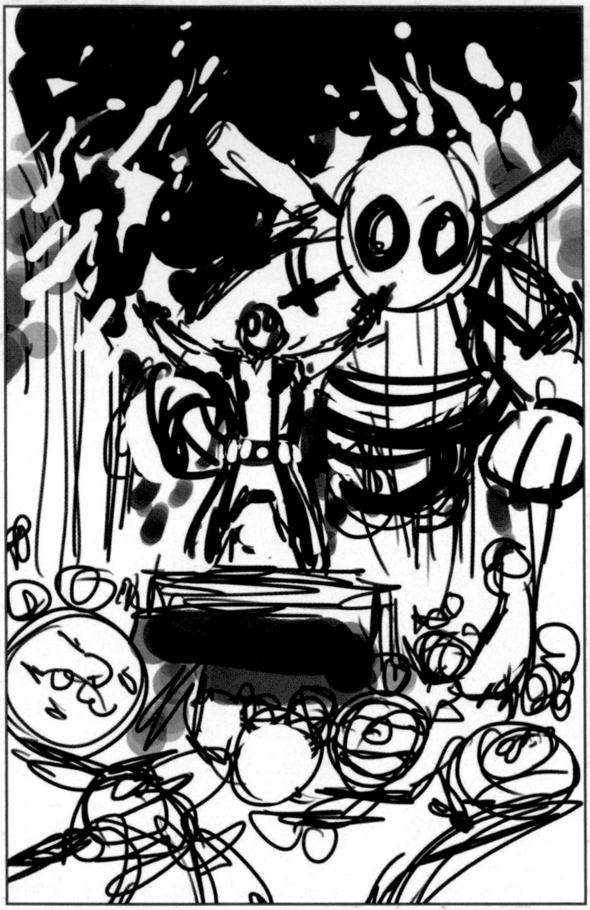

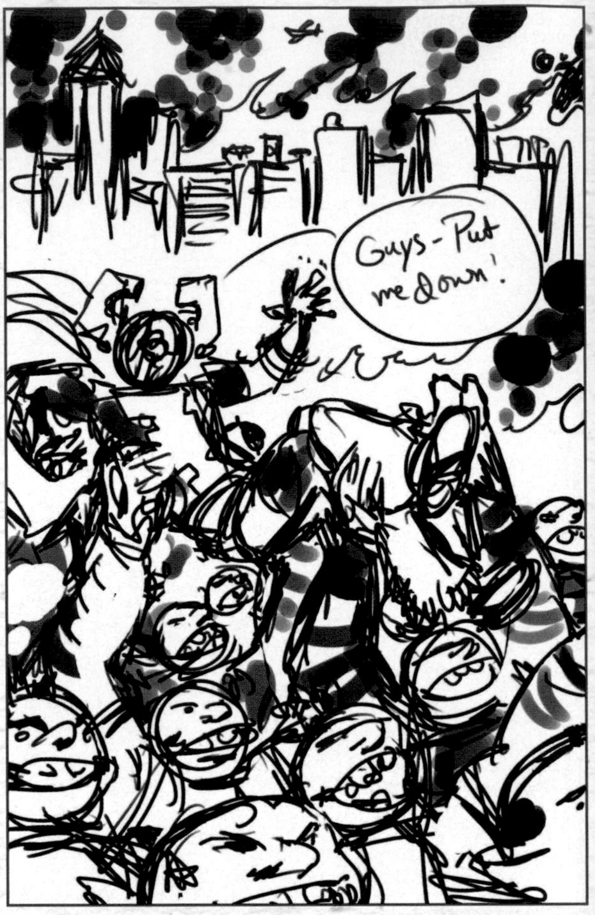
Guys - Put me down!

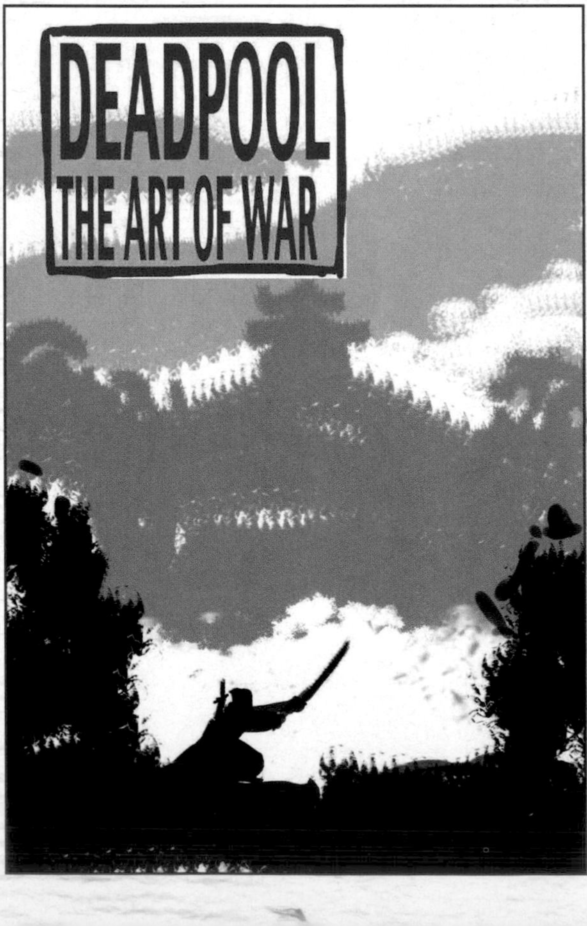
DEADPOOL
THE ART OF WAR

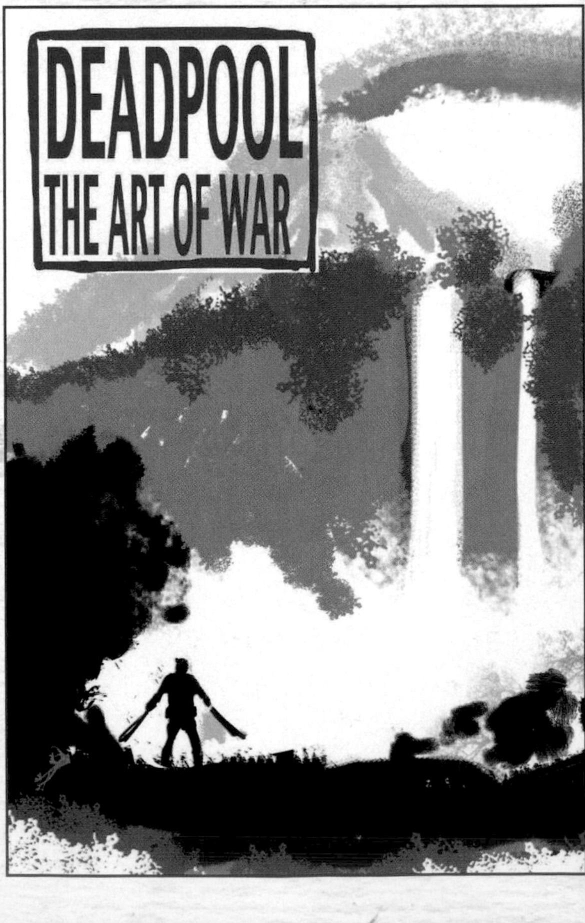
DEADPOOL
THE ART OF WAR

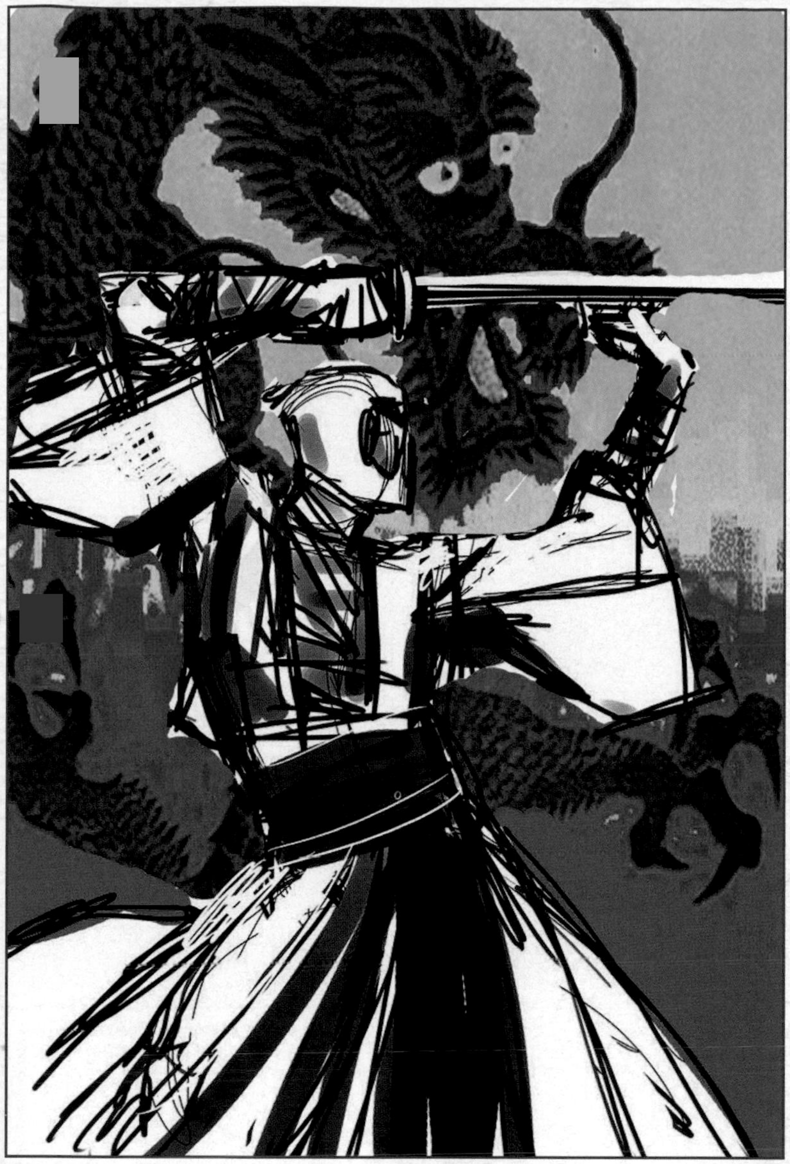

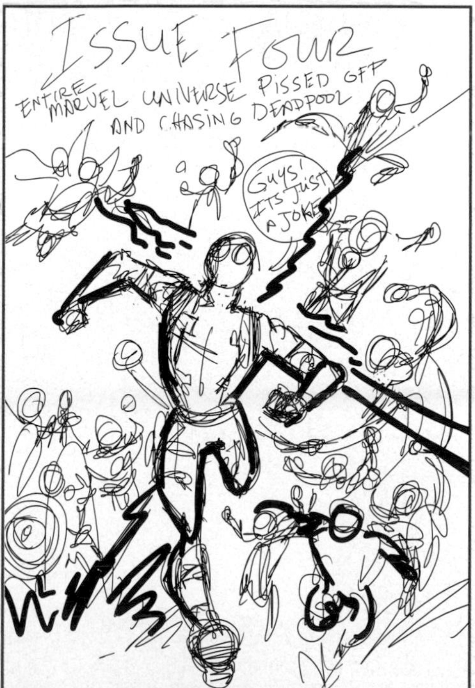
ISSUE FOUR
ENTIRE MARVEL UNIVERSE PISSED OFF AND CHASING DEADPOOL
GUYS! ITS JUST A JOKE

COVER SKETCHES FOR #1–4 BY **SCOTT KOBLISH**

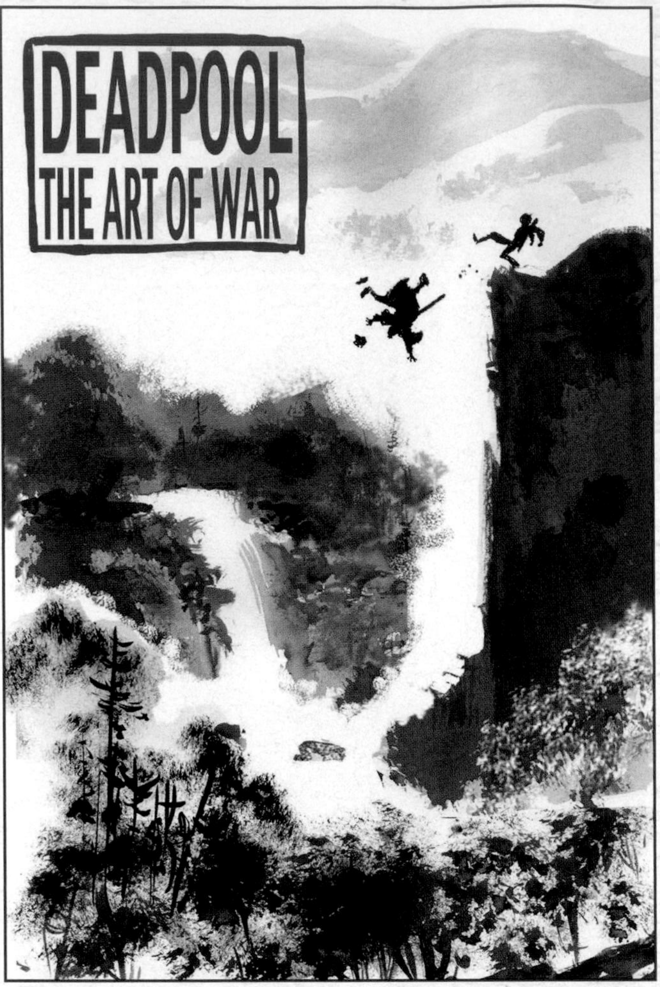
DEADPOOL
THE ART OF WAR

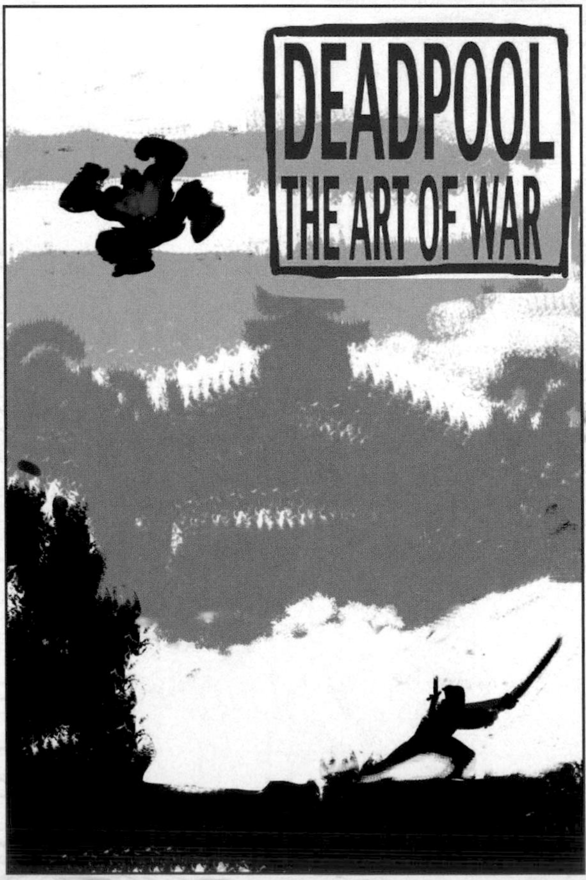
DEADPOOL
THE ART OF WAR

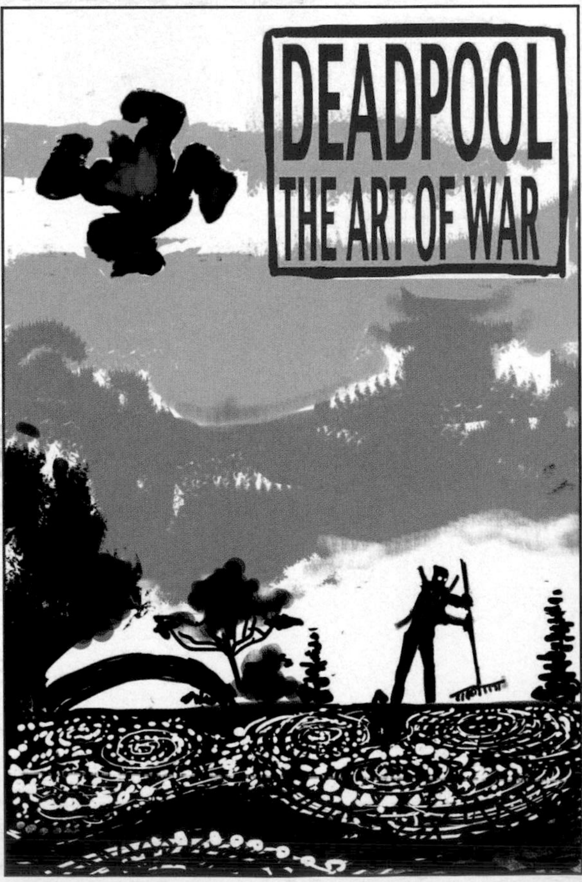
DEADPOOL
THE ART OF WAR

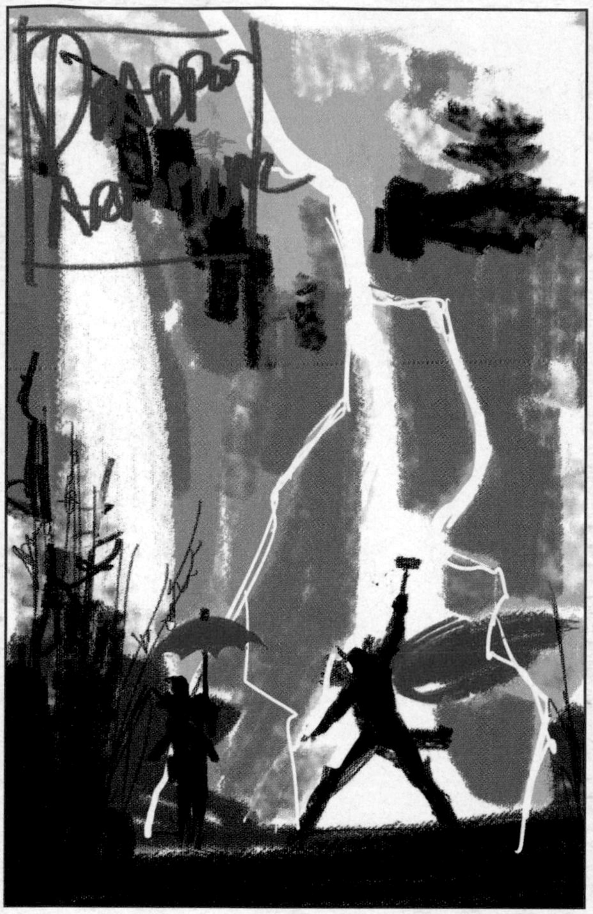

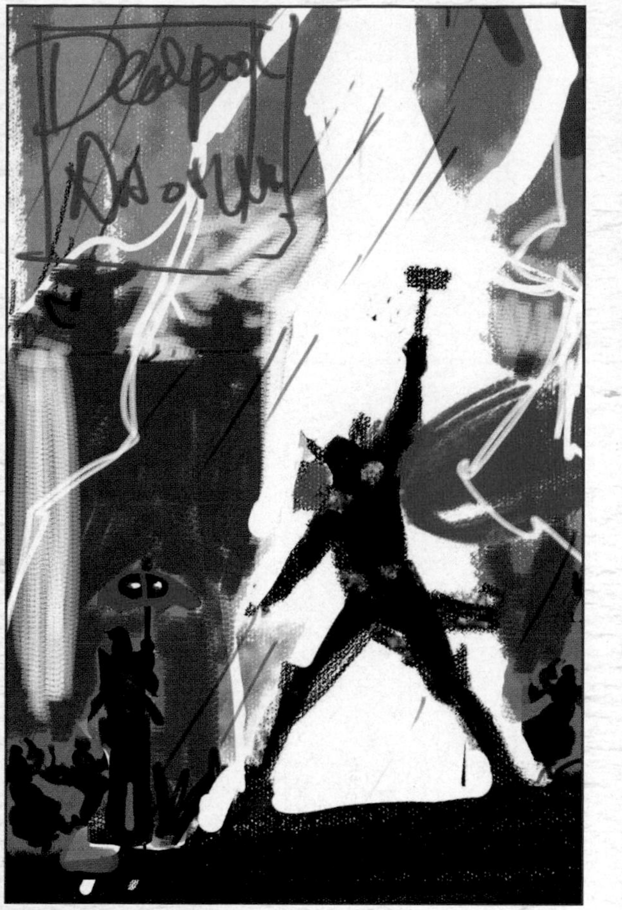
Deadpool

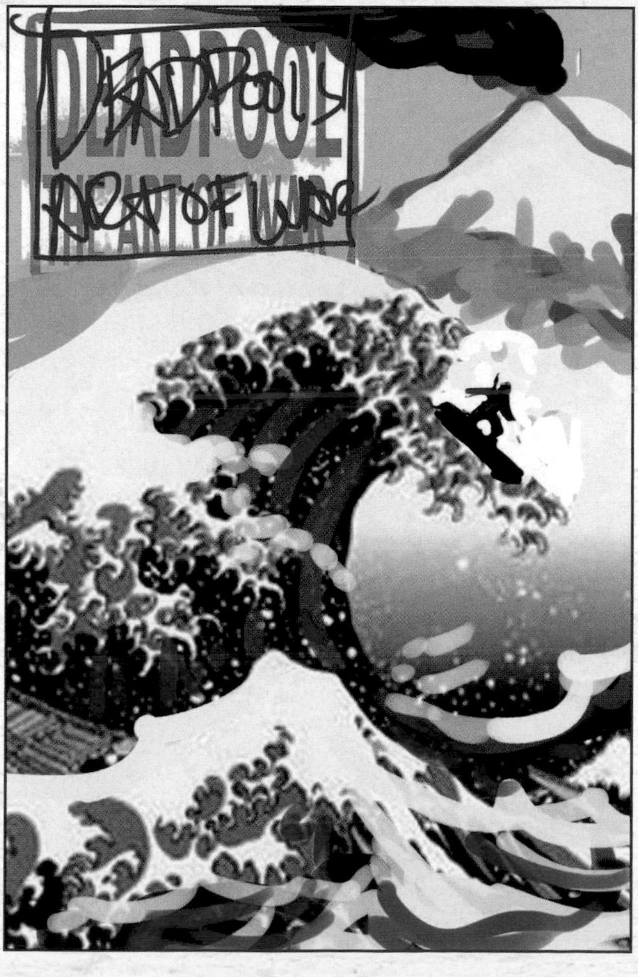
DEADPOOL
THE ART OF WAR

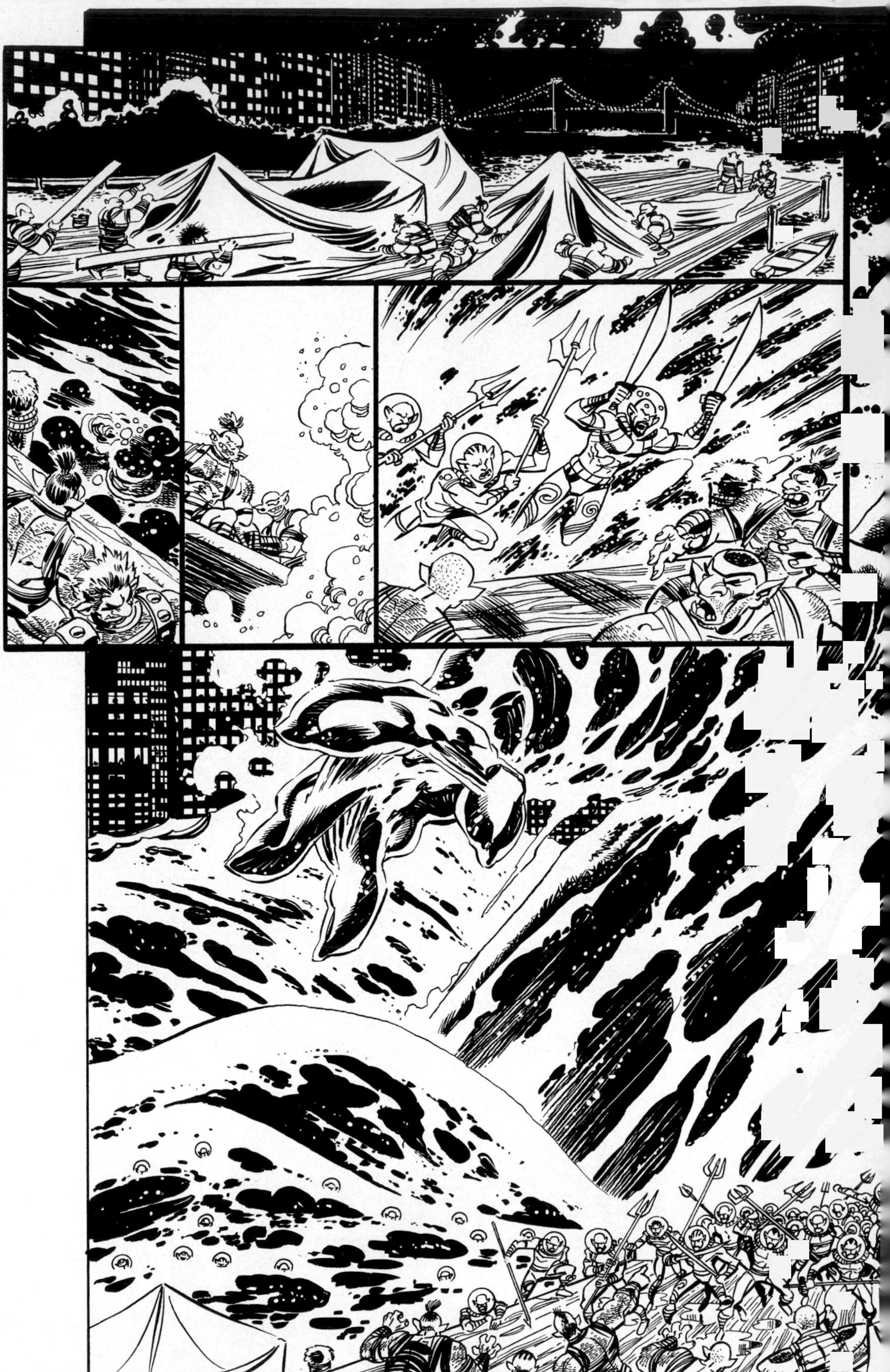

#3, PAGES 16–17. ART BY **SCOTT KOBLISH**

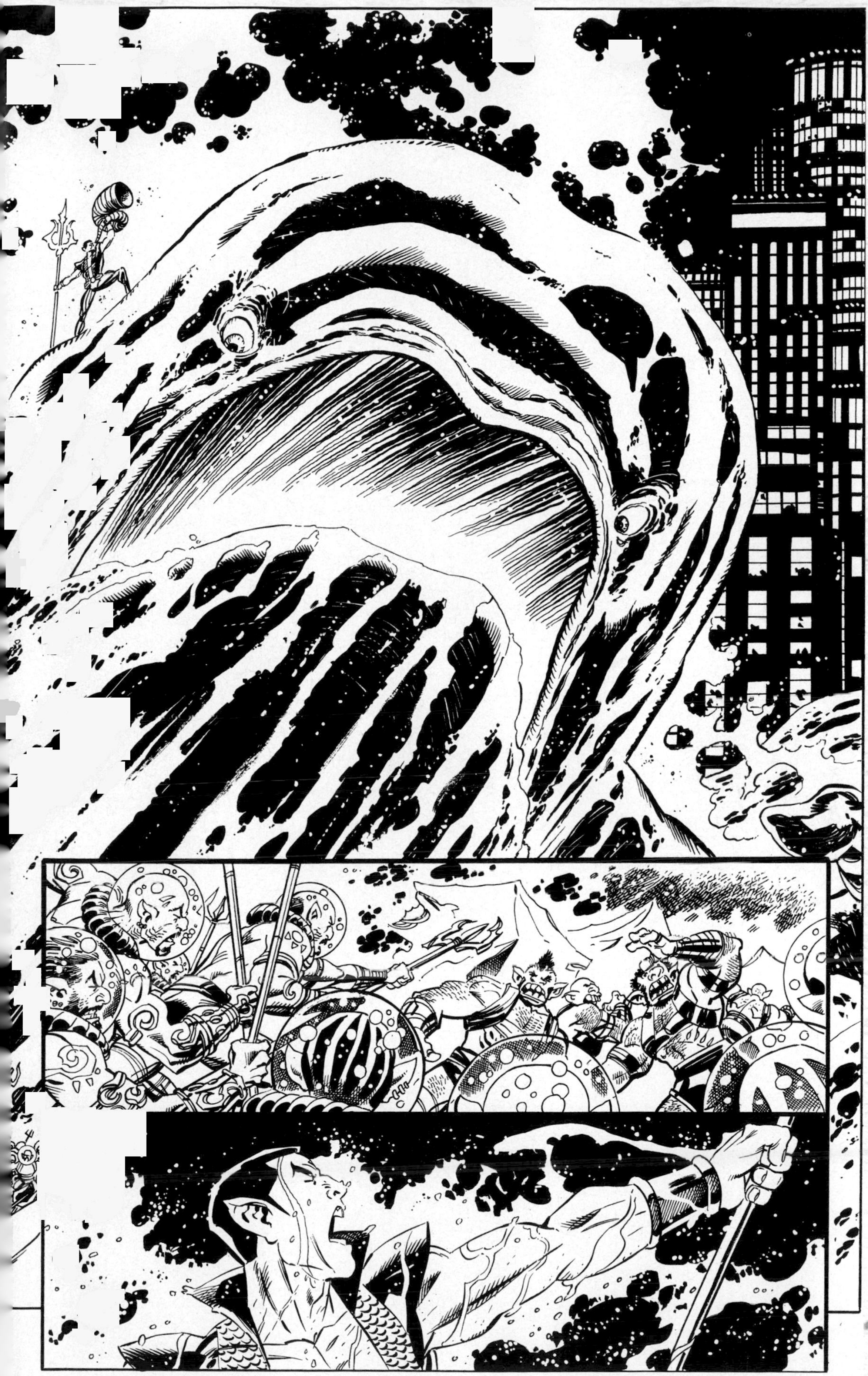